Chuck Palahniuk,
Parodist

Chuck Palahniuk, Parodist

*Postmodern Irony
in Six Transgressive Novels*

DAVID MCCRACKEN

McFarland & Company, Inc., Publishers
Jefferson, North Carolina

LIBRARY OF CONGRESS CATALOGUING-IN-PUBLICATION DATA

Names: McCracken, David, 1962– author.
Title: Chuck Palahniuk, parodist : postmodern irony in six
    transgressive novels / David McCracken.
Description: Jefferson, North Carolina : McFarland & Company,
    Inc., Publishers, 2016.
Identifiers: LCCN 2016026445 | ISBN 9780786479290 (softcover :
    acid free paper) ∞
Subjects: LCSH: Palahniuk, Chuck—Criticism and interpretation.
Classification: LCC PS3566.A4554 Z76 2016 | DDC 813/.54—dc23
LC record available at https://lccn.loc.gov/2016026445

BRITISH LIBRARY CATALOGUING DATA ARE AVAILABLE

ISBN (print) 978-0-7864-7929-0
ISBN (ebook) 978-1-4766-2738-0

© 2016 David McCracken. All rights reserved

*No part of this book may be reproduced or transmitted in any form
or by any means, electronic or mechanical, including photocopying
or recording, or by any information storage and retrieval system,
without permission in writing from the publisher.*

Front cover image © 2016 iStock

Printed in the United States of America

*McFarland & Company, Inc., Publishers
    Box 611, Jefferson, North Carolina 28640
        www.mcfarlandpub.com*

For Wendy.
Her assistance was invaluable.

Table of Contents

Preface	1
ONE—Chuck Palahniuk and Postmodern Parody	5
TWO—*Haunted* as Parody of Boccaccio's *Decameron*	19
THREE—"True fact": Hyperreality in *Snuff*	37
FOUR—*Pygmy* as Parody of 1970s Karate Films	54
FIVE—*Tell-All* as Parody of Hollywood's Golden Age of Gossip Journalism	72
SIX—*Damned* as Parody of Dante's *Inferno*	90
SEVEN—The Elephant Man in *Invisible Monsters Remix*	110
EIGHT—Empowerment	124
NINE—The Rhetorical Situation	137
TEN—Future Postmodern Parody	178
Chapter Notes	191
Bibliography	203
Index	213

Preface

While I prepared to read a paper concerning Chuck Palahniuk's *Snuff* at an academic conference a couple of years ago, I overheard someone sitting not far from the podium say rather loudly that Palahniuk was "antithetical to everything academically moral." I remember these words exactly because they instantly increased my already sweat-producing nervousness about reading a paper that addressed a pornographic record-setting gang bang.

The fifty-something female professor from a middle-sized Southern public university continued making disparaging comments related to Palahniuk and equally caustic remarks pertaining to why the conference organizers would grant someone such as myself the opportunity to express what would certainly amount to perverted opinions about Palahniuk's novel. I had not prepared for this reception, and I discovered twenty minutes later after I finished reading my paper that this woman was not alone. Scanning the audience, I could tell by facial expressions and body language that many people held similar attitudes toward the content of my essay.

There were, however, several participants in the room who declared they were loyal Palahniuk fans, and many told me afterward they enjoyed my interpretation of *Snuff*. Unfortunately, I gave this woman's negativity more of my mental attention than I did these positive comments, so her words stayed with me after my session and lingered with me throughout the conference.

On the following day, I almost followed this woman into a session that included a presentation about Kathy Acker's *Don Quixote*. I wanted to see how she reacted to Acker's parody of Cervantes's novel. If she did not like my paper about Palahniuk's *Snuff*, I doubted that she would like an essay about Acker's *Don Quixote*.

My goal in writing this book is to provide a response to people similar to this woman who question why anyone would study Chuck Palahniuk's fiction. A version of my *Snuff* essay is included as Chapter Three. No matter how much it may upset this population, transgressive fiction has staked a major claim in academic literary studies in the twenty-first century, and the popularity of this genre of writing will only increase. In many ways, transgressive writing has become the next major wave in American literary studies. To test this premise, one only needs to scan paper titles at any of the regional popular culture association conferences or, more revealing, to check programs at esoterically stuffy literature conferences. There will undoubtedly be numerous papers devoted to transgressive writers. The same is true for theses and dissertations. Scholarly attention is being devoted to transgressive fiction.

This does not mean my study will only provide academic interpretations of Palahniuk's novels. I realize that Palahniuk readers are indeed intellectual, but they are also cynical when it comes to the business of intellectualism. I am therefore aiming the scope of this book at two types of readers: those who couldn't care less about literary criticism and just want interesting information to supplement their understanding of Palahniuk's novels, and those who want some scholarship to add to their academic readings of Palahniuk's writing. I hope my explanations of the literary criticism do not distract those who want to know a little more about Palahniuk's fiction, but I also want the literary theory to help reinforce my ideas concerning Palahniuk's application of parody, which I contend satisfies what both academic and non-academic readers want out of reading his novels, the Palahniuk perception of the world.

I contend Palahniuk is an important contemporary author whose transgressive fiction will inevitably establish its place in the American literary tradition. In the first chapter, I define postmodern parody, focusing primarily on Linda Hutcheon's theories. In the subsequent six chapters, supplementing Hutcheon with other theorists, I explain how Palahniuk's *Haunted*, *Snuff*, *Pygmy*, *Tell-All*, *Damned*, and *Invisible Monsters Remix* are all in various ways postmodern parodies. In the next chapter, I discuss how Palahniuk treats cultural empowerment in *Fight Club*, his most famous work, and those six novels. In the longest chapter, I argue how Palahniuk effectively applies parody to address his rhetorical situation. In the final chapter, I mention Palahniuk's most recent works. Palahniuk confronts issues with which his readers relate, those directly associated with economic, social, and cultural marginalization and disenfranchisement.

My study demonstrates that Palahniuk is unafraid to question still largely held puritanical beliefs related to social propriety, personal salvation, and the American Dream. Contrary to what my colleague believes, Palahniuk helps to set the standard for what is "academically moral" by demonstrating that this domain is not controlled by one empowered type of person or connected with one privileged group, brought across the Atlantic to be either stuck next to Plymouth Rock or planted in the "city upon a hill," as something predestined to remain static and fixed, mandated by a few of the self-proclaimed scholastic elite.

In the following chapters, I discuss Palahniuk subjects that make people such as my colleague extremely nervous and uncomfortable, but I also demonstrate that these folks only fear what they do not understand. Palahniuk is actually more aligned with academia than most academics realize. Palahniuk is correct in his statement, "The fringe is the future" ("Foreword" 9).

ONE

Chuck Palahniuk and Postmodern Parody

Seth MacFarlane realizes that the success of his comedies—*Family Guy*, *American Dad*, and *The Cleveland Show*—depends upon his television audience's knowledge of popular culture. MacFarlane offers a succession of cutaways to references, comparisons, or allusions to culturally significant personalities, events, or situations that he counts on his viewers recognizing. There are references devoted to full-length episodes, as when *Family Guy* characters are morphed into the *Star Wars* cast or when *The Cleveland Show* mimics the first *Die Hard* movie, but most of the punchlines depend upon short clips referring to items with which viewers can readily identify in American popular culture. For the jokes to make sense, the audience must make the connections between what they see in the segments and the cultural references. If they do not, the jokes flop, the ratings fall, and the show is cancelled. MacFarlane has been very successful in making sure these connections are made, and proof of this is the omnipresence of his programs day and evening though widespread syndication. In other words, viewers appreciate how MacFarlane parodies American popular culture, so they continue to watch his shows.

The critical meaning of the term "parody" is going through revitalization. It has been associated with "remake," "adaptation," "allusion," "travesty," "imitation," "satire," and other synonyms for something that copies something else, and it has been linked with "mash-up," "pastiche," "montage," and similar concepts. The definition of parody in *A Handbook to Literature*, the undergraduate English-major bible, illustrates this transformation. In the fourth edition published in 1980, parody is defined as "a composition burlesquing or imitating another, usually serious, piece of work. It is designed to ridicule in nonsensical fashion, or to criticize by brilliant treatment, an original piece of work by another author" (319). The twelfth edition published in 2012, the most current version, omits the reference to burlesque and nonsense: "A composition imitating another—usually serious—piece. It is designed to ridicule a work or its style or author" (353). The omissions signal significant changes concerning the intention of parody, ones that influence how a viewer (or reader or listener) might perceive a text that is designated as a parody. In its general sense, a parody is a text that loosely refers to a previous text and may or may not be comic, although the tone is now accepted more as neutral. Along this line, there is broad academic agreement that a contemporary parody not necessarily "ridicule" a previous work, but instead it should call attention to that preexisting source and then take advantage of that previous meaning to communicate a new meaning. MacFarlane is truly a master at referring to something that his audience will recognize and then drawing upon that reference to make an innovative or insightful point. MacFarlane depends upon his viewers associating what he presents (e.g., through Peter, Cleveland, or Stan) with what they have previously seen (anything in American popular culture), and the merging of the two produces the meaning that MacFarlane intends for them to receive, granted his aim is usually to ridicule or to satirize.

Chuck Palahniuk understands all of this, maybe even better than MacFarlane, and he is fully aware of the literary benefits of parodying American popular culture as well as texts within the traditional Western literary canon. Palahniuk does not apply parody in the same manner as, for instance, James Joyce imitates *The Odyssey* through *Ulysses*, but he is more in line with how Homer's epic is remade through the film *O Brother, Where Art Thou?* or even how it is recast through the other Homer, Homer Simpson, in *The Simpsons*. Considering Palahniuk's aversion to the academic mainstream, he would probably shrug off any reference to T. S. Eliot's "Tradition and the Individual Talent," yet he certainly draws from the canonical literary heritage of established great books to craft much of his fiction. In *Tell-All*, Shannon McFarland comments, "*Nothing of me is original. I am the combined effort of everybody I've ever known*" (39). Palahniuk is undeniably an original thinker with a one-of-a-kind imagination who writes in an idiosyncratic style, and he has indisputably a trademark approach universally recognized toward often ignored subjects. Palahniuk is undoubtedly an American creative innovator. All this said, however, the argument can be asserted that Palahniuk borrows from his literary heritage and draws on previous creations to produce his own brand of American fiction. Shannon may state she is a composite of previous "efforts," but these "combinations" have definitely made her into a distinctive literary personality, and there is no other fictional character exactly like her. In this way, she serves as metaphor for

Palahniuk's art. Eliot contends in his essay, using Homer in his example, modern poets forge an alliance with their literary heritage, and through several of his novels, Palahniuk shows a similar fidelity to past texts—specifically to the ideas they include—and recreates them into something vastly different. Shannon McFarland is a unique fictional creation even though there are perhaps literary precursors before her, and only the imagination of Palahniuk could take those previous "efforts" and combine them into her.

Palahniuk takes advantage of the literary technique of parody to express his distinctive ideology in *Haunted* (2005), *Snuff* (2008), *Pygmy* (2009), *Tell-All* (2010), *Damned* (2011), and *Invisible Monsters Remix* (2012). Specifically, Palahniuk takes ideas from previous texts, processes them through his transgressive filter, and then presents them in different forms, often turning them upside down, inside out, and inverting or subverting their meaning. Stated another way, Palahniuk takes the packaging of ideas from previous sources and repackages them according to his own distinctive transgressive variety—the resemblance between the past idea and its present reincarnation is apparent but definitely colored by the Palahniuk influence. On the dust jacket of his recently published collection of short fiction, *Make Something Up: Stories You Can't Unread*, Palahniuk is advertised as "literature's favorite transgressive author," and in his introduction to *Burnt Tongues: An Anthology of Transgressive Stories*, Palahniuk writes that the "hallmark of a classic long-lived story is how much it upsets the existing culture" (3). In the six novels selected, Palahniuk reacts against current literary decorum and taste, but he does so by maintaining a connection to previous texts (and the ideas they purport) largely held as benchmarks concerning what is socially appropriate and culturally acceptable. He parodies these previous texts so that their established meanings serve his rhetorical purpose, which might be, as will be discussed later in the following chapters, to motivate his audience toward taking action in their own lives. Palahniuk gets essentially at the core of what it means to be marginalized and disenfranchised in America, and he deconstructs stereotypes perpetuated through the media related to these labels. Readers identify with the social and cultural outcasts in these six novels, no matter how dysfunctional or abnormal they seem, and this is why Palahniuk is such a popular writer since the beginning of the new millennium. Through parody, Palahniuk taps into central issues that his readers understand through approaches no other writer currently provides. Walt Whitman was the voice of American democracy and the advocate of the "divine average" during the nineteenth century, and Palahniuk extends this tradition and all that its heritage demands into the twenty-first century.

Because the definition of parody continues to evolve, an explanation is needed regarding how it will be used in this study in addition to what is meant by postmodern parody and transgressive fiction. This information will lay the theoretical foundation for the discussion of Palahniuk's six novels in the subsequent chapters. In terms of postmodern parody, John Barth has established the contemporary literary standard. In his 1967 essay entitled "The Literature of Exhaustion," perhaps the manifesto of postmodern literature, Barth contends that previous authors have depleted the creative reserves for original ideas, and all that is currently available amounts to duplications, reproductions, and replications. Barth draws upon Jorge Luis Borges to serve as the artist who understands this postmodern dilemma, and he explains how Borges draws upon parody as a response (*Friday Book* 69–70). Barth explains that Borges understands there is essentially no original literature—all the ideas have been theoretically "exhausted"—and points out how Borges applies parody to create new fictional versions of old literary ideas (*Friday Book* 73). In his 1980 article "The Literature of Replenishment," Barth retracts some of what he said previously, claiming he did not intend to offer a blanket statement that there are no new ideas (*Friday Book* 205), and he admits, agreeing with Borges, parody is indeed a way of producing new meanings (*Friday Book* 206).[1] In the 2011 essay "Do I Repeat Myself? The Problem of the Already Said," Barth returns his attention to literary originality. He mentions Umberto Eco's comments about Homer's "wine-dark sea" and "rosy-fingered Dawn" in *The Odyssey* as setting the precedents for how water and sky would be described through creative language for centuries, hence causing the problem of the "already said" when "nearly 3,000 years' worth of poets and storytellers have had to find other images for sea and sunrise—a task that must become increasingly difficult as the repertory of possibilities is exhausted" ("Do I Repeat"). Barth acknowledges, however, that Homer was not the first to express through these exact word combinations imaginative ways of looking at those natural occurrences, and he mentions the irony of a scribe named Khakheperresenb complaining that he could not in his art, twelve centuries before Homer, produce unique creative expressions. Barth concludes by wishing he could travel back in time to reassure Khakheperresenb that "originality, after all, includes not only saying something for the first time, but re-saying (in a worthy new way) the already said: rearranging an old tune in a different key, to a different rhythm, perhaps on a different instrument" ("Do I Repeat"). Thus, Barth inaugurates parody as the paramount feature in postmodern literature.

Whereas Ezra Pound proclaimed "Make it new" to serve as the

modernist mantra, Barth may be extending this into the postmodern dictum "Make it new by making it new again." Contemporary writers have used parody as an artistic strategy to refocus, to reconfigure, and to revitalize past meaning for a present historical context while also considering how it can effectively adapt that meaning to a current audience. Most scholars agree the etymology of the word "parody," Latin *parodia* and Greek *paroidia*, refers to a burlesque song or poem, but the meaning has typically been applied to anything that mocks through imitation, as the 1980 edition of *A Handbook to Literature* indicates.[2] Parody is considered now, however, to be much more inclusive as a dominant form in postmodern literature. Of the current theorists, Linda Hutcheon provides the most appropriate definition of postmodern parody for this study of Palahniuk's novels. Hutcheon contends parody is an essential quality of postmodern literature, and she clarifies, considering previous definitions of the term, contemporary parody is devoid of its characteristic mocking, comic, humorous, or similar intent. To be more exact, Hutcheon states, "Parody—often called ironic quotation, pastiche, appropriation, or intertextuality—is usually considered central to postmodernism, both by its detractors and its defenders. For artists, the postmodern is said to involve a rummaging through the image reserves of the past in such a way as to show the history of the representations their parody call to our attention" (*Politics* 93).[3] Hutcheon argues that the bridging of the present and the past serves to connect high and low cultures, and this in turn provides a revitalization of the original for a general audience. Hutcheon points out that parody is often related to kitsch (*Poetics* 31), but she perceives this reinvention of the original—the reconstruction of the past—as a positive "closing the gap" between the high and the low, the academic and the popular, and the elitist and the accessible (*Poetics* 44). Essentially, Hutcheon defines parody's function as demonstrating similarity but emphasizing difference, an extremely important feature that will be emphasized in the following chapters, and significantly she eliminates the component of "ridicule" in its definition: "What I mean by 'parody' ... is *not* the ridiculing imitation of the standard theories and definitions that are rooted in eighteenth-century theories of wit. The collective weight of parodic *practice* suggests a redefinition of parody as repetition with critical distance that allows ironic signaling of difference at the very heart of similarity" (*Poetics* 26).[4] Although much of Hutcheon's critical attention focuses on what she terms historiographic metafiction, her classification for distinctively postmodern fiction, her points about parody are just as theoretically innovative, academically respected, and professionally acknowledged in critical theory.[5]

In the following chapters, application of Hutcheon's theory will demonstrate how Palahnuik uses postmodern parody to establish similarity but more so to emphasize difference, predominantly through "ironic signaling," between six of his novels and various texts. Working from the assumption that irony is when the unexpected occurs or when the opposite is intended, Palahniuk takes advantage of irony as a key element in each of these six parodies. In *Haunted*, he draws upon Boccaccio's *Decameron* to present a similar frame narrative in which participants pass time telling stories while sheltered from the outside world. Whereas Boccaccio provides regal characters affluent enough to establish a country sanctuary from the Black Death, Palahniuk's personalities chase illusions of celebrity within an abandoned theater, only to realize that what was initially set up as a writing commune becomes a forum for them to express their present resentments toward their previous situations. In *Snuff*, Palahniuk provides layers of imitation, blending truth with fiction, to illustrate the different degrees that sometimes differentiate reality and fantasy. Using Cassie Wright's quest to become the gang-bang queen as the central plot, he shows how what is considered real can be copied, transformed, and replicated into other forms. In *Pygmy*, Palahniuk depends on his audience's familiarity with 1970s karate movies to serve as common knowledge. He plays with his readers' prejudices concerning Asian cultural stereotypes as Pygmy ironically transforms from outcast to superhero by protecting America against foreign terrorism. In *Tell-All*, Palahniuk provides a freeplay of signifiers through the boldfacing of celebrity names, and he uses gossip journalism as a vehicle to undermine power from those who have traditionally held it. Hazie Coogan's narration enables him to call into question current meanings related to these past personalities. In *Damned*, Palahniuk draws on both Dante's *Inferno* and Judy Blume's *Are You There God? It's Me, Margaret* to challenge traditional views about both hell and adolescence. By parodying two disparate texts, Palahniuk justifies Madison's motivation behind her actions. In *Invisible Monsters Remix*, Palahniuk establishes comparisons between Shannon McFarland, her brother Shane, and Joseph Merrick in *The Elephant Man*. Through this connection, Palahniuk addresses issues related to gender performance, personal identity, and self-empowerment. In each of these novels, Palahniuk takes an existing text and presents it in an innovative and a provocative new way for a contemporary audience. To accomplish this, Palahniuk must confront past ideologies associated with those texts and reconfigure them for his current readers. His strategy for this is literary transgression. Unfortunately, this approach is also the reason behind much of the negative criticism of his writing. Regardless, transgression

One. Chuck Palahniuk and Postmodern Parody

allows Palahniuk the artistic freedom to present postmodern parodies that truly speak to twenty-first-century readers.

Although Palahniuk is now attributed with the title of major American transgressive writer, he had many predecessors who developed this genre. In his 1963 "Preface to Transgression," Michel Foucault lays the foundation for transgression in a similar way to how Barth established seminal ideas related to parody. Foucault writes, "transgression prescribes not only the sole manner of discovering the sacred in its unmediated substance, but also a way of recomposing its empty form, its absence, through which it becomes all the more scintillating. A rigorous language, as it arises from sexuality, will not reveal the secret of man's natural being, nor will it express the serenity or anthropological truths, but rather, it will say that he exists without God" (30). In an influential 1993 *Los Angeles Times* article, Michael Silverblatt explains, "The underlying idea of transgressive thinking (as derived from Foucault) is that knowledge is no longer to be found through the oppositions of dialectical reasoning. Instead, knowledge is found at the limits of experience. The body becomes the locus for the possibility of knowledge.... AIDS is throwing everyone's sexual norms into disarray, and the already embattled nuclear family is under attack by the new rhetoric of incest, abuse and dysfunction." In a 1995 *New York Times* article, Rene Chun offers a more practical definition: "Subversive, avant-garde, bleak, pornographic—and these are compliments. Such words are used to describe transgressive fiction, books pitched to young adults, written by authors descended from William Burroughs and the Marquis de Sade, that explore aberrant sexual practices, urban violence, drug use and dysfunctional families in graphic detail" (49). In a 1996 *Atlantic* "Word Watch," Anne H. Soukhanov describes transgressive fiction as "a literary genre that graphically explores such topics as incest and other aberrant sexual practices, mutilation, the sprouting of sexual organs in various places on the human body, urban violence and violence against women, drug use, and highly dysfunctional family relationships, and that is based on the premises that knowledge is to be found at the edge of experience and that the body is the site for gaining knowledge." In the 2003 book *Transgression*, Chris Jenks states, "To transgress is to go beyond the bounds or limits set by a commandment or law or convention, it is to violate or infringe … that conduct which breaks rules or exceeds boundaries" (2–3).[6] He adds, "Transgressive behaviour therefore does not deny limits or boundaries, rather it exceeds them and thus completes them.... Transgression is not the same as disorder; it opens up chaos and reminds us of the necessity of order. But the problem remains. We need to know the collective order, to recognize the edges in order to transcend them" (7). These are just a few of those recognized as coining the contemporary usage of the label transgressive fiction, and each commentator undoubtedly describes a facet of Palahniuk's writing.

Through the transgressive genre, Palahniuk addresses marginalization and disenfranchisement, leading the attack on both from the unique perspective of working from the bottom upward. Instead of exposing marginalization and disenfranchisement in their various manifestations, harking to many of the negative socioeconomic and political ramifications, Palahniuk takes for granted that these are already understood (even internalized) by his contemporary readers, especially Americans well aware of issues associated with cultural diversity, political correctness, and human rights. Palahniuk's characters are usually affiliated with the socioeconomic have-nots instead of the haves, so they start from places where many readers identify themselves as sitting. These characters empower themselves not through government aid or social intervention (at least not all the time), but from self-exploitation, the marketing, commodifying, or promoting of themselves, following the basic premise why not do this first before allowing a system, an agency, or other people the opportunity. Palahniuk redefines the meaning of victim by enabling the marginalized and the disenfranchised—those who see themselves as left out but not necessarily victimized—to take charge of their own situations and in turn to take control of their own destinies. Palahniuk's characters manipulate societal and cultural mores pertaining to moral decency and therefore discover strategies to circumvent any probable retaliation or inevitable retribution (one only needs to consider Project Mayhem in *Fight Club* for an illustration). In the Palahniuk fictional universe, a victim is someone who refuses to accept pain, sacrifice, and inequity as essential components of life and dysfunction as the overriding principle that unifies seemingly diverse individuals into a cohesive community. Palahniuk's characters understand the opposite is true—dysfunction rules. The inhabitants within Palahniuk's textual territory possess the flexibility to adapt in frequently moral turned into amoral situations, and they survive by the ethic that everyone (not just a culturally diverse few) sits somewhere on the outside boundary of the traditional power circle. To get to the center, power is derived from exploiting that marginalization, and power is not necessarily attached to values, at least not those upheld by traditional institutions representing authority. If anything, institutions that advertise totalizing systems such as religion and politics are not trusted. Paradoxically, Palahniuk's characters understand realistically that to be abnormal is to be normal in contemporary American culture. Palahniuk recognizes that the transgressive is the perfect genre to present this ideology.

The Palahniuk ethic is predicated on self-knowledge. Characters who come out of a situation okay, without any moral or ethical qualification attached, are those who know who they are, tapping into that often elusive and seemingly complex intuitive sense of personal serenity. They exhibit a transgressive version of Ernest Hemingway's "grace under pressure." Those who do not adapt are left struggling to find this inner peace. They may have wealth, fame, and health, but they do not have individual serenity derived from the Socratic "know thyself" self-satisfaction. In a discussion of Palahniuk's religion, G. Christopher Williams cites a now famous interview Palahniuk had with Laura J. Williams in which he admits, "My characters are not people. They are machines that do a job. They are machines that destroy themselves.... Characters are just vehicles for telling a story. Devices. Mechanisms" ("Nihilism" 170).[7] After Williams presses Palahniuk about his philosophical leaning toward nihilism, a belief that life is meaningless, Palahniuk claims he is a romantic: "All of my books are basically romances; they're stories about reconnecting with community" ("Nihilism" 172). Although Palahniuk says this, he is not a romantic in regard to promoting an idealized vision of reality, nor is he espousing an anti-realistic/naturalistic view of the world, and he is definitely not writing in the vein of American Transcendentalism. *Haunted* is in many ways gothic, but most of Palahniuk's novels do not leave the first impression that they are associated with literary tenets of romanticism. Furthermore, Palahniuk surely does not present a Pollyannaish view of the world, nor does he offer melodramatic propaganda, sounding of "Kumbaya," tasting of saccharine, or feeling warm and fuzzy. None of this is Palahniuk. Sometimes inclusion into a community only guarantees not being alone, and Palahniuk's characters are frequently alone amidst a group.

A more accurate description of Palahniuk's philosophy is between pragmatism and existentialism. God is replaced with something comparable to the twelve-step Higher Power (think about Joe's frequenting these meetings in *Fight Club*) that helps those who help themselves. In "The Fringe Is the Future," the foreword to *You Do Not Talk About Fight Club: I Am Jack's Completely Unauthorized Essay Collection*, Palahniuk claims the church was "where people could go, a safe place where they could express their worst selves, then be forgiven and accepted back into the community," but now "to vent and exhaust their worst fears, people go to addiction recovery groups, political protests, fight clubs" (10). Characters are left with terrestrial options—just what is available on this planet, in this world—and nothing celestial can effectively be prayed to or drawn upon for divine assistance. The value of a belief is the practical application it provides and the tangible outcomes it produces. Granted, Palahniuk might appear nihilistic, but this may just be an inverted perception of good and bad, positive and negative, and other such qualitative binaries. Whereas most would assume life is a progressive pattern of good events, Palahniuk's characters eventually, through the tests inherent in human experience, discover that the bad events are the everyday occurrences, thus the good ones are the anomalies. This is not necessarily nihilistic as much as it is being pragmatically realistic. Those who expect the least usually gain the most, which is a kind of spiritual equilibrium, not happiness necessarily as it is a feeling of being comfortable in one's own skin or a sense of epistemological satisfaction, an aura of "I am who I am and I know what I know, and I am okay with both, no matter what they are." Those who do not reach this point are the self-deluded and self-deceived. Many scholars have addressed Palahniuk's philosophy, but the truth is that misery, loneliness, suffering, inequality, discrimination, and, most important, marginalization and disenfranchisement are what Palahniuk's characters can count on each day, and Palahniuk portrays how these people function bearing in mind this knowledge.[8] Palahniuk's parodies present these inversions (ones most readers would not want to embrace), and he demonstrates that pain is normal, frequently expected, surprisingly relished, and astonishingly appreciated. This view of pain is what so often unsettles and unnerves readers, but this reaction is also the nature of transgressive fiction.

Needless to say, not everyone likes Palahniuk's brand of parody, nor does every reader understand the significance of his transgressive style and appreciate how he empowers the marginalized or disenfranchised in his stories. An argument may be made that Palahniuk displays insensitivity toward the common person, whom he possibly dehumanizes by allowing base desires and raw instinct control emotion, compassion, and consideration. This would be only a surface reading of Palahniuk's words, and the deeper meaning is apparent after drilling down into the substance of "ironic signaling" in his works. Palahniuk's fiction is undoubtedly an acquired taste, and an apt comparison—apropos considering how some perceive Palahniuk—might be to when one first consumes liquor. First of all, one must have the maturity to drink and assume responsibility for the result of the drink. There is probably nothing pleasant or appealing about guzzling a shot of whiskey, and there is discomfort and irritation as that liquid travels down the throat, and if one does not have the intestinal fortitude for the reaction the liquid has with the stomach, the result will be a fierce and immediate counterreaction or gut reflex that will expel the alcohol and more than likely influence one not to attempt a repeat of this distasteful process. On the other hand, if one can keep the booze down and give it time to metabolize, the feeling is not so uncomfortable and perhaps the experience turns out to be pleasurable. This might be an appropriate analogy for reading Palahniuk's novels. His stories are for a mature audience that is prepared for the content, and those readers assume Palahniuk will push the limits of cultural diversity, political correctness, and social decorum. After perhaps an initial jolt, there might be some discomfort during the reading, but then there is an inebriating payoff, that delightful moment when one has that "aha" revelation figuring out some twist in the plot, and then there is the almost *deus ex machina* instance when one reads a Palahniuk ending. As will be discussed in the next chapter, readers undergo a similar process as those looking into the Nightmare Box. Afterward, they are unable to articulate in literal, concrete, direct language what they have seen, but they are obviously transformed by the experience. Readers get a glimpse into twenty-first-century reality (although hopefully not induced into a bout of depression as several characters are in *Haunted*). As loyal Palahniuk fans confirm, this glimpse into Palahniuk truth becomes addictive, if for nothing else just to see what the Palahniuk imagination will offer to top his last story, and readers can expect the extremely prolific Palahniuk to publish something new every year. Going back to the drink analogy, many readers will relish the Palahniuk reading experience—even if there is an unpleasant aftertaste—but some take that first gulp of his prose and never indulge in another of his books, and that is fine. Palahniuk's fiction is certainly not for everyone.

There are two reviews in particular that illustrate the less-than-hospitable critical reception Palahniuk often receives. In her scathing review of *Snuff* in the *New York Times*, Lucy Ellmann writes, "What in the hell is going on? The country that produced Melville, Twain, James now venerates King, Crichton, Grisham, Sebold and Palahniuk. Their subjects? Porn, crime, pop culture and an endless parade of out-of-body experiences. Their methods? Cliché, caricature and proto-Christian morality. Props? Corn chips, corpses, crucifixes. The agenda? Deceit: a dishonest throwing of the reader to the wolves. And the result? Readymade Hollywood scripts." After bashing Palahniuk for ostensibly shocking and nothing more, Ellmann concludes, "Instead of any real creative effort, Palahniuk chucks at us every bit of porno-talk he can muster. But not in a good way. This is no celebration of a field in which America excels—the hatching of new vocabulary—but an exercise in deadening the English language. Johnny One-Note, this book is shooting blanks." The other has been immortalized by its placement on the *Wikipedia* webpage for Chuck Palahniuk, regrettably serving as one of the first pieces of criticism viewers will read about Palahniuk's writing. The backstory surrounding the review may be more significant than the information because Palahniuk responded directly to the reviewer's commentary. In her review of *Diary* for *Salon*, Laura Miller writes admittedly one of the harshest indictments against Palahniuk's professionalism. The subheading sets the tone of the article: "The wildly popular 'Fight Club' novelist Chuck Palahniuk is back with more fodder for his army of disenfranchised Everymen, delivered with all the grace and poetry of a blunt object." In the subsequent critical tirade and literary chastisement, Miller describes Palahniuk's work using descriptors such as "crappy," "phony," and "sloppily," in addition to the phrases "hopped-up imperatives" and "posturing one-liners." Unsurprisingly, one of the most caustic sentences from Miller's review is quoted widely across the Internet: "these books traffic in the half-baked nihilism of a stoned high school student who has just discovered Nietzsche and Nine-Inch Nails." Miller goes on to point out logical inconsistencies in *Diary* and to question Palahniuk's artistry. As she unloads, "A great novelist excels on the small scale and the large, the individual leaf and root as well as the forest; good fiction convinces us that the imaginary is real by selecting exactly the right detail and rendering it perfectly. Reading Palahniuk is a revelation of sorts because it shows that bad fiction works exactly the same way: It's execrable on a sentence-by-sentence basis as well as in overall form and theme." Palahniuk responds with just a few sentences, notably, "Until you can create something that captivates people, I'd invite you to just shut up" (Letter).

The key word in this curt reply is "captivates." Palahniuk is not the first popular American writer to be bashed by critics who question his literary competency, and reviewers such as Ellmann and Miller only poke and jab Palahniuk into taking more creative chances and trying out more imaginative ideas that rebel against traditional expectations pertaining to literary taste and decorum. He thrives on these harsh attacks, and his creative responses will be innovative texts that consequently become the impetus for a new type of readership that will inevitably influence the production, the marketing, and the consumption of what is deemed "literary." Readers are definitely captivated by what Palahniuk writes, and Palahniuk will continue to cater to his wide fan base and to cultivate their needs while at the same time manipulating their impressions of those needs. Palahniuk's writing can certainly be seen as anti-academic, but there is nothing wrong with such a designation (this is viewed in some Palahniuk fan circles as a badge of honor). The following chapters should, however, disprove this thinking to some degree. Ernest Hemingway and Raymond Carver (among others) are not going to be exiled from the American literary canon because of their minimalist styles, proletarian themes, or dysfunctional characters. Actually, Hemingway's capricious nymphomaniac Brett Ashley, William Faulkner's sexual opportunist Caddy Compson, or Faulkner's sexual role-player Joanna Burden would be right at home in the Palahniuk world, as would other Yoknapatawpha residents such as Joe Christmas and Emily Grierson. Sherwood Anderson's character "grotesques" could also adapt in a Palahniuk setting (Wing Biddlebaum, Doctor Parcival, and the Reverend Hartman would easily acclimate). The irony at the end of Eugene O'Neill's *The Iceman Cometh* is not at all unfamiliar to Palahniuk fans. Any of the alcoholic working-class characters from Carver's stories—easily "Gazebo," "Careful," or "Chef's House"—would fit right into a Palahniuk location. Within this context, Palahniuk is naturally carrying out a literary legacy passed down from previous American writers, therefore continuing a truly indigenous tradition in American literature, although he presents a side of Americana, as Ellmann points out, that certainly is not that of Melville, Twain, and James. On Palahniuk's behalf, one must concede, using a bit of common sense, the American cultural landscape as well as the literary climate have fundamentally changed since the nineteenth century, which is Barth's point in his three essays. The best Palahniuk can do is to make what Melville, Twain, and James did in their fiction new for twenty-first-century readers. A current audience wants to read what relates to them, and Palahniuk captivates his audience because he serves this purpose, and he does so primarily through parody, essentially putting into practice Hutcheon's theoretical tenets to revitalize literature from the conservative old into the transgressive new. Looking ahead to Chapter Four about *Pygmy*, Americans have been promoting racial stereotypes since the beginning of its literary tradition. One only needs to read Mary Rowlandson's captivity narrative to see how she was an early promoter of the "red devil" racism toward Native Americans. Moreover, one only needs to consider the sensationalism of Rowlandson's published account, which went through many editions, when reading Chapter Five devoted to *Tell-All*. Concerning American fascination with romantic gossip, one just needs to refer to John Smith's embellished accounts of his encounters with the Powhatan and the famous intercession by Pocahontas, events which probably did not happen exactly as Smith alleges but surely supplied Disney and others content for countless media productions. Thinking about the continuity of the American literary tradition, Palahniuk is simply maintaining his unique connection with his literary past.

In an interview with Adam Lee Davies, one prompted by the publication of *Snuff*, Palahniuk says, "I want to explore what Tom Spanbauer [Palahniuk's writing mentor] calls 'dangerous writing,' which emphasizes that the only type of writing worth doing is the kind of writing that is confrontational and that is edgy. Anything else is a waste of time." In a response posted following Davies's interview, a respondent who obviously did not like *Snuff* scolds, "None of the usual intelligence or wit and it was obvious from the start what was going to happen." Another warns in capital letters, typographically shouting at the audience, "SNUFF IS A PATHETIC ATTEMPT AT TRYING TOO HARD." Earlier in that interview, Palahniuk mentions how the staging of the numbered men getting ready to go upstairs to meet Cassie is comparable to a scene in the movie *All That Jazz*: "I always thought of it as more like mortality: everyone being numbered but not knowing when their number would be called by Death—the woman at the top of the stairs in all the bright lights.... Barbara Hershey was Death, the beautiful woman dressed in white on the bed" ("Chuck Palahniuk Tells"). Knowing that Palahniuk possibly had *All That Jazz* in mind would probably not persuade the two respondents to like *Snuff* any better, but putting the novel in the context of this comparison (as a parody of the film) elevates the story above just something about an aging porn star wanting to become the queen of the gang bang. *Snuff* is much more complex than this reading. I hope the following chapters explain why Palahniuk's "dangerous writing" is, contrary to what some readers believe, anything but a waste of time and dispel the accusations against his style of fiction as just vulgar, obscene, or profane. Palahniuk is without question an extremely important contemporary American writer. The following interpretations of how Palahniuk applies postmodern parody will prove this declaration.

Two

Haunted as Parody of Boccaccio's *Decameron*

Initial reviews of Chuck Palahniuk's *Haunted* are not generally positive. Ken St. Andre writes, "Palahniuk casts aside all constraints in this twisted saga of antagonists without a protagonist. The short stories would work if taken singly and at intervals, but strung together they become a catalog of atrocities. Palahniuk is a clever and inventive writer, but this book is recommended only for public library readers with strong stomachs and morbid dispositions." A reviewer for *Publisher's Weekly* comments, "Palahniuk tells his story with such blithe disregard for these characters that it's hard not to wish he had dispensed with the novel altogether and published, instead, the 23 short stories that pop up throughout the book." A commentator for *Kirkus Reviews* warns, "Stomach-churning horror that takes a bit too much joy in its diabolic machinations." In an academic commentary, Sidney Sondergard recognizes the author's sociopolitical intentions but claims, "*Haunted*, then, presents Palahniuk's least individually developed cast of characters" (14–15). Of course, these types of reactions do not deter loyal Palahniuk fans from purchasing this book—they might even prompt them to get it—but the reviews are worth mentioning at the beginning of this chapter because they illustrate the critical reception Palahniuk often receives. For the most part, general magazine and trade journal reviewers do not seem to understand what Palahniuk is attempting to accomplish in his writing.

Recognizing Palahniuk's artistic inclination for experimenting with arrangement and form, *Haunted* is arguably, to disagree with these critics, Palahniuk's most elaborately constructed novel, although *Invisible Monsters Remix* competes for this distinction. This book may be his most intricate and complex, and considering *Haunted* was released as one in a series of three horror novels (along with *Lullaby* and *Diary*) and was marketed as a horror story, it also contains some of his most repulsive, disgusting, and offensive descriptions. Palahniuk frames the twenty-three stories with Brandon Whittier's three-month writer's colony in which nineteen participants describe true-life experiences as literary fiction, essentially blending realism and romance, calling into question what is true and what is imaginative.[1] Through a progression of introduction, poem, and story, each writer reveals a personal secret concerning individual dysfunction, matching his or her nickname with a perverse quality. As time during the retreat elapses inside an abandoned theater, the participants degenerate into self-mutilation and cannibalism, believing they can spin their collective experiences into fame and fortune once they are rescued and propelled into the media spotlight. Similar to many of Palahniuk's characters, they are obviously self-deceived, victims of their own solipsistic faith that they will be rewarded, with all the pomp and circumstance attached to celebrity, for their self-generated hardships and self-inflicted injuries. This is pronounced by the narrator in the book's final sentences, "For now we wait, repeating our story.... How Mr. Whittier trapped us here. He starved and tortured us. He killed us.... And someday soon, any day now, the world will come open that door and rescue us. The world will listen. Starting on that sun-glorious day, the whole world is going to love us" (404). Since the audience reads these words, at least the narrator's manuscript has survived the tragic enterprise of the writer's retreat, but nothing else is known concerning what ultimately happens to those remaining.

The stories are grotesque with excessive amounts of blood and gore, and the characters are stereotypical with predictable actions, but Palahniuk controls the interplay of the various texts rhetorically so that everything culminates into a unified theme concerning human motivation and self-exploitation. More to the point, Palahniuk displays the paradox associated with genuine self-introspection, the difficult job of digging deep into psychological repressions. The participants claim they want to look at themselves closely during the creative process while writing their novels, but this self-introspection results only in horrifically disastrous consequences: unfortunately, these characters get to see themselves for who they actually are. In this way, Tess Clark's "Post-Production" provides a thematic microcosm for all of the stories in *Haunted* when she sees through homemade porn how deformed, misshapen, and unattractive she and her husband actually are naked. As Mrs. Clark learns, people do not really want to see themselves for who they are, physically or psychologically. Through this setting, Palahniuk shows how famous-author aspirants believe that their so-called self-sacrifice—what they infer is selfless asceticism is only selfish flagellantism—will jump start their literary masterpieces, and all that they accomplish is the magnification of their insecurities and the exposure of their egotism. In short, the opposite of what they expect occurs: instead of producing their *magnum opus* pieces, they set up unrealistic expectations, reveal their worst character flaws, and are left with what might be the scariest results that they could ever imagine, the inner truths about themselves.

In the Palahniuk universe, this knowledge can be more of a curse than a gift. The 2005 book jacket advertises *Haunted* as "*The Real World* meets *Alive*. It draws from a great literary tradition—*The Canterbury Tales*, *The Decameron*, the English storytellers in the Villa Diodati who produced, among other works, *Frankenstein*—to tell an utterly contemporary tale of people desperate that their story be told at any cost." Although reviewers mention the apparent influence of Boccaccio upon Palahniuk, they do not explore in any depth the literary implications of Palahniuk's parody of *The Decameron*.[2] In an interview with C. P. Farley, Palahniuk admits that most of his ideas relate to common, ordinary, typical human experience, so he basically borrows content with which readers can identify and reproduces it through his brand of transgressive fiction: "I always think I deal with really typical things.... I really invent so little of what I put in my fiction. But finding ways to make it real in the world, or reinventing it and make it *seem* real again, I think I do that really well. But as far as overall originality, there's just not a whole lot there." Palahniuk's parody of *The Decameron* is an example of his signature transgressive "reinvention," and by recontextualizing the group of medieval storytellers in a twenty-first-century setting, Palahniuk portrays how no one can successfully rely on a geographical cure for soul-sickness, endorsing the message inferred through the aphorism "Wherever you go, you unfortunately take yourself with you."

In both *Haunted* and *The Decameron*, the participants escape apparently bleak and desperate situations for what they believe will be better alternatives. Most of Palahniuk's characters have committed actions from which they are fleeing either legal, political, or psychological consequences, and they take advantage of the writer's colony as an opportunity for a life change, to start over by becoming great writers. The only problem (and undeniably a major one) is that they really only want the stereotypically superficial rewards associated with this goal. They are both naïve and ignorant concerning the hard work the writer's craft demands. To escape the Black Death, Boccaccio's ten young people organize their own kind of storyteller's workshop to pass time by exchanging stories related mostly to the theme of love. Both Palahniuk's and Boccaccio's groups experiment with the transgressive by offering lustful, bawdy, erotically sensual stories, thoroughly provocative and decadent, relying upon sexual innuendo and farce, although the tellers never cross the line into overt pornography. In Boccaccio's stories, examples include the tenth tale on the third day in which a fourteen-year-old girl discovers sexually how to "put the devil into hell" and the sixth tale on the ninth day in which two lodgers "accidently" sleep with their host's wife and daughter. Palahniuk's most famous example (and his most notoriously grotesque one) is Saint Gut-Free's story "Guts," in which the speaker reports in graphic detail how his lower intestine was sucked into a pool pump while he was masturbating. Other examples in Palahniuk's stories include Mother Nature's account about being a high-priced foot-sex prostitute and Director Denial's tale about sex acts with life-like Russian dolls. In both sets of framed narratives, there are plenty of grossly and perversely provocative stories.

The settings for both *Haunted* and *The Decameron* serve as catalysts for the speakers to substitute their ordinary behaviors, ones that are in all likelihood socially appropriate and ethically moral, with actions that lend themselves to the transgressive. The introduction to *The Decameron* is renowned for its realistic depictions of Florence in 1348 during the bubonic plague, thoroughly describing with scientific precision the apple and egg-sized swellings associated with the physical manifestations of the illness in addition to explaining the diversity with which people tried at the onset to elude contamination and in the end to dispose of the dead. The narrator states, "In addition to this bestial behavior, they always managed to avoid the sick as best they could. And in this great affliction and misery of our city the revered authority of the laws, both divine and human, had fallen and almost completely disappeared, for, like other men, the ministers and executors of the laws were either dead or sick or so short of help that it was impossible for them to fulfill their duties; as a result, everybody was free to do as he pleased" (5–6). Consequently, many people sacrificed humble moderation for impulsive hedonism, satisfying their appetites rather than maintaining strict restraint, and the exorbitant amount of dead was provided irreverent burials lacking proper religious ceremony. In the theater, Whittier creates a similar environment. Not long after arriving, pregnant Miss America is the first of the volunteers to have second thoughts that this location will provide enough sanctuary from what she and the others were fleeing. As the narrator comments, "We'd walked into a trap. They worried someone might find us and.... They told Mr. Whittier they needed to keep moving, hiding, running to stay safe" (44). In *The Decameron*, the option for avoiding the Black Death is leaving Florence; in *Haunted*, the option for avoiding personal responsibility is joining the writing commune.

Both choices are equally deceptive and, in the long run, ineffective strategies. Although Palahniuk does not provide his characters with the same amenities Boccaccio's wealthy young people enjoy, there might be a rhetorical reason for the hardships his group faces. As Linda Hutcheon points out, postmodern parody promotes the similarities but emphasizes the differences between texts. Whittier's fake death provides the impetus for communal anarchy and triggers the physical self-mutilation and spiritual self-desecration, none of which appears in *The Decameron*.

The irony related to Palahniuk's characters' expectations demonstrates Hutcheon's theory of parodic irony. In *Irony's Edge*, Hutcheon states that irony is "the expression of an attitude" (40) and points out that "ironic meaning forms when two or more different concepts are brought together" (64). Palahniuk's characters construct, inadvertently as well as intentionally, their own dystopias. They may go into the writer's retreat assuming the experience will have romantically utopian qualities, but there is nothing but a naturalistic dystopian realty in what they receive. Whereas the participants of *The Decameron* flee disease—simultaneously their dis-ease with their boring lives as well as the bubonic plague—for a more comfortable holiday relaxing at their country homes, conversely the participants of *Haunted* choose to increase their hardships, their sacrifices, their internal psychological as well as external physical stresses for the glamor of exploitative sensationalism. Instead of fostering a utopian creative workshop, which they could have done, providing healthy opportunities to generate their literary masterpieces, they decide to manufacture their own artistic purgatories. They attempt to guarantee the requisite suffering for them to write cathartic confessions that will evoke instant cultural sympathy and popular stardom. Moreover, their tales frequently lack the comic, satirical, or humorous double entendre of many of those in *The Decameron*, especially Boccaccio's instances of sexual confusion, distraction, or coincidence. Palahniuk's stories are often funny because they are distasteful in the sick-joke way that Stephen King mentions in his benchmark essay published in *Playboy* about the horror genre, "Why We Crave Horror Movies": readers laugh and cringe simultaneously as they identify with the misfortunes of others (*Little* 686–87). In his conclusion, Boccaccio defends stories such as the one about the "Devil in Hell" for not containing any overtly obscene language (143–44), but this does not mean they are nevertheless crude or repulsive. On the other hand, Palahniuk never attempts to justify any of his descriptions in "Guts," which is obviously vulgar from the initial references to outrageous masturbation techniques to the final uncoiling of lower intestine as it is sucked into a particularly powerful pool device.[3] Consequently, there is no potential for a utopian happy ending (in the traditional sense) in *Haunted*. The participants' fate is bleak, and those who survive will face darker situations after the last page, even though they do not recognize this. As a result, Palahniuk's fiction is seemingly more pessimistic than even dirty realism along the lines of Charles Bukowski, Larry Brown, Denis Johnson, Raymond Carver, and Bobbie Ann Mason, or the topics of Paul Bowles or Palahniuk's favorites Brett Easton Ellis and Amy Hempel. And, of course, Palahniuk strives for what he terms "the hidden gun" or the "ticking clock" plot twists when the unexpected occurs, an ironic conclusion representative of existential reality or absurdist expectation when the outlandish and the far-fetched seem perfectly plausible ("Chuck Q&A").[4]

Palahniuk admits his stories in *Haunted* are drawn from various texts. In an interview with Sean O'Hagan, Palahniuk cites his primary inspiration as Poe's "The Masque of the Red Death." The epigraph for *Haunted* is taken directly from this Poe story: "There was much of the beautiful, much of the wanton, much of the *bizarre*, something of the terrible, and not a little of that which might have excited disgust." During the O'Hagan interview, Palahniuk comments about Poe, "He was obsessed with premature burial, for instance. I kept thinking, 'If Poe were alive today, what would be the everyday horrors he would write about?'" Palahniuk definitely creates the aura of entombment inside the windowless theater. Moreover, references to the Villa Diodati retreat of 1816 consistently remind readers of the famous ghost story party including Lord Byron, John Polidori (author of *The Vampyre*), Mary Shelley (author of *Frankenstein*), and Percy Bysshe Shelley, and this intertextuality is mentioned repeatedly throughout *Haunted*, but the underlying and understated comparison to *The Decameron* is much more significant. Poe likely borrowed ideas for his short story from Boccaccio's portrayal of how Florentines responded to the Black Death. Boccaccio's own story refers to Dante's *Inferno* in its subtitle. *Prencipe Galeotto*, or Prince Galehaut, is an intertextual reference to Lancelot's close friend who served as his messenger to Guinevere, and this relates to Canto V in which Dante fictionalizes a love tryst between Francesca and Paolo, sinners condemned to the level of the Lustful, who are reading the story of Lancelot and Guinevere (Bergin 160). This alludes to Boccaccio's assumed purpose in writing *The Decameron*, the promotion of women's rights, as well as sets up the motif of love in most of the stories.

A more likely reason for Palahniuk using the metaphor of Boccaccio's Black Death is to depict the existentially unsympathetic cosmos within which his characters live. In *Reading Chuck Palahniuk: American Monsters and Mayhem*, Cynthia Kuhn and Lance Rubin nail down the Palahniuk universe: "Buckle your seatbelt: to delve into Chuck Palahniuk's writing is to enter an unrelenting circus of pain. There will be blood and bruises, guts and gore. Palahniuk unflinchingly reveals the dark compulsions and actions of characters struggling to find fulfillment in a postmodern world where the Orwellian power of mass media and the crushing weight of the past make doing so all but impossible" (1). The frame constructed in both the "Author's Preface" and the "Author's Introduction" reveal Boccaccio's seemingly feminist agenda, summarizes realistically how citizens responded to the bubonic plague in 1348, and explains why ten young people would travel to their country homes in the Fiesole to spend ten nights over two weeks telling tales. The narrator states in the beginning, "Therefore, I wish to make up in part for the wrong done by Fortune, who is less generous with her support where there is less strength, as we witness in the case of our delicate ladies. As support and comfort for those ladies in love (to those others who are not I leave the needle, spindle, and wool winder), I intend to tell one hundred stories.... In these stories will be seen delightful as well as sad examples of love and other adventures" (2).[5] This introduction is famous for its candid descriptions of disease as well as its treatment of women as helpless without the guidance of men. On the other hand, Palahniuk's frame does not introduce such a defined purpose or refer to any biological epidemic (a surprise considering Palahniuk's penchant for informative factoids), although those who apply to the invitation posted on an Oregon café bulletin board for the writer's retreat are apparently afflicted with psychological and physical problems akin to disease, notably guilt, remorse, and shame, in addition to no lower intestines, no lips, and a pregnancy. Instead of fleeing the city to escape mass death, these participants volunteer to submit themselves to excruciatingly difficult self-examination. Even though Boccaccio relies upon an historical event as the stimulus for his characters' storytelling, Palahniuk's postmodern setting is just as caustic and debilitating as one dominated by plague. Although Palahniuk does not devote attention to a lengthy introduction as Boccaccio provides to set up the stories, there is ample information within the narrator's sections, the poems, and the stories to reveal the dismal circumstances from which the characters have fled.

Within both framed narratives, characters clearly portray what their names signify. Fans have discussed on the extremely active webpage *The Cult: The Official Chuck Palahniuk Website* the possible allegorical references in *Haunted*. One respondent attributes, for instance, qualities associated with the Seven Deadly Sins to the characters: all of the participants are avaricious; Guts-Free is lustful as well as gluttonous; Agent Tattletale is slothful; Miss America is envious in addition to vain; and The Chef is wrathful (Parkaboy). Unquestionably, the characters personify a variety of sins. Traditionally, Boccaccio's main characters have been delineated according to medieval numerological studies. In "The Frame Characters of the Decameron: *A Progression of Virtues*," Joan Ferrante asserts Boccaccio borrowed from Dante's *Purgatorio* Canto XXIX for signification, relating the Cardinal Virtues of Prudence, Temperance, Fortitude, and Justice to the seven women and the Theological Virtues of Faith, Hope, and Charity to the three men (214). According to Ferrante, "Pampinea represents faith; Fiammetta, Love; Filomena, Hope; Emilia, Prudence or Wisdom; Lauretta, Temperance; Nifile, Perseverance or Fortitude; and Elissa, Justice. Two of the men symbolize qualities which are also necessary to the proper development of the soul ... Filostrato, Despair or Dread; and Dioneo, Sensuality. Panfilo, the third man, is the embodiment of all the virtues, Nobility of Spirit or Virtue itself" (214). If Lady Fortune and her famous wheel are the organizing principles for *The Decameron*, fate is certainly the unspoken determinant for the circumstances in *Haunted*. Palahniuk's characters are at the retreat for what they hope to be good luck, and if they had been previously blessed with Fortune's gifts, those benefits were certainly fleeting. Boccaccio's arrangement has generally been based on sexual politics, the men telling lustful stories intended to woo and eventually to seduce the women, the women offering romantic stories tinged with moral principle to counteract the men's tales and to repulse their advances. According to this schema, if a story is particularly racy, probably a man tells it; if a story promotes caring and compassion, probably a woman narrates it. This story sequence has, of course, several deviations, and sometimes males tell stories not pertaining to sexuality.

Palahniuk is perhaps more straight-forward by allowing the name to dictate the gist of the teller's tale. For example, Lady Baglady narrates "Slumming" about her and her wealthy husband recreationally pretending to be homeless, only to witness the kidnapping of a Brazilian oil heiress. The key word "Baglady" connotes the basic meaning of the story, and the word sets up audience expectations. In *Illness as Metaphor*, Susan Sontag discusses how diseases were inaccurately interpreted as manifestations related to moral character traits, so cancer, for instance, could be a metaphor attached to a psychological problem, and if the problem were solved the metaphor and hence the illness could be erased. Whereas the storytellers in *The Decameron* flee the physiological devastation of the body by going into the country—they do not want Black Death, so they leave Florence— the participants in *Haunted* seem to cultivate their physical problems not only into subjects for their stories but as the means through which they are identified. In many cases, Palahniuk's characters have deformities (Saint Gut-Free's intestines, Clark's breasts, Baroness Frostbite's lips, etc.) that essentially serve as metaphors to reveal their character traits (and psychoses) in their stories, and they apparently embrace these abnormalities. In allegorical fashion, and imitating medieval tropes, Palahniuk reveals a character's personality through body type and name designation—the name fits the malady. Readers make assumptions, for instance, about Missing Link even before he begins his story. In short, both settings provide opportunities for readers to prejudge the characters solely based on their names. Considering Sontag's point, "Black Death" in Palahniuk's lexicon functions as a metaphor to describe his characters' spiritual aridity, and the characters do not relinquish ties to this affliction.

Both Boccaccio and Palahniuk provide exemplary models of transgressive fiction for their times. Boccaccio undoubtedly reacts against the organized church and clergy in many of his tales, and he presents fate as a secular rather than a religious entity. There is no wonder why many of his stories appeared in *Penthouse* magazine (as many of Palahniuk's have appeared in *Playboy*). Reacting against cultural, social, and political authority, transgressive literature typically straddles the line between the acceptable and the profane. As mentioned, many of Boccaccio's stories might lean toward the obscene. These include the seventh story on the second day when the Babylonian sultan's daughter claims she is still virginal after having sex with at least nine men, the third story on the seventh day in which a nun learns how to lie about her carnal experiences, the second story on the fourth day when Brother Alberto sleeps with a woman after pretending to be the angel Gabriel, among many others that deal with sexual liaisons, trysts, and mismatches. Palahniuk has sometimes been criticized for being too crude, too gross, and too disturbing in his sexual descriptions, and *Haunted* has plenty of instances to support these claims (the Matchmaker's cutting off his own penis is a vivid example). Although all of the stories in one way or another deal with human connectedness, sexuality is definitely a feature in most of them: Mrs. Clark's initial story is about a homemade porn movie plan that flopped, the Matchmaker's story describes how a German concentration camp officer slices off his own penis during public fellatio, Comrade Snarky's story addresses how a group of feminists assault a post-operative transsexual who attends one of their meetings, and even the retreat's organizer, Brandon Whittier, offers a story about his blackmailing caregivers who have sex with him out of sympathy for his progeria, which makes him appear elderly at only thirteen.

Both Boccaccio and Palahniuk have defended their transgressive depictions of sexuality against censorship. Boccaccio's apologia in the "Author's Conclusion" is a famous response against criticism that he used inappropriate language. Boccaccio writes, "There will, perhaps, be some among you who will say that I have taken too much license in writing these tales; that is, I have sometimes made ladies say things, and more often listen to things, which are not very proper for virtuous ladies to say or hear. I deny this, for nothing is so indecent that it cannot be said to another person if the proper words are used to convey it; and this, I believe, I have done very well" (143). Boccaccio offers points in his polemic that could invariably promote Palahniuk's own creative choices: "And if there should be a few expressions or little words in them that are somewhat freer than a prude might find proper … let me say that it is no more improper for me to have written these words than for other men and women to have filled their everyday conversation with such words as 'hole,' 'peg,' 'mortar,' 'pestle,' 'sausage,' 'Bologna sausage,' and other similar expressions" (143–44). Boccaccio argues these words might be misinterpreted by a maladjusted mind; therefore, indecency is basically an issue related to perception rather than content (144–47). Granted, many of the stories in *Haunted* are shocking, perhaps even revolting or distasteful, but what makes these so disconcerting is their relevance. Thomas Bergin asserts Boccaccio addresses the "middle-class contingent" and the "emergence of the proletariat" through his identification with women and with merchants (162). Palahniuk's own defense of his transgressive language is similar to Boccaccio's apologia, both writers arguing profanity, obscenity, and vulgarity are related more to readers' perceptions than writers' words. Palahniuk confesses in *Stranger Than Fiction* that a dominant theme in his work is "a lonely person looking for some way to connect with other people" (xv).[6] Palahniuk's appeal is that he writes to an expansive middle-class as well as working-class readership by presenting subjects that are significant to them. In the interview with O'Hagan, Palahniuk comments about his readers, "There are people out there who will not read books, but somehow they'll read my books. They serve them in a way most fiction doesn't. I give them a less filtered form of entertainment. I acknowledge some unacknowledged parts of our lives, which, as a culture, we don't tend to talk about." The sexual stories in particular resonate on an instinctual level with this audience, and many of the stories in *The Decameron* could be placed, with appropriate alterations, into *Haunted*. This is certainly true for the seventh story on the eighth day in which a scholar takes revenge upon a widow who has scorned him by forcing her to spend an entire July day naked at the top of a tower, brutally burned by the sun and incessantly stung by insects, or the numerous stories in which daughters and fathers have questionable sexual encounters or when there are all kinds of sexual shenanigans amidst wedding ceremonies. For the most part, both writers cater to readers who are marginalized and disenfranchised, and even though their stories contain both extremes of humor and horror, they also raise questions about personal empowerment.

In this sense, Palahniuk's parody of Boccaccio emphasizes the difference between divine justice and human self-determination. Boccaccio was interested in the Lady Fortune's role in maintaining the mysterious ebb and flow of fate that balances terrestrial good and evil. By fleeing the Black Death in Florence and establishing sanctuary in Fiesole, where wealthy Florentines maintained villas, the ten young people took the initiative to at least geographically, although the distance was only a few miles, separate themselves from the immoral atrocities precipitated by social collapse. The sophisticated ensemble could continue their sense of taste and decorum through ten days of carefully organized storytelling, and the tales reflect the social status of the authors as well as depict their belief in Lady Fortune's unequivocal egalitarianism. Examples of this trust include many of the stories during the second day that focus on happy endings, such as the third tale when a young man spends his wealth only to have it replenished after he unknowingly marries an English princess; the fourth tale in which a young man is poor, turns pirate, is shipwrecked, and becomes wealthy; and the eighth tale that depicts how a count who is wrongly accused is able to return to his rank. Other days include similar stories full of both good and bad consequences prompted by coincidence, accident, and serendipity. In fact, most of Boccaccio's tales deal with the theme of chance in one form or fashion. Palahniuk inverts the function of fate in his stories as characters move beyond global geographic relocation toward direct manipulation of their personal physical spaces by not only severing body parts but by sabotaging their supplies, breaking their plumbing, and wrecking their furnace. Palahniuk's characters take control of their destinies one step (maybe more) farther than their Italian counterparts, and they believe their Lady Fortune needs some assistance to ensure their fates are correctly fulfilled. Tragically, Palahniuk's group is predestined for failure, and even though the stories do not always have negative endings, none of them completely imitate the positive ones in several of Boccaccio's tales. There are just not many happy endings on Palahniuk's side.

A comparison of two stories demonstrate Palahniuk's opposite take on Boccaccio's view of fate, illustrating Palahniuk's parodic focus on difference rather than similarity. In the first story on the first day, during which Queen Pampinea decides on an open subject, Panfilo, one of the gentlemen, tells the story of Ser Ciappelletto. The narrator begins prepping his "Dearest Ladies" for a spiritual tale, one demonstrating an occurrence of God's "marvelous deeds" (18). Panfilo introduces his story as one about human limitation and the celestial nature of God's grace: "Nor should we believe that such special grace descends upon us and within us through any merit of our own, but rather it is sent by his own kindness and by the prayers of those who, like ourselves, were mortal and who have now become eternal and blessed with him, for they followed his will while they were alive" (18). The subject of this parable is a horribly nefarious notary whose sins include fabricating legal documents, giving false testimonies, instigating communal discord, in addition to the more heinous crimes of stealing, assaulting, blaspheming, and even murdering (19). In addition, there is the insinuation of homosexuality: "he was, in fact, more fond of men [than of women], more so than any other degenerate" (19). In short, Panfilo points out, "He was probably the worst man that ever lived!" (20). While Ser Ciappelletto was carrying out corruption for his client Messer Musciatto, he became ill and was forced to make death-bed decisions (20–21). At this point of the story, Panfilo describes how Ser Ciappelletto tricked a priest into believing he had never been lustful, gluttonous, avaricious, wrathful, mendacious, among other sins, and his greatest sin for which he was sincerely contrite was cursing his mother (23–25). Ser Ciappelletto's caretakers clearly recognized the deceit, but the friar took the confession at face value and raised the sinner's social currency upon death to saintly value: "he fixed Ser Ciappelletto so firmly in the minds and the devotions of all those who were present there that after the service was over, everyone pressed forward to kiss the hands and feet of the deceased, and all his garments were torn off his corpse, since anyone who could get a hold on a piece of them considered himself blessed" (27). Panfilo concludes, noting the saint is probably serving in hell, but "if this is the case, we can recognize the greatness of God's mercy towards us, who pays more attention to the purity of our faith than to our errors by granting our payers in spite of the fact that we choose his enemy as our intercessor" (28). To put the message bluntly, trust should be put in God, "Him who began our storytelling" (28), to see through the deceit into the veracity of the heart.

Palahniuk's version of this story does not conclude at such a romantically ethical place. The poem "Trade Secrets" foreshadows the Earl of Slander's story "Swan Song" by undercutting the value of his Pulitzer Prize in journalism by exposing the manner in which it was achieved: "A journalist has a right… / …and a duty, to destroy / those golden calves he helps create" (39–41). Whereas Panfilo begins with a description of Ser Ciappelletto's immoral character, the Earl of Slander introduces Kenny Wilcox, former child star Danny from *Danny-Next-Door* turned average veterinarian, as conservatively moral, possessing obvious humility and noticeable compassion. The Earl of Slander irreverently calls Wilcox "my savior" (92), elevating him as someone to save this dog Skip but at the same time preparing this "faded star" (93) for a fall. Instead of giving all power to a higher entity, the Earl of Slander emphasizes his potential as final arbiter concerning how Wilcox will be perceived by his peers, and this capability has nothing to do with religion or God. Whereas the priest listens to Ser Ciappelletto's confession, the Earl of Slander interviews Wilcox. In this way, Boccaccio allows Ser Ciappelletto to create a fiction full of preposterous lies to serve his spiritual agenda, and Palahniuk enables the Earl of Slander to construct a fiction that is a pastiche of clichés related to Hollywood child-star suicides. Ser Ciappelletto manipulates for religious sainthood; the Earl of Slander manipulates for journalistic fame. In both cases, truth is forfeited in favor of a lie that will lead toward gain, equally desirable salvation or stardom. While defining *schadenfreude*, the Earl of Slander confesses his motivation for bestowing the degenerate image upon Wilcox, "Our purest joy comes when people we envy get hurt" (94), and his preparation to carry this out is fueled by pure resentment: "For prep, the whole week before we talk, I surf the Internet. I download files from the former Soviet Union. Here's a different kind of child star: Russian schoolboys without pubic hair, sucking off fat old men. Czech girls still waiting for their first period, getting butt-fucked by monkeys. I save all these files to one thin compact disk" (96). After the Earl of Slander drugs Wilcox and then sets up the suicide, he becomes a strong contender for Ser Ciappelletto's title "worst man." The Earl of Slander writes a story that demonizes Wilcox, completely revising the veterinarian's identity. At the conclusion of this tale, Boccaccio has Panfilo question whether Ser Ciappelletto accomplished his goal; at the end of this story, Palahniuk leaves the Earl of Slander seemingly to question what he might have sacrificed for his goal. Both authors address truth, ethics, and morality, but Palahniuk's version leaves the door open for skepticism concerning the authority of divine justice. Several other stories in *Haunted* have comparable plots in *The Decameron*, and as in this case, they have been updated and subverted to fit a contemporary context and audience.

Palahniuk treats the nature of reality and art in perhaps the most chilling of the stories, Tess Clark's "The Nightmare Box," which actually provides a metaphor to explain the problems confronting all of the retreat's participants. In this story, Clark's daughter Cassandra has looked inside and seen something that takes away all of her energy, drive, and will to live. No specific description is given for what Cassandra sees, but Clark describes how her daughter starts to isolate herself, becomes increasingly despondent, and eventually succumbs to an apathetic death by just giving up. After Cassandra looked in the box, she participated in an earlier Whittier retreat, and Clark has joined the current one to find out what her daughter experienced. There is insinuation that inside the Nightmare Box is the reflection of the worst people could possibly see in themselves, or, put another way, a glimpse into what they actually are, either way apparently a devastating vision. A crucial point concerning the box is that its ticking is seemingly random—in fact functioning by a Random Interval Timer (212)—and the moment when it presents the opportunity for viewing cannot be predicted. As Clark mentions, "It could run for a month, always ticking. Or it could run for another hour. But the moment it stopped, that would be the moment to look inside" (214). Shopkeeper Rand reports the box had remained ticking for nine years without ceasing (215). There are two incidents cited during which a twenty-year-old college student looked into the box and became, by all functional standards, paralyzed with insects moving freely throughout his clothes and his nails growing long and yellow (215), and a former store owner hung himself after resisting a look into the box for as long as he could stand (217). Fate, fortune, or even destiny appears to control the availability of the vision in the box; no one has control to mandate exactly when a viewing will occur, as is evident by many people looking into the box unsuccessfully before Cassandra. Her moment seems fortuitous but could have been determined by design, inspired by a force operating within a universe that serves as a great equalizer, comparable to Dame Fortune, maintaining a balance of power. Cassandra looked into stark, unadulterated, blindingly harsh reality within her own soul, something that can only be felt in one's inner core and is too overwhelming to be articulated or expressed. In what might be the crucial spot in the novel, Rand attempts to explain that what he saw in the box "is a glimpse of the real reality": "It's something that goes beyond life-after-death. What's in the box is proof that what we call life isn't. Our world is a dream. Infinitely fake. A nightmare" (222). A possibility could be that all of the patrons of Mr. Whittier's commune are getting a glimpse into this reality through the nightmarish setting inside the theater, but only the nightmare box is capable of transmitting its raw truth, which none of the characters are capable of receiving. Metaphorically, the box compares to the theater, and to refer to Shakespeare's famous line in *The Tempest*, what is perceived as "a dream" is just the realistic stuff from which the dream is made, and, to carry this forward, there is no dream, only bare reality.

To reiterate, irony is a key feature concerning Palahniuk's imitation of *The Decameron*. As with the Nightmare Box, Palahniuk exposes humanity at its horrifyingly worst in *Haunted*. All of the stories seen in their entirety, as one collective vision, might provide the closest glimpse possible into the agent of paralysis lurking inside the Nightmare Box. This is communicated through Palahniuk's undisguised words at the end of the book. There is a reason why the two nameplates on the box are "The Nightmare Box" and "Roland Whittier," the same last name as the host. At the end, Brandon Whittier states, "Telling a story is how we digest what happens to us.... It's how we digest our lives. Our experience" (380). Later, the narrator, whose identity is never revealed, responds,

> Other events—the ones you can't digest—they poison you. Those worst parts of your life, those moments you can't talk about, they rot you from the inside out. Until your Cassandra's wet shadow on the ground. Sunk in your own yellow protein mud. But the stories that you can digest, that you can tell—you can take control of those past moments. You can shape them, craft them. Master them. And use them to your own good. Those are stories as important as food. Those are stories you can use to make people laugh or cry or sick. Or scared. To make people feel the way you felt. To help exhaust that past moment for them and for you. Until that moment is dead. Consumed. Digested. Absorbed. It's how we can eat all the shit that happens [380].

In terms of causality, the flash of "real reality" spurs Cassandra's desire to become a writer (347), and she apparently was motivated to express what Rand attempted through his analogy of releasing doves at a company picnic to what he witnessed in the box (221). Ironically, these participants fail to reconcile their past with their present through the telling of their stories. These survivors wait passively for someone to create a "Mythology of Us" (404), to manufacture almost a facsimile of what must have happened during their three-month ordeal. They wish for media coverage to broadcast how their severe deprivation served as a catalyst to artistic creative brilliance, but this report will only reflect a "Museum of Us" (404) showing that their tragic demise was only caused by their own vices. As a textual account of their experiences, *Haunted* reveals them for what they actually are, just a bunch of dysfunctional people trying to run away from themselves. Betrayal is perhaps the one theme that unifies all of the stories, and there is little reason to believe the survivors will not be betrayed one last time and, remaining self-deceived, die truly unfortunate deaths. Clark discovers the idea Whittier expresses at the end of *Haunted* in response to the question why all of those remaining will not leave the theater after they are released, after they are no longer essentially prisoners: "We always do this ... for the same reason our children's children's children's children will always have war and famine and disease. Because we love our pain. We love our drama. But we will never, ever admit that" (382). Clark writes in her notes that the Nightmare Box either hypnotizes, implants, sublimates, or reprograms a viewer's brain, infecting it in some manner so as to "make everything you know wrong. Useless" (220). Considering the paradox related to self-introspection, Whittier offers a profound comment, "You, the victim of yourself" (102). The Nightmare Box reveals a devastating self-knowledge that is so brutally honest it incapacitates and, in most instances, precipitates the viewer's self-destruction. In the Palahniuk cosmos, nothing ironically can be at the same time more awful or more exhilarating than "you" being the "victim of yourself," depending upon how one processes the revelation.

Palahniuk's speaker in the narrative's frame is never revealed, but either this person survived the ordeal or the entire manuscript was found. Relatively early in the novel, when Whittier supposedly eats what is comparable to ten turkey dinners (104), this narrator mentions how Whittier and Clark talked about the Villa Diodati and other topics "not to bore us to death" (100). This narrator realizes humans assess their actions based on faulty assumptions. People deceive themselves into believing their lives are laid out through a series of good, positive, and optimistic experiences. The truth is, however, these events are the anomalies: the bad, negative, and pessimistic moments govern human existence, and these are what determine the course of most peoples' lives. As the narrator states, "No, we love war. War. Starvation. Plague. They fast-track us to enlightenment" (100). This person comments, "It's the mark of a very, very young soul, Mr. Whittier used to say, to try and fix the world. To try and save anyone from their ration of misery" (100). *The Decameron* still resonates so well with modern readers because of its honest depiction of the human condition, and if there is one message that can be taken from all of the tales as a whole, this might be never to underestimate the importance of chance. Palahniuk is offering a similar commentary in *Haunted*. As the narrator proclaims, "No, the best story we'd bring out of this building would be just how we survived" (100). "Survival" is the key word because surviving might be good enough in the Palahniuk universe. If this book is indeed comparable to reality shows such as *Survivor, Big Brother*, even *Naked and Afraid* or any other similar program, what is forgotten is that help is always waiting in the wings during those episode tapings. Support staff will rush in if there are major problems. A better comparison to reality programming might be *Intervention*. Even though help is an option, some participants do not select it, and death is always the underlying reality in every episode. In *Haunted*, there is absolutely no support staff, so they must help themselves if there are any chances for their recoveries.

Regardless how *Haunted* was received upon publication, this work might be the most definitive in terms of presenting the Palahniuk philosophy related to the basic human paradox of perception and reality. Although the format for the book could resemble contemporary reality show situations and mimic the events at the Villa Diodati, the content of the frame narrative as well as within the stories delve much deeper into the conflicts of the psyche than any reality program, and references to Byron, Shelley, and Poe mostly serve as allusive diversions to construct the authentic literary crust on top of the pseudo-intellectual writing workshop that functions as the setting. Relating *Haunted* to *The Decameron* provides a more effective avenue to access Palahniuk's overriding theme in this book. At the end of Boccaccio's story, there is no declaration that the ten young people will live happily ever after. Logically, no one can really outrun disease, particularly one as deadly as the Black Death. In Poe's "The Mask of the Red Death," no one survives the disease from which Prospero believed he had successfully defended himself. Just as those in Boccaccio's and Poe's stories, Palahniuk's participants are only biding their time until the inevitable occurs. Boccaccio writes in his conclusion, "I must confess, however, that the things of this world have no stability whatsoever—they are constantly changing, and this might have happened with my tongue" (147). In comparison, Whittier comments, "You are permanent, but this life is not.... The irony is, if you can accept that—you'll never suffer again. Instead, you'll run toward torture. You'll enjoy pain" (103). The narrator adds, "Mr. Whittier had no idea he was so right" (103). Undoubtedly, Palahniuk assumes the role of Boccaccio as well as donning the persona of the narrator in his own work.

As *Haunted* begins, the narrator stresses how the participants have gathered to complete their perfect stories, their masterpieces, and as the individual stories are told, these take secondary importance to their primary plan of constructing their experiences held hostage in the theater. The ultimate irony is that they never realize that their stories, just as those of Boccaccio's characters, are more important than their actual existence, and they are, unfortunately, insignificant and expendable whereas their ideas (what readers view in *Haunted*) are not. Perhaps this is the true message inside the Nightmare Box. Cassandra only wanted to be a writer after looking into the box. Perhaps she saw a vision of the insignificance of her life in the universal scheme of things. This might sound pessimistic, but it is actually pragmatic. There is an old saying reminding people not to take themselves too seriously because, in the larger cosmic plan, they are just not as important as they believe. There is another saying that is relevant in this instance: "I may not be much, but I am all that I think about." The ideas in the stories have the lasting transcendence, and in this way, the participants of Mr. Whittier's writing retreat did accomplish something amazing: their stories outlasted them and resonate in ways that they could not. In this manner, they left their marks on the world.

Three

"True fact": Hyperreality in *Snuff*

Throughout *Snuff*, Chuck Palahniuk routinely states the words "true fact" immediately after any section that provides culturally arcane information. These sections include Palahniuk's characteristic factoids consisting of interesting but seemingly irrelevant encyclopedic minutiae. Of course, the adjective "true" attached to the noun "fact" is a redundant qualifier; a "fact" is already "true," and the juxtaposition of these two words does not increase the fundamental meaning of anything purporting to be valid, actual, or, in its essential form, real. In Palahniuk's fictive textual universe, however, the pairing "true fact" serves an extremely important epistemological function. Palahniuk applies "true fact" to address the theoretical issue at the heart of his novel, what constitutes the real or—to continue the adjectival redundancy—the emphatic real, or to apply a more appropriate postmodern term, the hyperreal. In a sense, information that is a "true fact" is one level beyond anything that is merely a "fact," and the descriptor "true" adds an extra layer of validation to convince readers toward unconditional acceptance of what is presented. In this way, Palahniuk repeats the phrase "true fact" to promote the hyperreality initiated in *Snuff*.

As mentioned in the previous chapters, readers often depend upon Palahniuk choosing subjects outside the mainstream, even counting on the offensive and the vulgar, and this gives Palahniuk the freedom to play with audience expectations. In *Snuff*, Palahniuk does not disappoint. He treats a subject that is definitely counterculture by tying it to forms of entertainment that are thoroughly mainstream. Most readers will know little about pornography, and Palahniuk relies upon this to both reinforce and revise traditional cultural stereotyping. He portrays the seedy, insensitive, exploitative porn industry most readers would anticipate, but he then undermines this presentation through intertextual references to the regular film industry, subsequently verifying these new presentations with his stamp of authenticity, "true fact." On the surface, *Snuff* is about aging porn star Cassie Wright retiring with a bang, literally a record-setting gang bang in which she will have sex on film with over 600 men. The narrative exchanges between the three male performers and the female coordinator focus on the likelihood Cassie will die during the event (thus the novel's title) and the possibility that Cassie's son (whom she supposedly gave up for adoption) is one of the participants. Critics have correctly pointed out the novel addresses mature content but is not pornographic—the sex described on almost every page is mechanistic, passionless, and pedestrian, without any sensuality or romance—and they have accurately commented that Palahniuk describes the production of pornography realistically. Keir Graff states there are "indistinct voices and characterizations, repetitiveness, and research that's not integrated but quoted from one character to another" (30); Neil Hollands writes, "Don't expect titillation here: every detail underlines the degradations of sexual obsession and the pornography industry" (78); a commentator for *Kirkus Reviews* reports, "After reading the novel ... it might be difficult for anyone to become aroused from watching pornography or find any redeeming social value in it"; and most of the others poke fun at Palahniuk and/or his plot.[1] There is nothing titillating or enticing about Cassie's oral, vaginal, and anal experiences during the sexual marathon or detailed in her previous films. In this novel, Palahniuk relates the action to porn culture as well as to Hollywood folklore, and these "true facts" in turn provide the construction of reality necessary for Cassie's own porn mythology to assume hyperreal status. The refrain "true fact" reminds readers that reality in the novel consistently must be validated by other referents (by references to what is "true" outside of the text), and this verification by proxy establishes hyperreality. Thus, Palahniuk applies postmodern parody to move beyond just a comparison between porn and mainstream film by showing the similarity but emphasizing the difference.

To understand how Palahniuk accomplishes this, a definition of hyperreality in terms of literary criticism is needed, and Jean Baudrillard provides the seminal theoretical framework. In *Simulacra and Simulation*, Baudrillard contends there is a four stage process by which art distances itself from its initial referent to become "simulacra," simulations of the original that have lost, through various reproductions, their inherent connection to the actual entity.[2] Any replication inevitably causes distortion, and the imitation is comparable in category or classification but may only vaguely resemble (if at all) whatever is represented. Because the reproduction is sometimes

Three. "True fact": Hyperreality in **Snuff** 39

perceived as an improvement, the simulation is often preferred over the original. According to Baudrillard, art first simulates reality. Second, art distorts reality. Third, art promotes the absence of reality. Finally, art assumes no relationship to reality, achieving hyperreality in which images are dependent upon their subsequent reproductions instead of upon the original referent. Baudrillard states, "It is no longer a question of imitation, nor duplication, nor even parody. It is a question of substituting the signs of the real for the real, that is to say of an operation of deterring every real process via its operational double, a programmatic, metastable, perfectly descriptive machine that offers all the signs of the real and short-circuits all its vicissitudes" (*Simulacra* 2).[3] In this view, there is a sequence of imitations emanating from an original, and the greater the distance from the original, the more distortion there will be in the imitations.

Palahniuk demonstrates this complex theory through his simulations of sexuality. The initial referent is basically the sexual act, and everything following emanates from this starting place, sexual copulation. The historic gang bang is, simplified to its primary components, comprised of reproductions of the human act of sexual coitus. The benchmark event serving as the first presentation of sexual intercourse chronologically in the novel is Branch Bacardi lacing Cassie's drink with betaketamine and Demerol and filming their sexual intercourse (185). The dysfunction of this event is exacerbated by Branch's remembrance of his sexual debacle with Brenda, a high school girlfriend he appears to have loved but lost by urinating in her vagina (per advice by his father as a no fault birth control method) after their first intimacy (155–58). Both sexual events are certainly anti-romantic, and they are the first two mentioned in Branch's and Cassie's sexual histories. In terms of sequence, this event initiates Cassie's sex-on-film career and sets the precedent for her subsequent sexual performances. Hence, all of Cassie's sex acts in her movies are reproductions of the first time that she was filmed with Branch, and these simulations from Cassie's films are shown continuously on overhead monitors in the performer bullpen to motivate the participants. Palahniuk intersperses within character dialogue references to actual porn stars and porn films in addition to inserting allusions to actual Hollywood personalities and major films, comparing the behavior of adult film actors to mainstream movie icons. This sets up the pattern that establishes the chain leading to hyperreality. Seen another way, Hollywood films introduce the first level of sexual simulation, and they are then imitated through porn film adaptations. In this sequence, Hollywood provides the screenplays that are transformed into porn scripts, and Palahniuk offers references to Hollywood actors who are imitated by porn performers. Moreover, Palahniuk has Cassie's sexual performances simulate ones previously depicted in both Hollywood and porn films, making the progression of copies move from real Hollywood to real porn to fictional Cassie, and, as will be discussed, there are additional copies of Cassie. Ultimately, Palahniuk presents what Baudrillard calls simulacra, when reproduction imitates reproduction and therefore achieves hyperrealism. By the end of *Snuff*, truth is no longer dependent upon reality but upon the simulations of simulations, and Palahniuk counts on the two words "true fact" to substantiate the validity of this hyperreality. The fusion of Cassie and Branch in the final scene is the epitome of hyperreality: the two symbolically become the sexual figuration that has defined their lives, metaphorically providing the consummation of all their previous sex acts, essentially physical distortions of their individual selves, indistinguishable as separate entities. In fact (pardon the pun), Palahniuk illustrates the total transcendence from the real to the hyperreal, and no other novel may more graphically display Baudrillard's theory.

To affirm this point, Palahniuk's presentation of Mr. 72's childhood sexual history reinforces his application of Baudrillard's theory. Mr. 72 only reveals his full name, Darin Johnson, when the gang bang is concluding. His identity as a number—as well as that of the other two major male narrators—emphasizes his function as just another worker on the man-meat line to manufacture the skin-flick product. As a teenager, he was caught masturbating to Cassie Wright porn on the Internet by his foster mother, who revealed Cassie is his birth mother (87). This set the stage (literally) for Mr. 72's obsessive belief that he is Cassie's notorious porn baby. Contrary to what most would do after discovering such information, Mr. 72 purchases a Cassie Wright replica vagina and constantly fondles the object while at school (82). He next purchases a replica of Cassie's left breast, pointing out it is the better one of her two (82–83). His comments are both hilarious and disturbing, and they illustrate how the imitation is almost as appropriate as the original for his purposes: "Nighttime, I'd squeeze my breast replica. Rub the dusty nipple against my lips. Lick it. Tweak it between my two fingers until I fell asleep" (83). Mr. 72's obsession with the fabricated Cassie, her mass-marketed reproduction, leads to his purchasing a plastic Cassie Wright sex doll, with which he is caught having sex while imitating Lloyd George in a pirated copy of *World Whore One* (86). The vagina, breast, and doll are simulacra serving as surrogates for the real Cassie Wright, sexual stand-ins toward which Mr. 72 can direct his desire. As Mr. 72 attempts to mitigate the fake with the real, however, he cannot achieve true intimacy (e.g., he simply cannot get, for obvious reasons, the plastic Cassie to function as the actual Cassie), but he is capable, nonetheless, of satisfying his carnal needs. When he performs in the gang bang, the real Cassie (the flesh-and-blood woman) takes precedence over the hyperreal Cassie (the manufactured sexual replacement). Mr. 72 is disappointed Cassie is not his porn-star mother, but he still has intercourse with her because she is an attractive woman, and, to be honest, he just wants to orgasm. He actually becomes sexually rapacious, so enthusiastic that Cassie begs her assistants to get him off of her (167).

In terms of reproductions of objects, Palahniuk offers several examples to call attention to the intricacies of simulation. Palahniuk stresses the attention to detail Mr. 72's father gave to his model train set (34–36). He also describes manufactured appendages: "Accurate down to Cassie's episiotomy scar. Bacardi's every vein and wart. The way people used to make death masks, casting plaster faces of celebrities in the hours between their demise and their decomposition.... How's it feel seeing your dick and balls, or your clit and cunt flaps, cloned a zillion times and sitting on the shelf behind some gum-chewing porn-store clerk? Or, worse, your most private bits heaped in some bargain bin" (41). Furthermore, Palahniuk refers to varieties of simulation through the Greek and Roman phalluses kept in the Vatican (44). Palahniuk clearly calls attention to the intricacies involved in the process of simulation, and evidence of synthetic phalluses and vaginas only demands an easy Internet search. To emphasize the utility of sex simulacra, Palahniuk mentions the vibrator was first marketed in the 1890s and was the third electrified appliance behind the sewing machine and fan. As Mr. 137 comments, housework is obviously less important than sexual satisfaction (44–45). Palahniuk also cites Hitler as the initial promoter of the modern sex doll, one with blond hair and large breasts, to satisfy Aryan soldiers far from females. Assistant and organizer Sheila points out the Allied firebombing of Dresden destroyed the factory before mass distribution. After this information, Palahniuk adds, "True fact" (49).

The first stage of simulation is related to Hollywood, or more specifically, how iconic celebrities imitated (or tried to imitate) reality both on and off camera. In this sense, art simulates reality. Palahniuk uses Cassie as a vehicle to explain how Hollywood icons struggled to maintain appropriate reflective images of reality. Cassie tells Sheila how Norma Talmadge, John Gilbert, Mary Pickford, and Karl Dane, among others, could not make the transition between silent and talking films because their voices were not suitable. Sheila notes that these powerful personalities just vanished because viewers did not want to hear their real voices, concluding with "True fact" (47–48). Cassie mentions how Terry who played Toto in

The Wizard of Oz broke his leg and was off the set for two weeks, following this detail with "True fact" (69–70). After offering information about Buddy Ebsen's allergic reaction to aluminum paint and losing his job to Jack Haley, Cassie tells Sheila that Terry, stuffed and mounted, was sold in 1996 for $8,000, afterward the words "True fact" (74). Perhaps the best illustration of how a Hollywood actress attempted to maintain her on-screen image is Lucille Ball. Cassie explains that Ball would not agree to alter her appearance surgically, so she wrapped her hair around toothpicks and then secured them to a wig cap that would tightly keep her facial skin pulled back. Cassie comments that Lucille Ball was in agony during many of the times audiences saw her laughing and smiling, following this information with "True fact" (122). Cassie mentions Lon Chaney blinded himself in one eye by fitting an egg membrane over his iris to appear blind in *Phantom of the Opera*, mentioning "True fact" (125). Cassie reports that when Rudolph Valentino died because of various health problems in 1926, an elevator boy at the Ritz Hotel in Paris poisoned himself, as did a London girl; two women outside the Polyclinic Hospital, where Valentino died, slit their wrists; and two Japanese women jumped into a live volcano. She adds, "True fact" (147–48). Cassie also describes the uncommon deaths and burials of Ernie Kovacs, Bela Lugosi, Walt Disney, Greta Garbo, Marlon Brando, Peter Lawford, Wallace Reid, and Marie Prevast—a star with no movie voice who drank herself to death only to have her dachshund Maxie chew on her corpse for days until management found the body (150–51).

All of these are presented as "true facts." After he explains how Rock Hudson was discovered, Mr. 137 confesses, "I love that Cassie Wright knew that bit of Hollywood history. The fact that we both knew so much of the same trivia ... that made me fall in love with her" (183). Additional references illustrate the abundance of Hollywood information in this novel. In 1952 Gene Kelly danced with a fever of 103° in *Singing in the Rain*; in 1973, Oliver Reed was stabbed in the throat on the set of *The Three Musketeers* and almost bled to death; and Lorne Greene had an alligator bite off his nipple in *Lorne Greene's New Wilderness* (72–73). In 1944, Marlene Dietrich bronzed her legs with copper paint for the movie *Kismet* and almost died from lead poisoning (120). Tallulah Bankhead and Lauren Bacall ground eggshells and mixed them with water to make their voices low and raspy, and Barbara Stanwyck rubbed Elmer's white glue on her face for the lactic acid to loosen dead skin cells (123). Dolores del Rio daubed grape Jell-O on her nipples to stain them dark, and Rita Hayworth used strawberry Jell-O to make her nipples pink. Betty Grable sprayed hairspray on her breasts and hips to keep her swimsuit on her body (124). Jeff Chandler died of complications involving a minor operation, and Eric Fleming died in the Amazon: the current caught Fleming, and the "piranha finished the job. Cameras still rolling. True fact" (149). Richard Burton was almost electrocuted touching a lizard in *Night of the Iguana*, "True fact" (176). Marilyn Monroe sat naked for hours in a tub of crushed ice to have "stand-up tits and ass" (183) for public appearances.

The second stage of simulation relates to actual porn stars and how their lives mirror those of their Hollywood counterparts. In this way, art distorts reality. Most pornography produced by the major companies— Vivid Entertainment, Wicked Pictures, Naughty America, New Sensations, to list a few—include developed plotlines that are often imitations of feature films or television shows. New Sensation remakes include *Scrubs*, *The Office*, *The Breakfast Club*, and *The Big Lebowski*, for example. Whereas romance in film depends upon psychological innuendo, suspense, and circumstance, romance in porn primarily concerns the physical sex act. Although there have been porn films known for their drama, adult movies that sacrifice dialogue and chemistry for plain old sex will probably not be profitable. Similarly, Palahniuk bases his fictional gang bang on actual porn productions. At the beginning of *Snuff*, Sheila tells Mr. 72 about the previous record-setting events (7), and Branch brashly defines a single sex act as oral, anal, or vaginal penetration lasting at least one minute (55).[4] Sheila mentions that in 1996 Candy Apples had 721 sex acts with fifty men, followed by "True fact" (7). She also cites Jasmin St. Claire's 300 sex acts, Spantaneeus Xtasy's 551 sex acts, and Sabrina Johnson's reported 2,000 sex acts, clarifying that after a royalty check bounced, Johnson confessed she only had 500 sex acts with thirty-nine men (7). To demonstrate how porn stars have died similar deaths to Hollywood celebrities, Palahniuk surveys recent porn tragedies. After Mr. 72 asks why Cassie would want to commit suicide through the gang bang, Mr. 600 summarizes the suicides of porn stars Megan Leigh, Cal Jammer, Shanna Grant, and Shannon Wilsey. Palahniuk is extremely detailed in Branch's summary of these deaths:

> Maybe for the same reason superstar Megan Leigh shot more than fifty-four films in three years and then bought her mom a half-million-dollar mansion. Only then did the star of *Ali Boobie and the 40 D's* and *Robofox* shoot herself in the head. Isn't a kid alive who doesn't dream about rewarding her folks, or punishing them. It's how come legendary woodsman Cal Jammer stood in the rain in his ex-wife's driveway and shot himself in the mouth. It's why pussy queen Shauna Grant died at the business end of her own .22-calibar rifle. And why one night, Shannon Wilsey, the blond high goddess of porn known as "Savannah," went out to her garage and put a bullet into her head [53–54].

Surprisingly, Palahniuk left out Alex Jordan, a contemporary of these actors, who killed herself reportedly after her beloved pet bird died. Concerning dead porn stars, there are several memorials available on *YouTube* dedicated to many of these people, such as "Dead Porn Stars Memorial Part 1" and "Dead Porn Stars Memorial Part 2." A list of deceased porn actors is maintained at "Dead Porn Stars" on the website iadf.com (Internet Adult Film Database). Addresses for all three websites are listed on the works cited page.

The most significant reference to actual porn is to Annabel Chong, who set the early record of 251 sex acts with eighty men (7). In several sections, Palahniuk emphasizes Cassie's fictional gang bang is predominantly based upon Chong's 1995 event. For instance, Cassie imitates Chong's decision to have groups of five men on stage at a time (22). In one of the most humorous of Sheila's trivia is her comparison between men and cows: "studies show that when males are placed together in close proximity before a sex act, their sperm count will rise. These studies are based on dairy farms ... basing porn films on modern dairy-farm procedures. Trade secrets that can destroy the romance of any good gang bang. True fact" (22–23). Sheila points out Chong, whose real name is Grace Quek, based her gang bang upon Valeria Messalina, a Roman empress with a voracious sexual appetite, and Quek's goal was to display female empowerment by assuming the persona of "stud" (24). As Sheila explains, "The set decorations, the white fluted columns and splashing fountains, a historical re-creation of Messalina's challenge to Scylla. The fake marble and Roman statues. The World's Biggest Gangbang. A student in gender studies at the University of Southern California, with a grade point average of 3.7, this film was Chong's tribute to Valeria Messalina. True fact" (95–96). This passage from Sheila is representative of Palahniuk's blending of objective information with subjective commentary. Sheila states specifically,

> You could cite Annabel Chong—real name: Grace Quek—who fucked that first world's record of 251 losers because, for once, she wanted a woman to be "the stud." Because she loved sex and was sick of feminist theory portraying female porn performers as either idiots or victims. In the early 1970s, Linda Lovelace was delivering exactly the same philosophical reasons behind her work in *Deep Throat*. The last thing today comes down to is personal growth. Do you respect someone's right to seek challenges and discover their true potential? How is a gang bang any different than risking your life to climb Mount Everest? And do you accept sex as a form of viable emotional therapy? It only came out later, about Linda Lovelace being held hostage and brutalized. Or how, before becoming a porn star, Grace Quek had been raped in London by four men and a twelve-year-old boy. Early adopters love Annabel Chong. The damaged love the damaged. True fact [24–25].

Three. "True fact": Hyperreality in Snuff

The progression from the actual Messalina to the mythic Messalina to Annabel Chong to other sex performers to Cassie Wright by itself illustrates the progression of simulacra toward hyperreality. As such, Palahniuk's Cassie is the last in a line of many sexual innovators.

The third stage of simulation relates to fictional porn films. This is when art begins to separate from reality. Palahniuk creates fictitious porn titles that refer to existing Hollywood, literary, and historical texts. But, the word "actual" is enigmatic because these porn films imitate media that are essentially themselves reproductions of reality. This blurring of fact and fantasy subsequently moves meaning from the real toward the hyperreal. The movies running continuously on the monitors help to place the meaning of the gang bang in a temporal context. They display Cassie's rise in porn from her first production—titled *Frisky Business*—to her signature world war films, and similar to the participants in the gang bang, readers are privy to Cassie's evolution as a porn actress. Moreover, Cassie's roles are historical parodies, farces, and satires full of anachronisms, misrepresentations, and revisions. When these films are introduced in the novel, Cassie is praised for her attention to accuracy. Critics supposedly raved over Cassie's depiction of Mary Todd Lincoln in the Civil War epic *Ford's Theatre Back Door Dog Pile*, re-released as *Private Box*, then re-released as *Presidential Box*. Mr. 72 comments to Mr. 137, "in the scene where Cassie Wright gets double-reamed by John Wilkes Booth and Honest Abe Lincoln, thanks to her research, she truly does make American history come alive" (10). Cassie is praised for adroitness with a speculum in *Emergency Room* (9–10), and Mr. 137 mentions she spent six months shadowing an endocrinologist for her role in *Titanic Back Door Dog Pile* (9). The porn films are obvious imitations of Hollywood classics, such as *The Da Vinci Load* (12), *To Drill a Mockingbird* (12), *The Postman Always Cums Twice* (12), *Chitty Chitty Gang Bang* (12), *The Wizard of Ass* (15), *On Golden Blond* (26), *The Blow Jobs of Madison County* (110), *The Italian Hand Job* (106), *Three Days of the Condom* (106), *The Miracle Sex Worker* (144), *Butt Pirates of the Caribbean* (40), and *Smokey and the Ass Bandits* (40). There are also references to literature, such as *The Gropes of Wrath* (15), *Moby Dicked* (16), *A Midsummer Night's Ream* (16), *Much Ado About Humping* (16), *The Ass Menagerie* (29), *Catch Her in the Eye* (29), *Bang the Bum Slowly* (29), *The Importance of Balling Ernest* (55), and *Slut on a Hot Tin Roof* (76). Cassie's best performances relate to world war: *World Whore One: Deep in the Trenches*, *World Whore Two: Island Hopping*, and *World Whore Three: The Whore to End All Whores*. In the World War II adaptation, scenes of Cassie's oral sex with Hirohito are shown concurrently with shots of the *Enola Gay* approaching Hiroshima (16–17). Palahniuk paid attention to accuracy in his duplicate titles. Even the rumor of Cassie's porn baby is contextualized within history depicted through the pornography as the father is named as Benito Mussolini, not Branch who played that role (17–18).

The fourth stage is the hyperreal in which the referent is another simulation. Or, to apply Baudrillard's term, the referent is a simulacrum, a simulation of a simulation. From the onset, Palahniuk attempts to deceive his audience by establishing two directions in the plot. The first leads readers toward finding out if Mr. 72 is indeed the porn baby of Branch and Cassie, and Palahniuk spreads general clues in the dialogues such as Mr. 72's resemblance to Mr. 600, Mr. 72's mother admitting Cassie is his birth mother, and Mr. 72's self-assurance he is the notorious progeny. The second is if Cassie has a death wish to martyr herself for the sake of the dubious gang bang milestone and a lucrative inheritance for her offspring. About three quarters into the novel, these two routes start to trail off, and as Mr. 600's dialogues gain more traction in the plot, Sheila's role becomes more important. After Sheila teaches Cassie about the Messalina mythology serving as the basis for Annabel Chong's famous 251 accomplishment and sees Cassie signing gang bang memorabilia, she comments, "Another last thing today comes down to is reality" (25). This is a crucial thematic statement. As the much anticipated moment approaches when Mr. 600 gets his turn, the tone of the narrative becomes more somber and serious. Even Mr. 72 becomes sincere, mentioning before Cassie shoves her nipple into his mouth that his being filmed makes the experience something permanent (165). The statement also foreshadows Mr. 72's realization Sheila is Cassie's daughter (175). After the two plot directions both point toward Sheila, Cassie admits during the novel's pivotal scene that she has known all along Sheila is her daughter, after this the refrain "True fact" (176). During Sheila's emotional recognition that Cassie has put her life in jeopardy to make her, as Cassie's only heir, wealthy, there is this confirmation, "True fact" (184). These epiphanies followed by "true fact" neutralize Sheila's anger toward Cassie for naming her Zelda Zonk, Sheila not knowing this was Marilyn Monroe's alias, the sexual icon's intellectual alter-ego (180). After these two significant realizations, Sheila admits, providing another version of what she said at the beginning of the novel but now with a much more reverent tone, "Another last thing today comes down to is reality" (184).

Shelia does not realize that this day is defined by hyperreality instead of reality, and the fusion, the literal melting together of Branch's and Cassie's bodies at the point of coitus, provides a tangible image (at least in the novel's context) to complete the sequence of simulations, although visualizing the mechanics of how the two are joined is not an easy task. The single spliced-together body also serves as a representation of the two famous actors' porn careers as well as the indelible emotional bond between them, in addition to all of the reproductions—remakes of Hollywood, literary, or historical texts—presented throughout the novel. Thus, the fusion of the two characters could point all the way back to the pre-porn incident (one dysfunctional moment imitating yet another) when Cassie and Branch had sex. Significantly, Branch notices how Cassie is presently only a simulation of a simulation of herself: "On the TVs, they're playing the first movie Cassie ever appeared in. Shot on video, maybe one step better than some security camera at the corner quick-stop grocery. On the TVs is her and me, young as Sheila and the kid 72. Cassie's eyes are rolled up to show only white, her arms flopping loose at her sides, her head rolling around on her neck so far the pull opens her mouth, drool sliding out the corner on her lips. Slack as a blow-up sex-doll version of herself" (185). The question whether or not they could possibly be burned together is irrelevant because simulation has been blurred beyond realistic representation. In other words, if readers have believed everything previously presented in the novel, they should accept the daunting image of Cassie physically welded by genitalia to the last gang banger. When Mr. 72 wildly thrashes on top of her, Cassie says, "You guys getting this?" (168), and when she decides to impale herself on technically dead Branch's Viagra-produced erection, she repeats, "Are you getting this?" (192). Cassie asks this of her film crew, but, in a sense, Palahniuk is also asking the same question to his readers. On the last pages of the novel, Sheila reflects, "But no, they didn't die. Branch and Cassie. Almost, but not quite. The stench of scorched pussy and balls comes from the kilowatt jolt that almost killed Ms. Wright— but brought Branch Bacardi back to life. The shock that fused their genitals together. Sealed together. True fact" (196). Sheila attempts to understand the hyperreality in terms of reality, confessing the two are her parents, followed by "True fact" (196), but she ultimately recognizes this is impossible: "For an instant, everything feels so important. Almost real" (197). In response to Cassie's last question, readers certainly got an ending they more than likely did not expect, one that definitely transcended into hyperreality. Readers might have foreseen Sheila as Cassie's daughter, but they probably did not anticipate the surrealistic fusion of Branch and Cassie. This is definitely one of Palahniuk's most incredible images, rivaling any of his other grotesque and flamboyant creations at the end of his stories.

Thus, the novel ends with Cassie setting the gang bang record and readers discovering Sheila is her long-lost daughter. Surprisingly, Palahniuk omits in his references to actual gang bangs that an actress in 1999 named Houston reportedly had sex with 620 different men in the film *The World's Biggest Gangbang 3: The Houston 500*.[5] Palahniuk must have known about Houston's record (this information is easily retrieved through an online search), and he is undoubtedly counting on some astute readers making the popular culture connection between Houston and Cassie. Granted, few readers will probably make this comparison, but those who do are rewarded with another interesting level of hyperreality. Ironically, Houston's mother is Disney Studios animator Clair Weeks, who animated the films *Snow White* and *Cinderella* ("Houston"). Baudrillard points out that Disneyland is where "the real is no longer the real" (*Simulacra* 13), a place renowned for its hyperreality. In "The Gang's All Here: Hope Flickers at the World's Biggest Gangbang," Kevin Bisch describes Houston's event similar to Palahniuk's fictional one. Bisch writes, "everything about Houston's physique is excessive, blown up. A surgically enhanced cartoon bombshell.... With her stressed-out silicon breasts, the store-bought tan, the lips hardened with lip liner, she looks like the love child of Jessica Rabbit and Bart Simpson." Porn superstar Ron Jeremy served as Mr. 620 for Houston's event. Jeremy was mentioned in *Snuff* for his celebrity-replica sex toy in the same discussion with Branch's and Cassie's genital reproductions (40). Bisch describes the excitement surrounding the final moments of Houston's gang bang: "Ron Jeremy steps up as No. 620 ... the crowd gets dense, packs in, stands on tiptoe just as before. But instead of the reverent silence during the fluffers' opening salvo, they issue a raucous countdown. 10, 9.... The old order is passing ... 6, 5 ... Jasmin [St. Claire] is stepping down ... 3, 2 ... a new world record! Ron blows his load on cue, as he has done countless times during the past 24 years." Afterward, and certainly anti-climactic (pardon another pun), Bisch offers the aside that Houston, Jeremy, and some of the crew went to TGI Friday's for mozzarella sticks. Admittedly, watching the film of Houston having real sex with over 600 men—the film is available free on various online porn sites—is not as interesting as Cassie's imaginary representation. The chances are slim that readers will surf porn sites to verify the fictional version against its realistic counterpart, nor will readers have any inclination to view anything remotely connected to something as politely inappropriate (or in blatantly bad taste) as a gang bang with 600 or more participants, but this neither diminishes nor negates the point, which might be Palahniuk's all along, that reality is sometimes simply not as believable as hyperreality, as paradoxical as this surely seems. Added to this is the unbelievable truth that gang bang queen Lisa Sparks had sex with an astronomical 919 men in 2004 ("Gang"), and Palahniuk must have known about this event as well as Houston's sexual extravaganza. Equally astonishing is Houston's body parts have been commodified into art. In a 2000 interview with George Gurley, Houston reports that Marc Medoff transformed three surgically removed pieces of her labia into art, presumably worth $100,000 ("Houston: An Intimate"). If anything, hyperreality may more effectively satisfy most peoples' expectations concerning what should occur in a situation such as a record-setting gang bang. A number for sex acts in one situation such as 919 just seems unfathomable.

Clues to Palahniuk's intentions are presented in how he and Doubleday Publishing promoted the novel. Of all places, the Internet is the perfect venue for Cassie Wright's mass-marketed reproductions. The Palahniuk fan-based site *The Cult: The Official Chuck Palahniuk Website* included parodies of *Snuff* when the novel was released, but more hyperreal is the set of three interviews Doubleday Publishing created between Palahniuk, imitating the interview style of any sensationalist reporter, and an actor playing Cassie Wright. The imaginary Cassie Wright, considering the context, would be more similar in reality to Christy Canyon, Ginger Lynn Allen, Amber Lynn, Juli Ashton, or any other forty or older porn matriarch who has stretched her longevity as an audio entertainer on Spice and Playboy satellite networks or who has cashed in on the new wave of MILF and GILF films. This Cassie Wright is a tall, hefty transvestite who lampoons the entire premise upon which *Snuff* is built as well as undercuts any seriousness attached to the novel. In one of the first questions, Palahniuk asks, "How does it feel to know that, that really, every woman in the world is measured against you?" Masculine Cassie responds without hesitation, "I think they have set an awfully high standard, certainly." Moreover, on Cassie Wright's *Myspace* page, headed with the announcement "Cassie Wright Lives," short trailers of three of Cassie's films are introduced with "Never before seen footage of cult classic adult film star Cassie Wright, star of SNUFF by Chuck Palahniuk." The site contains parodies of *The Twilight Zone*, *The Wizard of Oz*, and *Chitty Chitty Bang Bang*—appropriately retitled *The Twilight Bone*, *The Wizard of Ass*, and *Chitty Chitty Gang Bang* (addresses for locations of these on the Internet are listed on the works cited page). The pictures on *Myspace* and the star of each trailer is a young Cassie, with blue eyes, blond hair, thin body, without the Barbie-like measurements of current porn stars (such as Houston) but comparable to a young Marilyn Chambers of 1970s adult movies. Comments left on the web site around 2008 perpetuate the illusion Cassie Wright actually exists: "When I grow up, I want to be just like you," "I am your biggest fan! And I, I think I might be your son," and "Hey you little pornbot!!!" These online locations were obviously devices to market the novel, but they also increase audience desire for a hyperreal Cassie, and the viewer posts indicate a strong fandom presence to interact within the simulated universe where Cassie operates. Palahniuk clearly feeds this appetite for hyperreality, and he more than likely relishes audience participation, although this does not even closely rival fan reaction to his novel *Fight Club*.[6] To extend the progression of the factoids about *The Wizard of Oz*, a mentioning of *The Wizard of Ass* in the novel, and then the trailer spoof of *The Wizard of Ass* online, there was actually a big-budget pornographic production of *The Wizard of Oz* filmed in 2013 called *Not The Wizard of Oz XXX* (available online) starring porn matriarch Nina Hartley, whose physical appearance and professional life mirror that of the fictional Cassie Wright in many ways, most notably her muscle-toned athletic physique.

    A comparison between versions of *The Wizard of Oz* demonstrates the effectiveness of Palahniuk's levels of parody. Concerning Hollywood trivia, Cassie mentions Dorothy's dog Toto's broken leg and Buddy Ebsen's allergic reaction to aluminum dust when he played the Tin Woodsman. There are references to the porn adaptation called *The Wizard of Ass*. Palahniuk does not supply details concerning the porn remake, but he allows the Doubleday Publishing promotional clip portrayed as a 1980s movie trailer function as ancillary content to the novel. The trailer for *The Wizard of Ass* begins with synthesized music characteristic of that era's porn, and Dorothy is a young blond woman in her early twenties who looks surprised, in typical porn bad acting, that she is "not in Kansas anymore." Moreover, she has an equally amazed expression when the voiceover announces, "Cassie is not a virgin anymore." Dorothy is soon wearing just her bra and panties bouncing on a bed, and then the camera turns to Branch Bacardi who agrees to show Dorothy his "corn" and soon exclaims, "Shuck baby" while Dorothy does something to him below the line of the camera. The clip is obviously a farce of porn during Cassie's early years as an actress, but it offers significant visual information to supplement how readers and viewers construct Cassie Wright in their imaginations. This clip and the two others created by Doubleday follow a current trend by publishers to supply short videos of novels to entice readers into purchasing the products. If readers want a glimpse into the personalities of a novel's main characters, they only need to watch the promotional film (often a summary of a novel's main plot points). Readers do not have to rely on their imaginations to create mental images of the characters; they only need to watch a short clip to see actors supply the necessary mental models. Viewers of the Cassie clips might allow that particular actress to become embedded in their imaginations as Palahniuk's character. Everyone knows how difficult it is to separate a book character from his or her movie counterpart. For instance, Brad Pitt is Tyler Durden, Helena Bonham Carter is Marla Singer, and Meat Loaf is Big Bob to many people—they ARE the characters they portray. The actual porn film *Not the Wizard of Oz* adds yet another dimension to the imitation sequence. The Tin Woodsman is tin-plated just as in the original film, except, of course, his genitals are uncovered for most of the film. The Wicked Witch is completely green with body paint except for around her nipples and her vagina, and in this rendition of the story, she has sexual intercourse with the Tin Woodsman. A reader may have a flash of Buddy Ebsen come to mind, but neither Jed Clampett nor Barnaby Jones would probably replicate what this Tin Woodsman does in this film. In the first moments of the porn film, Dorothy catches Nina Hartley as Aunt Em giving fellatio to a caped man. After seeing this, Dorothy goes into her room to masturbate, not content included in the 1939 Hollywood movie classic. Actress Maddy O'Reilly playing Dorothy in this porn version does not resemble the Cassie Wright described in the novel, but Palahniuk's Cassie in the interview clips is also much different from what readers might expect. Cassie in the fake film trailers is the closest to "true" Cassie, which relates to Baudrillard's theory of simulacra in that this version of Cassie is technically only a simulation identified as the most "real." The actual porn film becomes the eventual vulgar duplication of *The Wizard of Oz*, and this film is an extremely professional and tasteful movie according to porn standards (with a reasonably large production budget). There are undoubtedly more profane and more obscene low-budget porn productions of the story available. If readers are unsure or uncertain exactly what the films on the overheard monitors are presenting, they only need to go online and watch just about a minute into *Not the Wizard of Oz*. Palahniuk illustrates through this process Baudrillard's theory, but he also has, plain and simple, a lot of fun stretching the elasticity of parody within transgressive boundaries.

There could be one more layer of simulacra attributed to Cassie as plans have been made for a film version of *Snuff*. According to *Empireonline* and other online film gossip sites, casting for the movie has been completed with Darryl Hannah as Cassie, Tom Sizemore as Branch, and Thora Birch as Sheila.[7] The signification of these stars provides even more deferment of meaning. Hannah is long past the innocence she portrayed in *Splash* and is now known for her edginess in the *Kill Bill* films. Sizemore is most famous for *Saving Private Ryan*, but he may be more recently associated with his stint on Dr. Drew's VH1 *Celebrity Rehab* programs. He has also been the star in his own supposedly leaked porn films and was long-time boyfriend to Heidi Fleiss, the notorious "Hollywood Madam." Thora Birch is the real life daughter of former porn star Carol Connors, known for *The Erotic Adventures of Candy* movies and an appearance in *Deep Throat*. In Birch's case, fact meets fiction (or conversely fiction meets fact). In a bit of a twist, the film actress portraying Cassie in the *Myspace* trailers resembles a young Carol Connors. Obviously, Hannah looks much different from the cross-dresser portrayed in the Palahniuk interview. The casting of Hannah is a much more realistic, believable, and expected portrayal of Cassie than the comic one in the promotional interviews. In the film, Cassie could be portrayed as victimized in a first-wave feminist account that could absolutely vilify everyone associated with porn, or she could be described as opportunistically self-promoting and taking full advantage of all her assets emblematic of third-wave or post-feminism. As with all movies based upon novels, the director's interpretation of the initial meaning determines the reproduction. In most cases, the change in media necessitates differences from the original to the remake, but what will be interesting in this instance is how the director will present the various levels of simulation in the novel. The strong feminist portrayals of Madison Spencer in *Damned* (2011) and Penny Harrigan in *Beautiful You* (2014) may also influence how Cassie is presented.

This production will probably not be an easy task. As a novel, *Snuff* illustrates the complex multivalent distinctions between reality and hyperreality. And, as always, Palahniuk makes a profound statement about the nature of American popular culture. Many readers may immediately be repulsed by the porn subject matter, immediately prepared to dismiss any cultural appeal or social worth for a text that from the beginning rejects any claim to tact or decorum. Granted, this novel could easily be admonished critically for its political incorrectness or gender insensitivity. Yet, there is little in *Snuff* that cannot be routinely viewed in programs appearing nightly on basic cable television. There is still a fine line today concerning what is and is not pornographic. Many women pose for pictorials in *Playboy* and other comparable magazines, many reality shows cater to sexual situations and mature content for ratings, and pornographic sites are supposedly the most visited locations on the World Wide Web. Americans still maintain conservatively puritanical stances while hypocritically satisfying their voracious craving for the carnal and the lascivious. As was stressed in the first chapter, critical theorists assert simulation in some form or fashion of the currently popular is standard practice in postmodern culture. Significantly, Baudrillard states, "pornography is a sexuality haunted by its own disappearance" (*Illusion*).[8] Palahniuk proves the accuracy of this statement in *Snuff*, and his accomplishment is what makes his novel so impressive. *Snuff* is not in the least a pornographic novel, and it demonstrates how pornography is sometimes not so much about simulations of sex as it is simulations of perceptions about sexuality. In this manner, Palahniuk plays with the elasticity of stretching the traditional into the transgressive and then allowing it to take the shape of the absurd. This is definitely confirmed in the spoofs of Cassie and her films that Palahniuk produced online, short clips that are obviously more preposterous than perverse. True fact.

Four

Pygmy as Parody of 1970s Karate Films

Most people would agree the KTVU News debacle concerning the crash of Asiana Flight 214 in 2013 was extremely careless journalistic broadcasting that perpetuated racist stereotypes toward Asians. The names of the pilots read by the anchorperson seem too outrageously in bad taste to be a part of an actual media event transmitted to thousands of San Francisco viewers. One would assume a KTVU employee with common sense would have noticed that the names of the pilots could not possibly be "Captain Sum Ting Wong," "Wi Tu Lo," "Ho Lee Fuk," and "Bang Ding Ow." The airing of these vulgar and offensive names amounted to overt discrimination against an entire ethnic population, and in a culturally diverse and politically correct America, this broadcast should not have occurred.

But, it did occur.

And, for all of its indecency, irreverence, and insensitivity, the event could have appeared in a Chuck Palahniuk novel.

A reader devoted to Palahniuk fiction would not have been surprised—let alone shocked, disgusted, or enraged—by the profanity associated with the names if they had come out of a Palahniuk story. In the Palahniuk literary universe, a gigantic gaffe on the level of the KTVU News broadcast is an aberration on network news but not necessarily anomalous plot content. Of course, readers would know Palahniuk is not in the least sanctioning such blatantly tactless and professionally irresponsible reporting (especially since he has a journalistic background). Palahniuk would just expose the event for all of its horrendous impropriety.[1] Palahniuk knows this kind of media solecism happens all too frequently in the real world, so he imitates it in his fictional world.

Palahniuk relies on a different approach to parody in *Pygmy* than he applies either in *Haunted* (referring to one previous text, *The Decameron*)

Four. Pygmy as Parody of 1970s Karate Films 55

or in *Snuff* (referring to various texts in different degrees). In this novel, Palahniuk depends upon his audience making the connection to a broader category of text, the B-movie martial arts films of the 1970s—with all of this subject's inherent racism, prejudice, and discrimination—and he counts on this recognition to drive the significance of his parody. This is not a nostalgic recollection of the past but rather a remembrance that functions as a reference point for the parody.[2] In *Pygmy*, Palahniuk is essentially counting on his readers' familiarity with 1970s karate films as seemingly innocuous entertainment in which a hero promotes all that is good and enforces his will through an exorbitant amount of exaggerated and hyperbolic physical violence (intensified by a lot of "pow," "bam," and "boom" and other pertinent onomatopoeia). Palahniuk wants this shared knowledge to be applied to his novel's version of the 1970s film archetypal hero, Pygmy.[3] After readers make the inference between those past films and this contemporary novel, Palahniuk can, to refer to Linda Hutcheon's theory of parody, draw on those similarities to emphasize the differences. Specifically, Palahniuk wants readers to respond to his story through the lens of the 1970s karate film genre so they can recognize the irony related to contemporary American culture. In Palahniuk's novel, for instance, instead of the hero brandishing a magical sword or some other standard implement of karate combat, Pygmy wields a fantastic super-dildo, not a typical tool in the hero arsenal, to defeat his enemies. Readers who identify Palahniuk's imitation of 1970s karate films will more fully understand the nuances of meaning in his novel and thus engage with the story at a deeper level. In other words, Palahniuk's plot decisions will simply make a lot more sense.

An example from another text doing something similar may be beneficial to understand Palahniuk's aim. In an episode called "Hawk and Chick," the cartoon comedy *Bob's Burgers* relies upon its audience knowing a little background about 1970s karate films. In this particular show, Bob Belcher and his daughter Louise recognize kung-fu film star Kojima while they are purchasing an onion at an outdoor market. Given Bob's curiosity and Louise's tenacity, they discover this Japanese ninja, named Hawk in his movies, has not spoken with his daughter Yuki, his film sidekick Chick, for several years. The rest of the episode is devoted to Bob and Louise reuniting the two (after they review their old VHS cassettes to make sure they have the right people) during a Hawk and Chick midnight screening of one of their adventures. Viewers do not need to know anything about 1970s karate films to understand all of the jokes in this episode, but having that shared reference point, being able to connect the allusions in *Bob's*

Burgers to that past style of movie, gives those jokes more punch. An example of this is the dubbing of the Hawk and Chick film that is discovered for the midnight viewing. Bob and his family provide the English translation of the Japanese, and, of course, the mouths of the characters on the screen do not sync with the words provided, and when Linda and Tina fight over who will do the voiceover for the mayor, a male role, Bob simply says, "It does not matter." Coincidentally, two male actors are the voices for Linda and Tina in *Bob's Burgers*. During the showing of the film, Bob and Tina must improvise the dialogue because the batteries in the tape recorder have died. Viewers familiar with 1970s karate films appreciate this detail because the dubbing of those movies into English was typically horrible. Again, viewers do not need knowledge of 1970s karate films to enjoy the "Hawk and Chick" episode of *Bob's Burgers*, but if they recognize how writer Rich Rinaldi and creators Loren Bouchard and Jim Dauterive parody those films, they might have a greater appreciation for the comedy. Palahniuk's purpose is comparable in *Pygmy*, and reader identification of this parody has a similar effect.

This is accentuated by Palahniuk's setting resembling 1970s Cold War America in which the foreign operative adolescents—not termed terrorists, freedom fighters, or other post–9/11 titles—are pitted against the capitalistic American adults. On the surface, Palahniuk's plot is full of serious espionage. The goal of Operation Havoc is for thirteen-year-old Pygmy to infiltrate middle-class American culture and ultimately detonate, with the aid of similar comrades portrayed as junior high students, a dirty bomb that will inflict wide-spread casualties through germ warfare. This might appear to be high drama, but the story is full of unmistakable satire and apparent comedy, and Palahniuk exposes Asian as well as American stereotypes to reveal the hypocrisies and prejudices that invariably sustain them. As Pygmy moves from the cultural outside to the inside, marginalized as a foreigner but then granted privileged status within the center of the ultra-conservative community, Palahniuk divulges the other characters' cultural solipsism and social provincialism. Assuming the role of Asian warrior, relying on superior mental acuity and physical agility, Pygmy tries his best not to succumb to the seductiveness of American capitalism with its inferior national infrastructure compared to his homeland, but he gives in nonetheless to the attractive Walmart, mega-church, public school, replete with capitalist excess, spiritual hypocrisy, and educational inadequacy. Through the course of events, Palahniuk elevates Pygmy to the role of this community's protector, savior, and redeemer, propelling Pygmy from his initial function as the destroyer of those egotistical Americans and everything for

Four. **Pygmy *as Parody of 1970s Karate Films*** 57

which America stands to the extreme opposite, the embodiment of the American Dream and the personification of American rugged individualism.

Palahniuk must introduce Pygmy as someone not initially trusted or accepted before he can place him inside the power center, and he accomplishes this through Pygmy's language, presenting how the way he speaks precipitates cultural prejudice and ethnic discrimination. Readers never learn the actual name of the narrator, who adopts the nickname attributed to him by the bully Trevor and promoted by the Cedars, his host family. The name Pygmy (sometimes spelled Pigmy) is an ethnic term usually referring to natives in various regions of Africa, but it is frequently associated negatively with colonialism, synonymous with someone who is diminutive, smaller and/or shorter than the normal or average (European) size. From the start of the novel, Pygmy is characterized as atypical and "less than" the Americans with whom he interacts. Although Palahniuk does not clarify, Pygmy's language, his martial arts prowess, and the names of the other operatives refer to a Chinese totalitarianism that maintains a strong hatred toward anything American, although he could be from any Asian country, North Korea possibly, ruled by a dictatorship that fosters a strong anti–American ideology. The Chinese affiliation is also suggested by the perceptible irony underlying Pygmy's gifts, the "Property of Jesus" t-shirt and the American flag, both being manufactured in China (6). Palahniuk's names are far from being as racist as those in the KTVU News broadcast, but they are still pejorative considering social etiquette and decorum, as the Cedar children go without proper names and are identified by Pygmy as Pig Dog Brother and Cat Sister, and the parents, although attributed last names, are called Cow Father and Chicken Mother. The initial reviews of the novel focus primarily on the main character's obvious English language difficulties. Corey Redekop writes, "Presented as ongoing communiqués from Agent 67 to his masters, *Pygmy* is written in a pidgin-English dialect that is initially off-putting.... The concept is not entirely successful (why would Pygmy write reports in English rather than his native tongue?), but it can lead to some offbeat and memorable descriptions of western culture." Cameron Woodhead states, "Pygmy's voice is so robotic and sloppily imagined that it deadens and oversimplifies, as well as proving an annoying distraction from, Palahniuk's satire." A reviewer for *Publisher's Weekly* comments, "read aloud, Pygmy's peculiar speech patterns sound like bad beatnik poetry." These critics do not understand the purpose underlying Pygmy's distinctive way of communicating and therefore do not recognize how Palahniuk crafts Pygmy's language as a part of a more important objective, exposing American jingoistic prejudice and xenophobic racism. Palahniuk deliberately and methodically designs Pygmy's sentence syntax and word selection to serve his particular rhetorical purpose, and these critics unintentionally confirm that Palahniuk has succeeded.

Palahniuk uses language as the primary means to differentiate Pygmy from the Cedars and other stereotypical Midwesterners. In his dispatches, Pygmy writes in broken English associated with Asian speakers in popular culture, a speech unfortunately mimicked in the KTVU News reporting of pilot names. Pygmy's language is characterized by inverted subject/verb arrangements, omitted articles and infinitives, and graphic adjectives and adverbs. The following passage from Pygmy displays this language, as well as exhibiting his resistance to assimilate into American culture: "Making all effort resist absorption into American cult of the individual, traditional method entrenched oligarchy so maintain own power: Fracture citizen isolated into different religion, different race, different family. Label as rich cultural diversity. Cleave as unique until each citizen stand alone. Until each vote invested no value. Single citizen celebrated as special—in actual remaining no power" (129). In several sections, Pygmy describes objects because he is unfamiliar with the appropriate words, such as "silver floating bladder" (5) for balloon, "thinking machine" (69) for brain, "foot shod boot associated profession boy of cows" (81) for cowboy boots, and, one of the most creative, "force compelled to sing how yearning for location on top arched spectrum of light wavelengths created by precipitate" (47) for rainbow. Palahniuk is counting on his readers noticing the similarity between Pygmy's speech and the language in English-dubbed karate films. Words on a page cannot duplicate the auditory sound of language in these films, let alone describe the characteristic problem related to syncing the dialogue with the actors' mouths (a notorious problem mocked often in popular culture), so a better option is to go online via *YouTube* to view trailers of these films or to watch the full-length presentations. These brief compilations definitely offer a taste of the flavor of the full productions: "Kung Fu Trailers 1970's," "Kung Fu Movie Trailers of the 1970's," and "Favorite Martial Arts Movies in the 70's."[4]

Palahniuk undoubtedly understands the double-edged nature of playing with language. On the one hand, he could be derided in a similar manner as KTVU News for racism; on the other, if readers identify the parody—considering the 1970s karate film referent—they should recognize his rhetorical purpose. Audience recognition of the rhetorical reason is crucial. In *Reading Race*, Norman K. Denzin mentions the following stereotypical speech patterns attributed to foreigners: "Vocal excess emphasized the inability of the ethnic other to speak ordinary English. Garbled, slurred speech and racially coded phrases connected to each minority group were developed, including, for blacks: Yo, git, jest, Bro; for Hispanics: thick, impenetrable accents, the use of Spanish phrases ... for Asians: pidgin English" (23). Concerning these speech patterns in B-films, Denizen states the following:

> As early and intensively as this tendency [to characterize language]—particularly pronounced in genre films from 1907 forward—emerged, the B-picture productions of the 1930s and 1940s are today the best known aspect of an overtly standardized cinema. B-pictures differ from A-cinema primarily in that the former were initially created as somewhat shorter movies for the double features then common in American cinemas. Shot with low budgets and at regularly scheduled intervals, B-movies appeared as explicitly standardized products, and they were much less concerned with a *distinctive* aesthetic style, the spectacular, *production value*, or the literary quality of the original story than were the expensive A-pictures. However, the latter also consistently displayed the use of standard techniques. This principle of standardization culminated in genre films, serials, and series, which constituted the core of the B-pictures [101].[5]

These are exactly the stereotypes Palahniuk wants to expose and subsequently explode. Contrary to what some readers may contend, Palahniuk is not a writer of exploitation novels, catering to violence, sex, and obscenity just for shock—although he certainly counts on some of this to get his points across to a consumer population that demands these ingredients in the fiction that they consume. *Pygmy* could resemble the "chopsocky" 1970s films that relied on exploitation of the marginalization of Asians, and an argument could be made that the references to vibrators could place the novel along the lines of sexploitation, but there is nothing sexually provocative or titillating in the sexual references, and Pygmy is not a stock character, although he may compare with the Other or subaltern described in postcolonial studies. Pygmy achieves power at the end of the novel, and this divorces him from exploitation film characters. Palahniuk's Pygmy fights all insinuations, assumptions, and references concerning his so-called diminutive status, and by the end of the novel, he asserts his essential role within the American community. In this way, Pygmy transcends the label of cultural outcast or social outsider.

Palahniuk is familiar with 1970s karate films and the nature of their production, and he must have researched them—as he is a tenacious and meticulous researcher for all of his novels—similar to perhaps how director Quentin Tarantino researched this genre to create his own parodies of them in the *Kill Bill* films, which definitely exhibit a loyalty to previous kung-fu movies. In *The Ultimate Guide to Martial Arts Movies of the 1970s*, Craig Reid explains in his concise yet thorough introduction how hundreds of martial arts films were produced in Hong Kong by Shaw Brothers Productions and an off-shoot company Golden Harvest Productions. As Reid mentions, the term "kung fu" is taken from the Cantonese dialect and means "working man" or translated refers to "hard work" (12). The heroes of the kung-fu films allowed an audience to identify with a more realistic character than ones previously portrayed in Asian marital arts films of the 1920s-1940s that included supernatural, mythic, or historical heroes (12). In other words, viewers could more readily identify with this seemingly working-class and hard-working hero. Reid points out plotlines featured traditional battles between good versus evil, conflicts generated out of revenge, or fights against foreign intruders (13). He comments that American audiences recognized the similarities among the sword-swinging samurais and the gun-slinging outlaws in the popular spaghetti westerns (13). Notably, Reid offers reasons why the dubbing of these films imported to the United States were so horribly bad. Distributors did not care about the quality, so dubbers were often not professional actors. These dubbers could not translate the languages yet were responsible for creating several voices for different characters. They completed this task most of the time without scripts, so they had to guess what characters were saying and fill in gaps sometimes with gibberish (14), which Reid claims accounts for the frequent conversation-extender "but still" in these movies (14). He recounts this process in his job: "because we each had three to five different voices to forge per film, we quickly ran out of voices to parrot after the second film. So we would develop a good-guy voice, a villain voice, an innkeeper voice, etc. and that is why the films all sound alike. There were also no rehearsals. We would watch the scene in Chinese with sound, then once without sound, then dub the scene. Speed was of the essence" (14). Distributors were satisfied if spoken voices generally synched with the screen actors' mouths moving (14). Although Reid does not discuss this point, these voice-over people gave their characters the choppy, child-like, syntactically jumbled dialogue that characterizes these films and consequently perpetuated the linguistic stereotypes attached to how Asians supposedly articulate English. In this way, they reinforced the already established negative stereotypes governing how Asians spoke in English.[6] An interesting example of this dubbing worth viewing is "Dense The Ten Extreme 1978 English Dubbed-Kung Fu Movies" available via *YouTube* (the address is on the works cited page).

Palahniuk understands the characteristically masculine protocol necessary to establish Pygmy as his hero. In *The American Martial Art Film*, M. Ray Lott notes that these films were extremely popular among American teenage males, and Bruce Lee was unquestionably their superstar pop icon (10). Lott states that Golden Harvest Productions started sending its

Four. Pygmy as Parody of 1970s Karate Films

martial arts films to the United States after they became successful for the Asian audience, and they instantly became popular among boys (10). He adds that Bruce Lee did not follow the Asian stereotype of "humble and unassuming" but came across as "a reserved but self-assured man who goes about his mission with a cynical, detached cool, the same way Charles Bronson and Clint Eastwood, both top stars at the time, did in their respective films" (14). Lott points out Lee "chopped his way to stardom" in films such as *The Big Boss* (1971), *The Chinese Connection* (1972), *Enter the Dragon* (1973), and *Return of the Dragon* (1973), besides starring as Kato in the 1960s television show *The Green Hornet*. At the same time, American films such as *Billy Jack* (1971), *Walking Tall* (1973), and *Death Wish* (1974) were financially successful; the television show *Kung Fu* (1973–77) was widely watched; and Carl Douglas's "Kung Fu Fighting" (1974) was a popular hit. Although Lee was undoubtedly the official face of the Asian karate hero, many devoted patrons of these films viewed the B-movie productions not for the star-quality of someone like Lee but for strange-looking characters who spoke with odd accents. In other words, viewers just wanted to see the good-guy Asian hero jumping, kicking, punching, slapping, chopping—all while snorting and grunting—against obvious villains and evil-doers, just as Billy Jack, Buford Pusser, and Paul Kersey fought against adversaries in their films.

These American macho fighters as well as Pygmy are modeled after the epic hero. P. T. J. Rance explains the traditional kung-fu film hero framework:

> The key elements of these stories are martial arts—wu—and the valiant knight-errant—the xia. Across their pages, heroes and villains battle for control and martial power. China's troubled history under a series of corrupt political regimes, rife with assassination and intrigue, had undermined the people's faith in the rule of law and made them look elsewhere for protection. The xia heroes, both male and female, came to represent justice, dealing out vengeance for wrongs done to the people from their position outside the system [23].

Rance also describes the standard heroic elements: "Drawing from the ninth century, these popular tales of martial chivalry draw on Chinese mythology, chronicling the adventures of heroic knights who travel the land righting wrongs. Set in an undefined period in China's distant past, they involve magic, swordplay, outlawry and lots of flying" (23). Rance notes that "events of the early 1970s changed the face of martial arts films forever. In the decades that followed, Hong Kong became the powerhouse of Asian filmmaking, and its main currency was kick flicks" (63). Pygmy imitates many of these traditional heroic qualities. A criticism concerning Pygmy is that he might be underdeveloped as a character, but Palahniuk intentionally wants his narrator to be so uncomplicated that his audience clearly notices these traditional heroic traits. Palahniuk wants Pygmy to be simple yet deep, and this quality also describes Billy Jack, Buford Pusser, and Paul Kersey as well as Charles Bronson and Clint Eastwood, men of action not words.

Cognizant of the Marxist implications in these films, Palahniuk is familiar with how they market American capitalistic ideology. Ariel Dorfman provides an excellent explanation of how propaganda and literature converge in his two sociological studies, arguing that American capitalists mask their ideology through the disguise of popular media and indoctrinate those who are exposed to it.[7] As a result, readers accept the ideology as their own, causing them to suppress their cultural identity and to disregard their national history. Although Dorfman analyzes this indoctrination process in relation to the Third World, primarily Chile, and investigates the subversive effects underlying literature as inane as Disney comics and television westerns, his insight sheds light on how 1970s karate films influence perception toward Asians by promoting racial and ethnic stereotypes. In *How to Read Donald Duck*, Dorfman discusses America's exportation of imperialist propaganda to justify its abuse of the Third World by perpetuating the stereotype that countries should be subservient to the United States, particularly related to industry and agriculture. In this 1971 publication, Dorfman specifically accuses the seemingly innocent and inculpable Walt Disney as the primary perpetuator of this ideology. Third-world readers of Disney's comics learn to comply with the stereotype presented in the literature and begin to treat the material as culturally iconic: "adults set out to prove that this literature is essential to the child, satisfying his eager demands. But this is a closed circuit: children have been conditioned by the magazines and the culture which spawned them. They tend to reflect in their daily lives the characteristics they are supposed to possess, in order to grow up properly and integrate into society" (*How* 30). Disney supplies third-world readers with the reality that they were supposed to believe and imitate, and he assumes a responsibility similar to the one that a parent has over a child by epitomizing the American work ethic and moral fortitude, qualities which make him an ideal spokesperson for capitalist ideology. As obedient children, the third-world audience obeys literally the instruction that appears figuratively in the comic. Disney's stereotypes restructure history so that the past justifies the present, and consequently, this effectively erases any history which contradicts or disputes contemporary American policy in the region.[8] Dorfman continues his analysis of

Four. *Pygmy* as Parody of 1970s Karate Films

popular media in *The Empire's Old Clothes*, a critique of Babar, the Lone Ranger, Mampato, and *Reader's Digest*. In the first chapter, he mentions "how easy it is for those in power, once they feel threatened, to make use of that arsenal of ready-made ideas to convince and mobilize potential followers.... These are the values of a social class: Its members impose their views on their subordinates" (10–11). Dorfman believes that the stereotype of the third-world population as mostly illiterate and childlike is the impetus for the infiltration of capitalist ideology through children's literature and, although the writing is simplistic, the message is quite powerful. Through popular media, the United States brainwashes the third-world population into dreaming a false vision of itself. The "illiterate and childlike" caricature was also promoted toward those in Asian countries, and Pygmy is confronted with this stereotype immediately when he joins the Cedars in the United States.

In an example of how strongly people are affected by media allegory, Dorfman explains that after reading an individual chapter of *The Empire's Old Clothes*, a Chilean lieutenant was so infuriated that someone had deconstructed his myth and had committed something close to cultural heresy that he arrested a janitor who worked in the shop where the article was printed. Dorfman comments that propaganda is instilled to such a degree that similar to the officer, "there are many who dream they are Superman, the Lone Ranger, or any of the free, Christian, occidental world's countless other saviors, those who dream they are the guardians of family, property, and public decency, those who dream—without a chink in their armor—that they are the nation's protectors" (*Empire's* 70). This false sense of security is reinforced in the media by publications such as *Reader's Digest*, which teaches its third-world audience that patriotism, spirituality, and conservatism benefit society, albeit these values are defined by American standards. Readers receive a sugar-coating of reality that emphasizes complete obedience to those in-charge and stoic devotion to American right-wing principles. Dorfman mentions that "in just such a way must the practical effects of this knowledge be distributed in the real world, with the very same wisdom and security that the magazine utilizes.... Everyone ends up on the same stratum; everyone knows the same thing; they've all been exposed to identical purifying opportunities by reading the magazine" (*Empire's* 155). By this method, a capitalist history is standardized and distributed as fact.

All of this information about 1970s karate films or the propagandistic packaging of American ideology is not necessary to enjoy Palahniuk's novel, but the background enables a reader to appreciate the effectiveness of Palahniuk's parody. When he meets the Cedar family, Pygmy is seen not only as "illiterate and childlike" but also non-Christian and primitive. Pygmy is extremely perceptive, as he first associates the family with the manufactured drugs they consume: Donald Cedar smells like Viagra and Propecia (2), "pig dog" brother smells like Ritalin (4), and the "chicken" mother smells like Zoloft, Xanax, and estrogen supplements (4).[9] Only the daughter, the "stealth cat" (6), is not type-cast by product at the initial meeting. This family's goal of Americanizing Pygmy is apparent by the mother's jingoistic pronouncement after giving Pygmy the American flag: "'We'll make an American out of you' ... 'Or, swear to our Lord almighty God, we are gonna die trying'" (7). Pygmy's reaction demonstrates his reluctance for this to occur: "Fingers of operative me pinch wood stick like stem of stinking weed. Wave stripe flag to fan away reek of host family air. Butter fat stench. Chemical hair soap stink. Such filthy reek American cash money" (6). Pygmy also considers how he would physically respond to any aggression, and these sections relate directly to the physical violence in karate films. In one instance, Pygmy thinks, "Operative me ready. Could be simple two pointed elbows to father's chest, one-two, *kam-pow*, Flying Eagle maneuver, and three days, but after next today, will father be vomiting both lungs, turned inside out with massive blood, dead. Fast as easy, young child able do" (3). In another part, he reflects, "Easy fast could be, feet of operative me hitting pig dog, *pow-pow*, Flying Giant Stock Death Kick, collapse inside of pig dog zygomatic arch, driving bone back direct to spear brain, *jab-boom*, dead before make next stink breath" (4). After meeting greeter Doris at the Wal-Mart, Pygmy thinks, using colorful onomatopoeia, "Could be, *zing-wring*, hands of this operative pounce in rapid Bird Wing Gentle Embrace to twist parrot neck, backbone *twist-snap*, to bring mercy instant soft death" (10).[10] Readers later discover that Doris is deceptively one of the operatives.

The first actual fight scene pits Pygmy against the representative racist in the novel, Trevor Stonefield, unmistakably the villain in the context of the kung-fu hero story. Pygmy's first encounter with him illustrates his loyalty to his host family as well as affirms Trevor as his archenemy: "Clear-yellow bully, foot stand on cowering pig dog, yellow hair swing across fire blue eye, bully say, 'You a gook? A nigger? A sandflea?' Say, 'Exactly what breed of wetback bitch are you?'" (12). Pygmy's response is swift and fierce, and, to be honest, a little puzzling (probably not what Bronson or Eastwood would have done): "Could be, this instant, elbows of operative me fly and drive fast, *wham–pow*, to soft corners of head temple, stun brain of yellow bully. Blackout. Foot of this agent stomp down trouser waist of bully to pool around bully feet. Next then turgid weapon of operative me, violate stunned anus, humiliate with seed the forced screaming pain of clear-yellow bully. All dry friction" (12). Pygmy has been instructed by his field marshal mentor to rape his adversary, so there is irony in that Trevor's initial taunts ultimately backfire on him. When Pygmy rapes Trevor, readers may be understandably baffled why this occurs. Later in the novel, Palahniuk provides the rationale:

> According explain field marshal, former past history, all American citizen hidden homosexual. All hungering clandestine masturbation within orifice fellow citizen identical gender. Best most enjoy so private mutual degradation. Thus for top method gain access government, attain power over individual, must operative merely engage enjoined sodomy within American. Next then, subsequent threaten expose said citizen as surreptitious pervert. Under past strategy must victim supply said operative government confidential information, supply currency. Fulfill all such requests from terror for being named publish sodomite [174].

Pygmy recounts, "Since modern era, explain renowned field marshal, depraved United State nation embraces such degenerates" (174–75). In a comic note, Pygmy describes the field marshal's unorthodox teaching agenda, which is clearly Palahniuk satirizing authoritarian power: "This today, study location prostate. Next today, clitoris. Second next today, nipples. Study stimulation lips. Stimulation scrotum. Craft best effective service of pervert penis and vagina. In vengeance against American predators must total operative graduate expert in pleasing all pedophile for extortion" (177). Pygmy writes, "Bully say, 'You come from one of those dick-mutilation places?' Say, 'Whip it out, pygmy.' Say, 'show me what the witch doctor done to you'" (16).[11] In Palahniuk style, this leads to Trevor's unconventional love for Pygmy and his orchestrated death—knowing Pygmy will kill him—during the massacre at the United Nations party (225). Characteristic of 1970 karate films, Pygmy assumes the role of the self-appointed protector of the clan, and Trevor positions himself as the primary threat. Ironically, how Trevor describes third-world populations foreshadows how the students identify themselves as representatives from those countries. The students perpetuate the negative stereotypes.

Similar to heroes in many 1970s martial arts films, Pygmy maintains an allegiance to an ideology advocating violence, obedience, and asceticism, and in this novel, these seem (at least from the actions of the Cedars and their friends) antithetical to American versions of Christianity, democracy, and education. And, as readers would expect, Palahniuk satirizes everything bureaucratically religious: the Cedars attend an ostentatious mega-church, one that includes capitalist luxuries such as tanning beds, coffee bars, and movie rentals (77); Magda attacks her soon-to-be lover the Reverend Tony during her chaotic baptism (27–29); and the Reverend Tony is poisoned by sniffing Magda's panties laced with a neurotoxin (193–94).[12] The dodgeball games and the spelling bee are described as mock-epic battles in which Pygmy views the other students as dogmatic adversaries, and Pygmy admits that he reluctantly participates in these scholastic rituals in order to infiltrate the American youth culture: "In order gain training organic chemistry or nuclear particle flux statistics, must engage too many idiot ritual: paint picture, volleyball, make waltz, craft poetry, participate dodgeball, scream idiot songs, torture violin or piano using many false note. Total most today, many useless task. Worst ever torture to watch youth wasted" (47). Obviously, dodgeball and spelling serve the function of kung fu. During the "battle of inflated balls" (159), Pygmy describes what is comparable to epic fighting: "Amid skirmish, landing hail infinite stinging bladders, rampant battlefield speeding missile, operative Tanek take position near elbow this agent. Tanek say whisper, keyed low so audible only ear of operative me, say, 'Attention, comrade.' Say, 'Become no seduced by silly adoration of American devils'" (160). Similar description is applied to the spelling bee: "All American student dismissed from battlefield, relegated into sets of audience, able only witness remainder word skirmish. Displayed onstage no one except operatives, Magda, Ling, Chernok, Oleg, Bokara, Mang, Tibor, Tanek, in addition this agent" (71). Pygmy has been trained, through events such as watching a rodent ground in a garbage disposal (39–43) and the public execution of Oleg's parents (93–99), that aggression is necessary against "corrupt, degenerate America" (155), but there are many features of Americana that he does not understand. For example, much to Pygmy's amusement, military prowess is associated with fried chicken in the form of Colonel Sanders. This is demonstrated in how he views Colonel Sanders as a military leader: "Along returning journey, encounter frequent memorial honoring American battle warrior, great officer similar Lenin. Many vast mural depicting most savvy United States war hero. Rotating statue. Looming visage noble American colonel. Courageous, renown of history, Colonel Sanders, image forever accompanied odor of sacrificial meat. Eternal flame offering wind savory perfume roasted flesh" (63). The comparisons between the school events and actual combat are appropriate ones, as these metaphors are frequently reinforced in American sports culture (as any fifteen-minute viewing of ESPN's *SportsCenter* would prove).

The section devoted to the model United Nations session is Palahniuk at his most politically profane and sarcastically satirical. In an America where media broadcast pathetic images of third-world populations suffering through poverty and famine and report the greedy exploitation of agencies claiming assistance to these people, Palahniuk presents how late Millennials/early

Four. Pygmy *as Parody of 1970s Karate Films*

Homelanders, a post–9/11 generation that has only known America at war against various anti–American threats, feel about this new world order. Demonstrating the opposite xenophobic or jingoistic attitudes of the Cedars, surprisingly none of the students want to represent the United States or its subsidiaries. Cat Sister tells Pygmy that absolutely nobody has volunteered to be the United States delegate (78), so he, as one of the least likely candidates suited for this role, is groomed for this job. Paradoxically, he becomes the emissary for the country that he was sent to terrorize. Pygmy's costume for this performance is taken straight out of a John Wayne film, western attire complete with ten-gallon hat and cowboy boots. The other students also assume their personas based on national and ethnic stereotypes or, being teenagers, take advantage of whatever cultural apparel allows them to dress provocatively, finding suitable reasons for putting on loincloths, inking on tattoos, and gluing on flies. Of course, inebriation on booze and drugs is expected. Pygmy takes the exercise seriously by apologizing for American abuse and neglect, amid "Fuck you, Uncle Sam!" (85) and other anti–American sentiments. As Pig Dog Brother films *Nations Gone Wild* (85), which is an apt reference of the event to the *Girls Gone Wild* spring-break hedonism, American students openly blame and ridicule their own country for international corruption. The irony is, of course, they are in fact the privileged Americans enjoying all of the perks bequeathed to the powerful, and the impending massacre has absolutely nothing to do with global or national politics but just plain, unadulterated resentment for being ignored. Before this school-sanctioned rave, Pygmy states, "Oleg allege no American student desire represent Western nation, American youth strictly aspire serve as delegate third-world government, racial ethnics, marginalized former colonies subjected imperial powers, striving achieve self-ruled" (73–74). The power inversion is complete with Pygmy saving the survivors against what is, if the exercise is kept in its context, an act of terrorism, as Trevor murders metaphorically a gym full of political representatives.

During his surveillance of American culture, Pygmy is also motivated by his libido, and in several instances, he is driven by sexuality rather than politics. His initial impression of all American females is that they are nymphomaniacs. As he reports in a very sexist and politically incorrect manner, "This agent, eye of operative me suffering fire pain, say how in America told all ladies glad liberated to always expose many fragrant vaginas. No ever possess maidenhead. Develop hobby of enjoying many frequent abortion. Always hungering to fashion moist lady mouths tight around gentlemen genital" (15). His misguided perceptions are unfortunately reinforced by Pig Dog Brother's fascination with female breasts and genitalia—this is how Pygmy learns American phrases such as "Madam Sweater Meat," "Madam Jugs," "Madam Party Pillows," and "Madam Blouse Bunnies" (58)—and by Mrs. Cedar's "Fukkerware parties" (33) and her obsession with electric vibrators. Worth noting is how Cat Sister thinks creating an uber-vibrator is a good idea, which foreshadows the topic of Palahniuk's 2014 novel *Beautiful You*: "'From battery sex toys to ones that plug into outlets,' say host sister. Solder draw into pattern, link diode, transistor, transducer, mystery project, host sister say, 'Build a better *vibrator*, Pygmy, and the world will beat a path to your door' … eye blink against white smoke, cat sister say, 'What scares me is how the Chinese are light-years ahead of us in the sex toy race'" (34). All of this might appear sexploitation on the surface, but in actuality, Palahniuk satirizes Chicken Mother's cordless vibrator addiction and male adolescent breast obsession as common practices in the American experience, as functional rather than dysfunctional behaviors. To Pygmy, this is all normal, everyday Americana.

In Pygmy's view, the school dance is an event preemptive to intercourse. He offers this impression of dancing during the school choir meeting: "all agent attempting shake from heads idiot lyric word of songs, infected worthless language of corrupt Western poetry. Useless American poetry and music no celebrate sacrifice lifetime to preserve state. No herald shining future of bright nuclear weapon, abundant wheat, and shining factory. No, instead most American song only empower to enjoy premature actions necessary for reproduction, grant permission commingle egg and seed among random partner occupying padded rear bench automobile" (46). The sexual orgy during the United Nations party only confirms Pygmy's assumptions about the promiscuity of American women. If dancing functions as a physical substitute for 1970s karate film hand-to-hand battle, Pygmy sees both the combative as well as sexual benefits of the action. In one situation, Pygmy thinks to himself how easy it would be to impregnate an American via a karate move: "Pumping Rabbit Maneuver, *squirt-squirt*, empty contents testicle awash viable American eggs" (111). In this way, Palahniuk takes advantage of establishing common ground with his audience through the 1970s karate film genre and, noting Hutcheon's theory of parody as showing the similarity but emphasizing the difference, moves forward to making statements, satirical as well as simply humorous, about contemporary American culture. True, this generation may have a different view of patriotism from their parents, and, granted, adolescents (both male and female) think about sex, but Palahniuk illustrates this ingeniously through his parody. Moreover, Palahniuk's doing this in transgressive fiction sets him apart from any other contemporary writer, and the end of *Pygmy* confirms this premise.

During the conclusion, Pygmy asserts his role as knight-errant hero featured in 1970s karate films. He is no longer the cultural Other, ethnic subaltern, or social outsider but is integrated effectively into the American community. His once fervent and zealous animosity toward everything American is replaced with cultural assimilation. This acceptance is partially based on his notoriety after killing Trevor, but it is, behind the scenes, also based on his decision to sabotage Operation Havoc by not tainting the money in the "Peace Machine" (198) with the "superdeadly mold" (207) that Donald Cedar has produced at the Radiological Institute of Medicine (140). Most of Palahniuk's novels have far-fetched endings, but this is definitely one of his most spectacular, rivaling the fusing of Cassie Wright and Branch Bacardi in *Snuff*. In fact, this conclusion is similar to the frequently unbelievable and outlandish endings presented in most 1970s karate films. After Pygmy is praised by the community for saving the mock UN session participants, Mr. Cedar decides to adopt him, and his statement drips with typical American cultural hubris: "Now, you might think an ignorant, backward child could never repay the generous gifts our community has granted him—the gifts of medical care, nutritious food, safe and secure shelter, free education, religious guidance and love—above all our love—but this child has repaid the debt" (121). Pygmy's hero stature is stressed during the hilarious scene in which Pygmy drugs the family, takes batteries from a vibrator inside Mrs. Cedar's vagina, and almost pokes out Mr. Cedar's good eye (since the prosthetic eye is needed for identification to get into his office) (168–72). Pygmy's defection is evident in this scene, and the other operatives then attempt to kill Pygmy during the school dance. Luckily, Pygmy is saved by the other students who (go figure) interpret the foreigners' karate actions as innovative dance moves (186–87).

This knight-errant role is also seen in his fight against technology. Pygmy sabotages Cat Sister's super-dildo, but then he is the only one who can disable the machine when it literally attacks the other students (202). At the time of the science fair, Pygmy reveals his decision to defect: "In greater afraid ... within thinking machine operative me, this agent ponder if entire being operative me pitted for destroy American, annihilate homosexual, crackpot Methodist religion, Lutheran and Baptist cult, extinguish all decadent bourgeoisie—subsequent successful total such destruction: Render this agent obsolete? Of no worth?" (206). The descriptions of the destructive vibrator going haywire is definitely trademark Palahniuk writing. Pygmy describes the scene: "Crowd all present retreat one stride, recede safe distance during phallus sprout miniature flame, red, yellow, blue flame. Sound screaming wail, no pretty music. Wailing demon phallus spring from table, bolt about exhibition floor, pursuing terrified judges. Trailing acrid black smoke, comet trail orange flames, screaming killer phallus spit molten plastic, pounce in chase wailing students. Stalk howling youth. Squalling inflamed phallus hunt squealing children" (202). This is similar to the final scene at the National Science Fair: "Killer phallus providing aerial cover, bombing hot plastic. Obscuring conflict with black smoke screen. Choking soot and smut" (237). During the novel's climactic ending, imitating the standard kung-fu free-for-all scene, Pygmy uses the "killer attack phallus" (236) to defeat the bad guys and save the day. In standard denouement, there is a happily-ever-after moment as Pigmy realizes that what he was taught was "actual outdated": "Admitting here failure of this agent. Operative me, traitor guilty of committing treason. Operation Havoc rendered utter aborted. Total disappointed of no result" (240). As Pygmy concludes, "Begins here new life of operative me" (241). Reminiscent not only of 1970s karate films but many heroic action stories (for that matter, some one-hour 1970s detective dramas), Pygmy moves from being the marginalized outsider to assuming his rightful place in the power center. Ironically, the technological innovation of Cat Sister's vibrator helps to foil the technological terrorism of the Peace Machine.

A reader can undoubtedly find this novel entertaining without knowledge of 1970s karate films, but one familiar with these movies cannot help but notice how Palahniuk parodies the Asian stereotyping that dominate those kick flicks. In transgressive fashion, Palahniuk blasphemes the socially moralistic sanctity of serious topics such as teen bullying, male-on-male rape, and school shooting through his hero story of Pygmy defending American good over anti–American evil. In fact, Pygmy might be too good. A reader wonders if Mrs. Cedar does not speak for all when she comments to Pygmy, "Well, if you jumped the first plane back to your native homeland, I wouldn't blame you one little bit.... This family ... our whole country is a total wreck" (228). Pygmy is in many ways a stock heroic character similar to ones in the 1970s karate films, but Palahniuk gives him a personality concerning how he confronts typical adolescent problems (typical at least in a Palahniuk definition of the term, and problems later also addressed by Madison in *Damned*). Superficially, the novel might just seem to be about an incredible dildo, domestic terrorism, and racial stereotyping, perhaps in horribly bad taste similar to the KTVU broadcast of the crash of Asiana Flight 214. More important, Palahniuk may just expose the "total wreck" of contemporary American culture. In the Palahniuk fictional universe,

Four. **Pygmy** *as Parody of 1970s Karate Films*

dysfunction rules, and readers just need to refer to actual events to see how life often imitates art. Incidentally, the 1970s karate films are regaining popularity. The El Rey Network is reviving these movies and might be potentially reinforcing the previous cultural stereotypes. As the El Rey Network advertises on its website, "Cinematic TV. Badass flicks. Killer opportunities. We serve it all up for rebels, aficionados and passionate creators." Concerning kung-fu films, there is this promotion, "He's lean, he's mean, he's an ass-kicking machine. He's the kung-fu hero and he's out to avenge his family, his fallen masters, and all that is righteous. Kung-fu movies take the everymen and make them supermen, fighting with fists, swords, flying guillotines and dragon blades to defend everything that is honorable." Readers just need to look at actual events to see how life often imitates art.

FIVE

Tell-All as Parody of Hollywood's Golden Age of Gossip Journalism

At the end of most check-out lanes in American grocery stores, there are racks filled with tabloid gossip magazines such as *Us, People, In Touch, Life & Style, OK!*, or the infamous ones, *Star, National Examiner,* and *National Enquirer*. Once herded into these lines, customers often cannot resist the flashy headlines (with a lot of exclamation points) accompanied by provocative photos (many probably photoshopped) and flip through these publications to find out the proverbial scoop about Hollywood celebrities. As of July 2015, there are plenty of stories about star divorces (a big one is Ben Affleck and Jennifer Garner splitting), star marriages (a hot one is Ashton Kutcher and Mila Kunis), and star problems (omnipresent are those dealing with the Kardashians: Kris's secret meltdowns, Kylie's weight gain, Kim's possible pregnancy, Kourtney's possible separation, and Khloe's basketball-player romance, not to leave out Caitlyn Jenner's diva escapades). Most shoppers thumb through the pages, wince, maybe wince again, and return these magazines before getting to the cashiers. One might be sucked into an article about Bristol Palin's recent pregnancy, for instance, and wonder like thousands of other people who could possibly be the baby daddy. People like gossip, and even though much of what is in those pages—or on television through *Access Hollywood, Entertainment Tonight,* or *Inside Edition*; or online through TMZ.com, *The Drudge Report,* or *The Smoking Gun*—could be less than 100 percent true, the ideas nonetheless influence how people perceive those personalities. Harry Levin, Perez Hilton, Christopher Hutchins, and others are trusted with reporting the truth, for verifying the dirt gathered that could stain the celebrities, and these gossip gatherers are given tremendous responsibility because they influence public

Five. Tell-All *as Parody of Gossip Journalism*

opinion concerning those who function as members of America's regal elite.

Chuck Palahniuk parodies this gossip industry in his novel *Tell-All*, and because of lightning-quick litigious reactions, and the lawyers who earn lucrative incomes for inspiring these responses, he chose to go back a few decades, 1940s and 1950s, within the golden age of gossip journalism, to address the tremendous power these entertainment journalists possess to either increase or decrease the value of a celebrity's current worth. Just like kings and queens in the past, celebrities have an important role in the American cultural psyche, and the gossip journalists have the ability to determine how this pseudo-royalty will be perceived at any given moment, through one article today in a tabloid magazine, and then through another piece tomorrow on an online site. As in *Pygmy*, Palahniuk does not focus on one or several texts but instead parodies an entire genre of writing, and in *Tell-All*, he understands the importance of veiling his own attack behind the names of deceased celebrities. From his own personal experience, Palahniuk certainly understands how media influence popular opinion. He has been the subject of gossip journalism on several occasions, and this unwanted and unwarranted attention has more than likely inspired the creation of this book.

Palahniuk may use Lillian Hellman and her exploits almost to frame his story (references to her often begin sections) because Hellman also addressed the issue of using past and present celebrities in her fiction. During an interview in 1973 with Nora Ephron, Hellman responds to a question about characterizing actual people she has known, particularly fictionalizing former acquaintances in her memoir *Pentimento*: "Oh, my, everybody's dead. But you feel freer that way.... It's too hard to write about the living. I'm not talking about pulling your punches, that's not it. It's hard to tell the truth about the living. It's hard even to know it" (133). Later, when asked about her apprehensions concerning what biographers might say about her after she is gone, Hellman comments, "I hope I've protected myself by choosing a few friends who will fight for me. It's a silly point, because what do you give a damn when you're dead. Any life can be made to look a mess of. Mine certainly can" (137). Hellman would have truly appreciated Palahniuk's colorful depiction of her in his novel. Besides finding the nearly demi-god status Palahniuk bestows upon her amusing, Hellman would have surely understood why Palahniuk decided to write a novel about celebrity, power, and gossip in Hollywood using past personalities. Palahniuk depicts Hellman as anything but "a mess," and he confronts the problem Hellman notes, that truth can be difficult to discern at times. Hellman understood all too well the fickleness and capriciousness of Hollywood fame, and she often maintained a love/hate relationship with those who served as Hollywood's reporters, the print media entertainment columnists. It is safe to say that Hellman benefitted from the best press publicity she received, but it is equally true that she was frequently wounded from the worst her tabloid enemies threw at her. There is little doubt that Palahniuk makes Hellman one of his novel's characters just for this reason. Although the portrayal might be considered negative, that she is lampooned or ridiculed, Palahniuk elevates Hellman because she stood up to Hollywood gossipmongers and did not allow them to dictate her creative and social decisions. If anything, Hazie Coogan's story could easily find a place in Hellman's *Pentimento* with the chapter entitled "Katherine Kenton." Actually, a more appropriate one would be labeled "Hazie Coogan."

Comparable to his other novels, most of the initial reviews of *Tell-All* are negative, and the inherent paradox is that these reviewers represent the entertainment media that Palahniuk satirizes. Gloria Maxwell states, "Diehard Palahniuk fans and those with a penchant for old-time Hollywood references will likely want to give this a chance. Others will find it tedious, needlessly redundant, and annoying—certainly, it's no ... Fight Club." Neil Hollands comments, "Palahniuk still has considerable linguistic firepower and satirical humor, but here he puts it in service of a repetitive, predictable story, never fulfilling the promise of a great premise. Constant, bold-faced references to Tinseltown obscurities become annoying long before the end of a short book. Palahniuk is coasting." A writer for *Publisher's Weekly* claims, "Palahniuk drops names from the famous to the headscratchingly obscure, peppers the narrative with neologisms supposedly coined by famous gossip columnists ... and, annoyingly styles the text so that nearly every name, brand name, and fabulous venue appears in bold. Unfortunately, the gossipy fantasia is a one-joke premise that, even at its modest length, wears out its welcome well before Miss Kathie's final fade-out" ("Tell-All"). Jonathan Shapiro admits, "Tell-All is a bomb.... A giant gasbag of a book, an unwieldy genre mish-mash, more confusing than entertaining, it lands with a thud as what the cigar-chompers in Hollywood used to call a 'feathered fish'—a story with so many disparate parts that it neither flies nor swims."[1] These critics make valid points, and there is no question the extensive highlighting and name dropping could intimidate some readers into not even giving this book a chance, let alone grapple with trying to figure out what Palahniuk is attempting to accomplish through the narrative. Many of these critics do not recognize (or at least fail to acknowledge they identify) that Palahniuk is essentially taking a poke at their own profession.

Five. Tell-All *as Parody of Gossip Journalism*

As always, Palahniuk experiments with form as well as content in *Tell-All*. Through Hazie, who narrates her tell-all confession about film star Katherine Kenton in the design of a screenplay, Palahniuk demonstrates how the socioeconomic marginalized and disenfranchised—in addition to possibly those lacking talent, charisma, or beauty—can gain celebrity status by way of subversion, deception, and manipulation. Hazie provides proof of this through her own type of gossip journalism, which takes the shape of the entire document (the novel itself) readers are presented. Palahniuk's application of boldface and constant name-dropping allow him to construct what is called a "carnivalesque" atmosphere in which the names play off of one another in terms of meaning, or put a more critical way, there is a dialogic between the codes or signifiers inside and outside the confines of the text. The theories of Mikhail Bakhtin help to explain this literary strategy.[2] In his study of Rabelais's *Gargantua and Pantagruel* entitled *Rabelais and His World*, Bakhtin develops the ideas of carnival and grotesque realism. Bakhtin claims the carnival frees people to transcend their normal, ordinary lives; they can become whomever or whatever they desire in a festival setting free of social or cultural restrictions. As Bakhtin states, carnival is that which "offered a completely different, nonofficial, extraecclesiastical and extrapolitical aspect of the world, of man, and of human relations" (197). He contends the carnival in Rabelais's time "celebrated temporary liberation from the prevailing truth and from the established order; it marked the suspension of all hierarchical rank, privileges, norms, and prohibitions. Carnival was the true feast of time, the feast of becoming, change, and renewal. It was hostile to all that was immortalized and completed" (199). According to Bakhtin, during the carnival, grotesque realism replaces the spiritual with the carnal, and the grotesque body gives social abstraction a human form. This transference is demonstrated through Hazie's etchings of Kenton's portrait on a mirror in the Kenton crypt below St. Patrick's Cathedral. Hazie meticulously marks the glass with a six-carat, marquise-cut Harry Winston diamond to "record the moment" (26). She states, "wielding the diamond, I get to work, drawing. I trace any new wrinkles, adding any new liver spots to this long-term record. Creating something more cumulative than any photograph, I document Miss Kathie's misery before the plastic surgeons can once more wipe the slate clean" (27). The mirrored grotesque Kenton assumes Dorian Gray qualities with the actual living Kenton, recording the spiritual and psychological decay unable to be erased through plastic surgery. This is especially evident when the glass finally shatters. Hazie remarks, "The lifetime of her scars and wrinkles, every distortion and defect she ever suffered, it's my own burden for the moment. The mirror itself sags with its collection of so many scratched insults. Every single one of Miss Kathie's faults and secrets" (174).

Palahniuk creates this carnival environment through the boldfaced names. He groups these historically and professionally different names within the boundaries of his paragraphs to interact and bounce off of each other, and consequently status and rank are eroded or erased through this interaction—everyone is equal within the linguistic contexts of Palahniuk's pages. Hazie is credited with generating this content—of putting them together—but readers attribute meanings to the numerous boldfaced names, associating the celebrity identities with information probably heard or read through gossip journalism (or technically to any previous references outside the text), and they compare that information to Hazie's insider stories about Kenton and her lover Webster Carlton Westward III. The result of all this is a crafty parody that mocks the integrity of entertainment criticism and a novel that is more complex and multifaceted than what critics claim.

In terms of grotesque realism, Hazie's ridiculous descriptions of lovemaking in the manuscript of *Love Slave* provide physical embellishment reminiscent of Rabelais, but the references to Hellman's incredibly superheroic abilities are more hyperbolic. Hellman's sections provide Palahniuk the perfect platform to parody historical events, and Hellman's reputation for stretching the truth corresponds with Hazie's own psychic self-delusion. Chris Talbott points out *Tell-All* "is a slim book based on a kernel of an idea the author was left with after hearing stories about the fabrication of Lillian Hellman's memoir." Oddly enough, the veracity of the content in Hellman's memoirs *An Unfinished Woman*, *Pentimento*, and *Scoundrel Time* is still being debated, and much of Hellman's cultural legacy is certainly related to her possible fabrications. In her defense, Hellman always claimed she combined fact and fiction, romance with realism, to recreate past experiences within the parameters of their significance to her present situations, and she was simply ahead of her time in terms of temporal vision. In Palahniuk's version of her theatrical production, besides putting together the blockbuster film *Unconditional Surrender* in which she serves as the heroine, Hellman saves Jewish babies from a Nazi death camp (1), helps to create the A-Bomb with Albert Einstein (18), confronts Lee Harvey Oswald in Dallas (63), and rescues John Glenn in outer space (91). An example of Hellman's physical prowess is in the beginning of the novel: "Lilly throws the terrified, make-believe Hitler into the center of tonight's dinner table, her teeth biting, her manicured fingernails scratching at his Nazi eyes. Lillian's fists clamped around the invisible windpipe, she begins pounding the invisible Führer's skull against the tablecloth, making the silverware and wineglasses jump and rattle" (5). Rewriting the historical scripts to serve her own egotistical agenda, Hellman functions as Hazie's model artist, one who has not only the creative acuity to redirect the course of events but the position to benefit from her placement inside of the action. Hellman writes herself into the role of the super-feminist during the era of first-wave feminism; therefore, she empowers herself within a male-dominated society and projects the strong feminist gender qualities Hazie wants to possess. Hazie notes about Hellman's blockbuster rendition of the war, "The critics were willing to forgive **Lillian Hellman** a few factual inconsistencies concerning the **Second World War**. As presented here, this was history—but better. It might not be the actual war, but this was the war we wished we'd fought" (144). This is Hellman's artistic perspicacity in a nutshell.

Palahniuk could not have selected a better mentor for Hazie. Hellman's 1973 *Pentimento*, which contains the chapter "Julia" that was developed into the 1977 Oscar-winning film *Julia*, was scrutinized for its authenticity in portraying events, but Hellman confessed, as Deborah Martinson points out in *Lillian Hellman: A Life with the Foxes and Scoundrels*, she had written a book of portraits instead of a straight autobiography (321).[3] Martinson defends Hellman's artistic decisions in *Pentimento*: "Unsurprisingly, amid the mélange of innovation within the book, critics began to quarrel bitterly over the ethics of autobiography.... Clearly *Pentimento* was not autobiography but something new, causing much critical angst. Thousands of readers, however, loved the book, and their readership made Hellman an American icon" (322). During a 1979 appearance on *The Dick Cavett Show*, Mary McCarthy lambasted Hellman's literary reputation. As Martinson describes, "Asked by Cavett to name overrated authors, McCarthy's response was quick and more political than literary: 'the only one I can think of is a holdover like Lillian Hellman, who I think is tremendously overrated, a bad writer, and dishonest writer, but she really belongs to the past, to the Steinbeck past'" (353). Hellman responded by suing McCarthy and Cavett for $2.25 million (Martinson 355). In Hazie's screenplay, theater and life merge as Hellman intercedes at just the right moment to save Kenton from being shot by Westward. As Hazie mentions, Westward "did nothing except fall deeply in love—passionately in love—[but] now he must play the villain for the rest of this silly motion picture we call human history" (177). Just as Hellman manufactures new realities through her historical remakes, Hazie manipulates the realities of Westward and Kenton to ensure her own happy ending. Palahniuk's Hellman took center stage, dominated everyone's attention, and thrived on self-publicity, not all that different from the actual Hellman. In contrast, Hazie lurks backstage, behind the curtain, yet she clearly controls the events passive-aggressively through falsifying documents—through Westward's own memoir mostly—and by serving as the duplicitous confidant undermining those who entrust her with their secrets.

Palahniuk's parody of the 1950 Oscar-winning film *All About Eve* underscores this theme of deception. Thinking about the obvious comparison between the film and her own situation, Hazie points out explicitly, "I was **Thelma Ritter** before **Thelma Ritter** was **Thelma Ritter**" (88), as well as declaring, "The Webster specimen's got it backward, I tell him. **Thelma Ritter** is a copy of me. Her walk and diction, her timing, and delivery, all of it was coached" (90). Hazie calls Joseph Mankiewicz one of the "damned copycats" for basing "Birdie" on her and stealing her dance moves and singing style (88). Hazie also accuses Mankiewicz of caricaturing Tallulah Bankhead for Bette Davis's role of Margo Channing (89). Hazie's affiliation with Thelma Ritter is relevant for a few reasons. First, Ritter's character is seen mostly in the first half of the film, and Birdie has little to do with much of the plot after Eve Harrington subversively assumes power. Granted, similar to Hazie, Birdie is sarcastic, witty, and pragmatic, but she never displays any motivation to usurp Margo Channing's authority. Perhaps this comparison exposes Hazie's self-perceived ethical position as the one who has, similar to Birdie, the moral compass to guide her friend through amoral diversions. The truth is, however, Hazie is much more like Eve in that she sabotages Kenton's success and eventually assumes her position, not garnishing the acting accolades as Eve does but taking her place in the Hollywood spotlight nonetheless. Second, Hazie's pride is apparent in how she takes the credit for serving as the model for Thelma Ritter's mannerisms and Marilyn Monroe's singing (ignoring that Ritter's and Monroe's idiosyncrasies made them famous). This place in the novel clearly demonstrates Hazie's deep psychosis as well as exhibits the fierce resentments she holds toward Hollywood networking. Palahniuk's entire novel could have been a parody solely of *All About Eve* if Hazie had identified more with Eve than Birdie; nevertheless, Hazie's testimony in this section functions as evidence to confirm the narrator's self-delusion. In an interview with Nicole Powers, Palahniuk admits *Tell-All* is influenced by *All About Eve*, but he also confesses inspiration from *Sunset Boulevard*. Palahniuk states, "I always loved [*Sunset Boulevard*], that Max is the one who orchestrates so much of that story, and Max the butler, Erich von Stroheim, is the one that's left at the end, not dead and not insane. In a way, part of me always thought Max set all of this up so that it would happen. It could easily have been done." Powers responds, "Ah, so Hazie Coogan is your version of Max," and Palahniuk answers, "Exactly." Hazie gloats over Mankiewicz's characterizations of her behaviors, but she also reveals psychologically how she believes she is staying behind the scenes in Kenton's life story and is not taking control from Kenton as Eve does from Channing. Third, from what is presented, Birdie may be the sexual antithesis of Channing, as Birdie does not seem sexually active or sexually interested in anyone. Hazie's alliance with Birdie may also broach a gender question. She may not see herself as Eve because she is not attracted to Westward, nor does she seem to desire Kenton, at least not romantically. Considering Hellman and Ritter, Hazie perhaps sees herself as the composite of two interesting forms of power, feminine aggressiveness and feminine passive-aggressiveness. Regardless of gender, an alliance with Hellman and Ritter makes Hazie a formidable adversary in Hollywood or elsewhere.

Palahniuk's use of highlighting establishes the carnival in *Tell-All* as well as reveals Hazie's psychological self-assessment concerning her relationship with Kenton and the other characters. During an interview with Paul Donoughue, Palahniuk refers to the inspiration for all the name-dropping: "I was in New York with Sam Rockwell, and he was talking about having been in a Jesse James movie with Brad Pitt. He suddenly caught himself and got very self-conscious, and made fun of himself by saying 'Listen to me: all I say is blah, blah, blah Brad Pitt. It sounds like I have some name-dropping form of Tourette's Syndrome.' And it was just a perfect way of defining the way that name-dropping happens in conversation." Rockwell's statement eventually became a line in *Tell-All*: "Lilly's drivel possibly constitutes some bizarre form of name-dropping **Tourette's syndrome**" (3). As a literary technique, the names serve as signifiers for celebrity denotation and connotation. For instance, as Hazie plans a dinner party, certainly a carnival-like situation, readers assign meaning to the words that in turn provide significations for the famous Hollywood personalities. Through the interpretative process, or intertextual wordplay, readers provide meaning to the first celebrity, relate that meaning subsequently given to the next celebrity, and so on until the semiotic process enables readers to view the entire passage as a collective unit of significations. Take as an illustration the following section: "Seat **Desi Arnaz** to the left of **Hazel Court**. Put **Rosemary Clooney** across from **Lex Barker**. **Fatty Arbuckle** always spits as he speaks, so place him opposite **Billie Dove**, who's too blind to notice. Using my own pen, I elbow into Terry's work, drawing arrows from **Jean Harlow** to **Lon Chaney Sr.** to **Douglas Fairbanks Jr.**

Like **Knute Rockne** sketching football plays, I circle **Gilda Gray** and **Hattie McDaniel**, and I cross out **June Haver**" (41). Desi Arnaz signifies meaning that is related to Rosemary Clooney's meaning, which is then applied to Fatty Arbuckle's meaning. Each of these names functions as a linguistic mask representing the star-quality attributed to that celebrity. Furthermore, by demystifying the celebrities in this social setting—making them "real" by showing them interacting with others at a gathering—these Hollywood big shots are knocked down to the common level. In a carnivalesque way, these elevated personalities are portrayed as normal people. On the other side of this, Hazie assumes power during this one social event to exert her authority over those who typically would not give her this right. In short, she is the one determining where they will sit and next to whom they will sit, thus controlling their places at the table, and where one sits is emblematic of the power that one holds. In a sense, Palahniuk provides a textual game of "Who would you invite to dinner?" As one knows from playing this game, names are chosen based upon purely subjective reasons, but that subjectivity is drawn from information associated with those peoples' names, the social or cultural value those names hold to the person selecting them.

Interpreting the names within this carnival environment, readers attribute meaning based upon their individual perspectives, which are influenced greatly by popular sources that include gossip journalism. Significantly, this is pure semiotics in that readers are focusing on the names as signs, attaching meaning to those signs, and then making connections between the structural placements of the signs. The dialogic is the relationship between the names on the page and the previous meanings readers assign to them based on how those names are defined through other sources, connecting how they are presented in the current text to how they were portrayed in previous texts. Hazie even admits that names boil down to linguistic markers: "Even the most illustrious names, once they're dead long enough, are reduced to silly animal sounds. *Grunt, bark, bray* … **Ford Madox Ford** … **Miriam Hopkins** … **Robert Ayrton**" (178). Hazie still controls this signification process within the carnivalesque situation. One of the best examples is when Hazie compares Kenton to cultural paragons of beauty, as *Paragon* appropriately becomes the title of Hazie's memoir about her relationship with Kenton:

> This woman is **Pocahontas**. She is **Athena** and **Hera**. Lying in this messy, unmade bed, eyes closed, this is **Juliet Capulet**, **Blanche Dubois**, **Scarlett O'Hara**. With ministrations of lipstick and eyeliner I give birth to **Ophelia**. To **Marie Antoinette**. Over the next trip of the larger hand around the face of the bedside clock, I give form to

Lucrezia Borgia. Taking shape at my fingertips, my touches of foundation and blush, here is **Jocasta**. Lying there, **Lady Windermere**. Opening her eyes, **Cleopatra**. Given flesh, a smile, swinging her sculpted legs off one side of the bed, this is **Helen of Troy**. Yawning and stretching, here is every beautiful woman across history.

My position is not that of a painter, a surgeon or a sculptor, but I perform all those duties. My job title: **Pygmalion** [48].

Essentially, Hazie orchestrates through name-dropping a carnivalesque atmosphere in which she can subvert social authority and undermine celebrity power. In an age of omnipresent electronic access to *Wikipedia* and other information retrieval possibilities through the Internet, reading just one paragraph such as this could become an interactive fact-finding exercise, comparable to a linguistic treasure hunt, juxtaposing the knowledge (denotative with connotative) gathered about these identities and then constructing an interpretation based upon the accumulation of this data. Furthermore, the privileging of the historical values of these personalities is significant. For instance, readers will interpret the beauty of Pocahontas, of Athena, of Helen of Troy, and of the others and eventually synthesize all of this into one vision of beauty. Moreover, all of these feminine icons of beauty are equal, at least within this prose selection. Readers may subjectively give priority to Cleopatra, for example, as the most beautiful, but others may give this distinction to Jocasta. Significantly, readers will make these decisions based upon their current frames of reference, previous sources of information, and the textual positioning of the names. Hazie does not necessarily rank these icons in order of attractiveness, but the sequence in which she presents them in the paragraph influences how they are perceived by readers.

In this way, Hazie compares herself to the gossip columnists, the dubious social delegators of cultural power.[4] Donoughue reports that Palahniuk researched this novel extensively: "Palahniuk trolled through the many catty, scurrilous newspaper gossip columns that gave the town its harshest reputation. In the words of Hedda Hopper and Walter Winchell he found the tasteless commentary that informed the Hollywood he would depict." Unquestionably, the major gossip columnists set forth the tell-all tone of the novel, and Palahniuk surveys their statements to cultivate the tell-all nature of Hazie's story. This cataloguing of names is not necessarily for signification as it is to develop Palahniuk's parody of pulp criticism in the guise of reputable journalism. For example, Hazie drops names of major reporters while describing Kenton's performance in Hellman's *Unconditional Surrender*:

> From any closer than row fifteen, Miss Kathie's dyed hair looks stiff as wire. Her gestures, jittery and tense, her body whistled down by fear and anxiety to what **Louella**

Parsons would call a "lipsticked stick figure." Despite the constant threat of murder, she refuses to involve the police out of fear she'll be humiliated by **W. M. Mooring** in *Film Weekly* or **Hale Horton** in *Photoplay*, depicted as a dotty has-been infatuated by a scheming gigolo. It's a choice between the devil and the deep blue sea: whether to be killed or humiliated by **Donovan Pedelty** or **Miriam Gibson** in *Screen Book* magazine [139].

Hazie later mentions more about these columnists, "For once, the critics weren't her worst fear, not **Frank S. Nugent** of the *New York Times* nor **Howard Barnes** of the *New York Herald Tribune* nor **Robert Garland** of the *New York American*. **Jack Grant** of *Screen Book*, **Gladys Hall** and **Katherine Albert** of *Modern Screen* magazine, **Harrison Carroll** of the *Los Angeles Herald Express*, a legion of critics take rapturous notes, racking their brains for additional superlatives" (146). And, of course, there are more: "Also, columnists **Sheilah Graham** and **Earl Wilson**, a group that any other show, any other night would constitute what **Dorothy Kilgallen** calls 'a jury of her sneers,' this night those sourpusses would clamor with praise" (146–47). Critics who said Palahniuk just throws out names might have a point late in *Tell-All*, but Palahniuk needs to mention one critic after another to call into question the habitual name-dropping of the gossip industry. In other words, this is exactly what the gossip journalists did, list names and expect readers to fill in the gaps, almost as if readers walked past them during a social gathering, glancing at one, then another, and then another. These gossip journalists also provide sexual double-entendres, which would have clearly been transgressive for the time. For instance, Hazie states, "Despite popular speculation, Miss **Katherine Kenton** and I do not enjoy what **Walter Winchell** would call a 'fingers deep friendship.' Nor do we indulge in behavior *Confidential* would cite to brand us as 'baritone babes,' or **Hedda Hopper** describes as 'pink pucker sucking'" (10). Several examples of 1940s and 1950s gossip columnist neologisms and witticisms are included is this lengthy list: "silver-framed photographs of men whom **Walter Winchell** would call 'was-bands'" (13); "A rogues' gallery of what **Walter Winchell** would call 'happily-never-afters'" (21); "Each romance, the type of self-destructive gesture **Hedda Hopper** would call 'marry-kiri'" (21); "What **Louella Parsons** would call 'moping mechanisms'" (24).[5] These often seem to be chances for Palahniuk himself just to drop several clichés one after another, almost as a series of non sequiturs, but they definitely serve his purpose.

There are places, however, when Palahniuk takes advantages of Hazie's citations from gossip columnists to express profound statements about truthful reporting, and these are especially interesting remembering Palahniuk graduated college with a journalism degree, was a practicing professional journalist, and still writes journalistic articles. For the sake of illustrating these and not simply stringing together quotations, there are insightful gems of wisdom cited by Hazie. She comments, "Professional gossip **Elsa Maxwell** once said, 'All biographies are an assemblage of untruths.' A beat later adding, 'So are all *autobiographies*'" (144). Considering Westward the writer of the Kenton biography, or "the type of tome Hedda Hopper always calls a 'lie-ography'" (96), Hazie offers this statement about the gossip industry: "To add insult to injury, the lies he'd written about my Miss Kathie and her sexual adventures, they would eventually be cherry-picked by **Frazier Hunt** of *Photoplay*, **Katherine Albert** of *Modern Screen* magazine, **Howard Barnes** of the *New York Herald Tribune*, **Jack Grant** of *Screen Book*, **Sheilah Graham**, all the various low-life bottom feeders of *Confidential* and every succeeding biographer of the future. These tawdry, soft, sordid fictions would petrify and fossilize to become diamond-hard, carved-stone facts for all perpetuity" (105). After this, Hazie states the most profound line in the entire novel, one particularly applicable and certainly true concerning gossip journalism: "A salacious lie will always trump a noble truth" (105). This last statement undoubtedly reflects Palahniuk's personal opinion about the entire entertainment media industry. Just as the gossip writers claim truthful reporting but then spin a story to serve their needs, Hazie attributes meaning to Kenton as she chooses, and thus influences how readers perceive the film star within the carnivalesque textual environment. More important, Hazie also assumes personas at will and takes advantage of their unobtrusive yet integral purposes to support celebrity status: "Because, I say, the life of **Katherine Kenton** is my work-in-progress.... Still writing, still scribbling away, I say that Miss Kathie is my unfinished masterpiece.... My job title is not that of nanny or guardian angel, but I perform duties of both. My full-time profession is what **Walter Winchell** calls a 'star sitter.' A 'celebrity curator,' according to **Elsa Maxwell**" (129–30). Hazie has the ability to determine how Kenton will be perceived as *Paragon* serves as the tell-all memoir full of the facts about Kenton's life. Just as Hellman hoped she was protected from malicious and slanderous assaults on her reputation, Kenton is unknowingly at the mercy of Hazie concerning her professional legacy.

An actual example of this power could be Sheilah Graham's relationship with F. Scott Fitzgerald, although Fitzgerald obviously never gave Graham near as much power as Kenton sacrifices to Hazie. While Fitzgerald struggled with wife Zelda's frequent hospitalizations in North Carolina, his daughter Scottie's starting college at Vassar, and his new job in Hollywood as a script writer, Graham provided much needed stability and served as Fitzgerald's confidante and caregiver when he was running out of friends. Besides serving as his lover, Graham bolstered his confidence and was the beautiful female accoutrement necessary in Hollywood society. This relationship was probably built more on status rather than emotion, and Fitzgerald benefited from Graham's companionship as much as she prospered from his notoriety. After Fitzgerald's death, Graham made a second gossip-journalist career out of her relationship with Fitzgerald, seizing upon the opportunity in several tell-all books to present herself as Fitzgerald's Florence Nightingale and his saving grace, particularly concerning his battle with alcohol, which she suggests she helped him to win during the months preceding his death. Graham provided the media with the particular details, for instance, of Fitzgerald having his fatal heart attack in the living room of her home, and nobody really knows if the dialogues she creates in her books are accurate. Considering Graham's background as a social climber, most are probably embellishments, stretching the truth to her advantage, but unlikely flat-out falsehoods similar to Hazie's fabrication in *Love Slave*. Graham published several gossipy books from the 1950s all the way to her to her death in the 1980s: *Beloved Infidel: The Education of a Woman*; *Confessions of a Hollywood Columnist*; *The Garden of Allah*; *How to Marry Super Rich*; *For Richer, for Poorer*; *Rest of the Story: The Odyssey of a Modern Woman*; *A State of Heat*; *The Late Lily Shiel*; *College of One: The Story of How F. Scott Fitzgerald Educated the Woman He Loved*; *The Real F. Scott Fitzgerald, Thirty-Five Years Later*; *My Hollywood: A Celebration and a Lament*; and *Hollywood Revisited: A Fiftieth Anniversary Celebration*. Her son, Robert Westbrook, published *Intimate Lies: F. Scott Fitzgerald and Sheilah Graham: Her Son's Story*, seeming to borrow generously from Graham's *Beloved Infidel* to provide almost identical accounts of the past, adding another layer to the gossip. Graham's celebrity ambitions radiate in the famous photos taken in a nightclub in 1953 displaying her and Marilyn Monroe. Monroe is in the spotlight, but Graham almost shines as dazzlingly.

E. Ray Canterbery and Thomas Birch claim Graham was the perfect audience for Fitzgerald. She laughed at his jokes and listened to his instructions, and Fitzgerald was the educated social charmer she had always wanted (307). They note that the "prospect of romance always seemed to revitalize Fitzgerald" (307), and Graham provided a needed stimulus at a crucial time in his life. Graham, who by her own testimony "remained in a state of heat since her early teens" (qtd. in Canterbery and Birch 294), did not really consider herself a mistress because she and Fitzgerald kept separate residences, and Fitzgerald did not finance her lifestyle (Bruccoli 435). Two events indicate Fitzgerald might have given priority to the sexual nature of the relationship. Returning from Chicago with Graham, Fitzgerald made a drunken spectacle of himself by telling a fellow airplane passenger that Graham was a "great lay" (Canterbury and Birch 318). Westbrook writes about a similar occasion when his mother found Fitzgerald in a bar: "Sheilah was more amazed than angry, for this was a man who when sober visibly winced at the word *damn*. They ordered more drinks, then Scott started bragging about her to his new friend. Chortling and grinning, he said what a great cunt Sheilah was, a fabulous lay. Sheilah refused to take him too seriously. He seemed to her almost a parody of adolescence" (*Intimate* 185). This was, of course, not the spin that Graham put on her relationship with Fitzgerald.

Just as Graham insinuates in her memoirs about her relationship with Fitzgerald, Hazie ingeniously establishes a role that appears subservient but is actually one of control. As she states, "I am not merely a woman who works in a factory producing the ever-ravishing **Katherine Kenton**. I am the factory itself. With the words I write here I am not simply a camera operator or cinematographer; I am the lens itself—flattering, accentuating, distorting—recording, how the world will recall my coquettish Miss Kathie" (9). The thirst for power and control is obvious in Hazie's own statements about Kenton. Hazie introduces herself directly: "If you'll permit me to break the fourth wall, my name is **Hazie Coogan**. My vocation is not that of a paid companion, nor am I a professional housekeeper. It is my role as an old woman to scrub the pots and pans ... those pots and pans have always belonged to the majestic, the glorious film actress Miss **Katherine Kenton**" (7). Likewise, she asserts, "My purpose is to impose order on Miss Kathie's chaos ... to instill discipline in her legendary artistic caprice" (8). Hazie clarifies, "My position is not that of a nurse, or a maid, or a secretary. Nor do I serve as a professional therapist or a chauffeur or bodyguard. While my job title is none of the preceding, I do perform all of those functions. Every morning, I pull the drapes. Walk the dog. Lock the doors. I disconnect the telephone, to keep the outside world in its correct place. However, more and more my job is to protect Miss Kathie from herself" (10). The reference to *What Ever Happened to Baby Jane?* is supposed to be obvious to readers, and Hazie makes sure to correct any misinterpretation. In a crucial passage, Hazie adamantly defines her role: "You talk about art imitating life, well, the reverse is true" (91). Hazie adds, "When I met her, Kathie Kenton was nothing. A Hollywood hopeful. A hostess in a steakhouse, handing out menus and clearing dirty plates. My job is not that of a stylist or press agent, but I've groomed her to become a symbol for millions of women. Across time, billions. I may not be an actor, but I've created a model of strength to which women can aspire. A living example of their own incredible possible potential" (91). Hazie has the control over the names she presents on the pages of her screenplay, and in this way, she is the puppet master who sets these characters in motion during semiotic word play. As she states in these lines, Hazie has the power to influence how others are perceived. This is the case with those in Hollywood who interpret Katherine Kenton's acting abilities; this is also true of readers who give meaning to the names within the contexts of the paragraphs. Hazie wants, however, the total control that she believes only stardom will provide.

This desire for more power is manifested in Hazie's installments of *Love Slave*. Hazie is quite astute at sophomoric sexual embellishment, and she could rival any beginning romance novelist at describing love-making at its most inanely intimate moments—Hazie certainly has a gift for R-rated soft porn. As a pragmatist, Hazie understands how sexuality can be turned into a weapon and used exploitatively. In a revealing line that differentiates how she and Kenton view sexuality, Hazie comments, "Katherine Kenton remains among the generation of women who feel that the most sincere form of flattery is the male erection. Nowadays, I tell her that erections are less likely a compliment than they are the result of some medical breakthrough. Transplanted Monkey glands, or one of those new miracle pills" (15). When Hazie describes loves scenes between Kenton and Westward, they are extremely phallocentric. As Hazie assumes the persona of Westward, she writes in one passage, "Abandoning the sudden glory of her puckered shelter ... I spewed my streaming tribute, gush upon jetting gush, the pearlescent globules of my adoration and profound admiration spattering Katherine's unutterable beautiful visage'" (115). Later, Kenton states, "Webster, my darling, the pints of love essence you erupt at the peak of oral passion taste more intoxicating than gorging on even the richest European chocolate.... All women should taste your delicious emissions" (124). This scene continues, "Lowering her silken sensual legs with infinite care ... Katherine immersed her spattered thighs, her acclaimed pubis descending into the scalding clouds of iridescent white. The hot liquid lapped at her satiny buttocks, then splashed at her silken bustline. The misty vapors swirled, perfume filling the sultry bathroom air" (124). In another section, while she looks at an adjacent tall building, Kenton states, "you stupendously virile male animal, this majestic tower is your only phallic rival in the world ... and I'd gladly climb a million steps to sit atop both" (133). In another scene, before she succumbs to an assassin, Kenton pleads, "Honor and remember me by sharing your incredibly talented penis with all the most beautiful but less fortunate women of the world" (143). Hazie's depictions in *Love Slave* imitate romantically melodramatic drivel, perpetuating masochistic female subservience, the opposite of Hellman's aggressive feminism in her scripts. In this way, Hazie's fabricated memoir, which is technically lies passed off as Westward's own falsehoods serving as his alibis, counterbalances Hellman's narratives.

Moreover, the outside static produced through all of the name-dropping, and the subsequent signification and word-play that almost functions as white noise, serves as chatter to verify the authenticity of both Hazie's and Hellman's stories. Through all of this, readers judge Hazie and decide on her culpability. In the 1940s and 1950s, readers underwent a similar experience when they read the gossip columns, and, to put this in perspective, today's readers do the same when they look at multifarious gossip magazines, programs, or sites. There is no way a reader of *Tell-All* will know every celebrity mentioned, let alone understand why Palahniuk has placed each celebrity in his or her location on a page, but similar to a Bakhtinian carnival in which power is subverted and roles are switched, readers navigate the best they can through Hazie's script. Hazie really gets at this when she speaks with Terry about her framing of Westward: "The nib of my fountain pen scratching, looping, dotting lines and sentences across each page, I say that no memory is anything more than a personal choice. A very deliberate choice. When we recall someone—a parent, a spouse, a friend—as better than they perhaps were, we do so to create an ideal, something to which we, ourselves, can aspire. But when we remember someone as a drunk, a liar, a bully, we're only creating an excuse for our own poor behavior" (128). The point is actually that Hazie builds up Kenton and Westward solely to knock them down, and she never, not in a single place in her script, excuses any of her poor behaviors. In her eyes, celebrity notoriety and fame can easily be torn down and taken away.

Hazie's comments at the novel's conclusion reveal that she believes the fictional reality she has created for herself, and she justifies her actions in the name of stardom. Even as she explains what she considers the truth about her relationship with Kenton, she continues to look at her life as a screenplay, a theatrical production that can be staged, directed, and ultimately criticized, not a life lived outside the strictures of the Hollywood film industry. As Hazie admits, speaking of herself in the third-person point of view as being shot through the camera lens, "Even as she watches those present unconsciously mimic the lovely girl, the ugly one considers a plan. As a possible alternative to becoming an actress herself, perhaps the better strategy would be to join forces—combining her own skill and intelligence with the other girl's beauty. Between the two of them, they might yield one immortal motion picture star" (162). Right before this, Hazie summarizes all the plots to kill Kenton: "Now, in the event Miss Kathie falls under an omnibus, bathes with an electric radio, feeds herself to grizzly bears, tumbles from a tall building, sheathes an assassin's sharp dagger with her heart or ingests cyanide—then **Webster Carlton Westward III** will never get to publish his terrible 'lie-ography'" (159). The beginning of the quotation reads, "In this flashback, the ugly girl has almost given up hope. She's studied her craft with **Constance Collier** and **Guthrie McClintic** and **Margaret Webster**, yet she still can't find work. The homely girl does possess an innate, shrewd cunning; none of her gestures is ever without intention and motivation. In her underplaying, the ugly girl displays nothing short of brilliance" (162). Hazie is indeed brilliant in how she carries out her scheme, but she does not really understand the ramifications of what has occurred.

Ironically, she gets away with murder and is praised for her tell-all memoir, but she is not truly satisfied or happy. If she were, she would probably take ownership of all that she reported. As Hazie notes, "Seated to my right, **Charlie McCarthy** congratulates me on the success of my book. As of this week, *Paragon* has been at number one on the *New York Times* best-seller list for twenty-eight weeks" (178). Or, maybe this is not so ironic given the nature of the beast. Perhaps, this is what readers should expect. In a Palahniuk universe, this ending seems appropriate. The naming of the adopted child Norma Jean Baker emphasizes the illusiveness of the situation. The child could not possibly become Marilyn Monroe, but the mentioning of the name still points toward this film star's tragic life. As Hazie notes, "No, none of us seem so very real. We're only supporting characters in the lives of each other. Any real truth, any precious fact will always be lost in a mountain of shattered make-believe" (179). Hazie's last instructions concluding this screenplay, within the rolling credits and the cutting of film, command that none of the preceding information should be traced back to her: "Please promise you did *NOT* hear this from me" (179). The ending calls into question the entire nature of truth, and Hazie appears to be negotiating with readers, taking credit for the information but also relinquishing possession of it. Nonetheless, Hazie has written herself into the spotlight, and the only truth that matters is the one that gives her power and control.

Palahniuk is clearly responding to the social duplicity and cultural chicanery of contemporary popular criticism, the type of reviews similar to the negative ones written about *Tell-All*. William Henry III, Jeanne McDowell, and Naushad Mehta assert gossip journalism has flourished, not decreased, since its golden age:

> Decades after Walter Winchell, Louella Parsons, Hedda Hopper and their ilk went the way of the dodo, their patented elixir of career hype, marital comings and goings, feuds, fortunes and celebrity pratfalls has become the journalistic cocktail of choice. In the great public circus of American life, gossip is back in the center ring. New York City, the U.S. media capital, has become a metropolis where most of the newspapers offer not just one gossip page but three or four. They feature glimpses of everyone from sitcom heroes and sports stars to obscure if self-important entertainment and publishing executives, social-climbing plastic surgeons and dress designers, deposed royalty, offspring of outed dictators and legions of the nouveaux riches or, rather, nouveaux gauches. Gossip columns may even feature other gossip columnists.

These writers describe a situation similar to the one in *Tell-All*: "Americans were encouraged to live in daydreams about the life-styles of the rich and famous, to emphasize the material over the spiritual. Gossip can be marketed so as to make the listener feel smugly superior to those being talked about. But in the gossip journalism of today, Liz wants to be Ivana, Ivana wants to be Liz, and nobody even pretends to want to be the gentle reader." Bakhtin believes the carnival provides the opportunity to revitalize the existing social hierarchy, although this only lasts as long as the duration of the festival. As he contends, carnival not only allows peasants to ridicule and taunt royalty and clergy, but it empowers them, the marginalized and disenfranchised, to initiate genuine social reform (*Rabelais* 199). The gesture unfortunately is only symbolic. Hazie has become a celebrity, but this power is certainly as mercurial and as indiscrete as the gossip gods who bestow this dubious honor. Palahniuk understands this process well, and he has the last laugh at those critics who call, for instance, *Tell-All* a "giant gasbag" or a "feathered-fish" of a novel. These critics underestimate Palahniuk's brilliant ability to satirize, ridicule, and, most important, parody.

Six

Damned as Parody of Dante's *Inferno*

Chuck Palahniuk is obviously not the first person in American media to transform Dante's medieval vision of hell into something a lot less frightening. Films such as *Little Nicky* and *Bill & Ted's Bogus Journey* have presented hell as not such a horrible place. There are the famous *South Park* episodes in which socially canonized good people—those honored for their compassion, courage, and philanthropic, humanitarian, or altruistic contributions—are placed into Satan's domain, and these personalities surprisingly include Princess Diana and John F. Kennedy Jr. (when their unfortunate deaths were recent news), Michael Landon, Mahatma Gandhi, and even Mother Teresa. There are also the notorious personalities one would expect to occupy the fiery depths such as Ted Bundy, Jeffrey Dahmer, and John Wayne Gacy, and, of course, this hell includes America's number one nemesis during the peak of *South Park*'s appeal, Saddam Hussein. There are countless other examples in American popular culture of hell not necessarily being all that bad. In fact, Adult Swim's *Your Pretty Face is Going to Hell* depicts hell as a region similar to Palahniuk's version in *Damned*. There are relatively normal jobs for those facing eternal damnation, flying demons and other nuisances constantly harass the inhabitants, and the same bureaucracies bothering the living irritate the dead. As has been mentioned in the preceding chapters, Palahniuk addresses a widely general audience in his novels, and he certainly gives his readers unique perspectives from which to view the influences of past texts on current ones in American culture. Palahniuk continues this through *Damned*. As with most parodies of a fire-and-brimstone hell, readers can identify the influence of Dante in the novel, but Palahniuk takes his remake of *The Inferno* (the first section in *The Divine Comedy*) to another level through his adolescent main character, Madison Spencer. Palahniuk's adolescent twist on Dante's hell distinctively sets his version apart from all of the others.

Six. Damned *as Parody of Dante's* Inferno

Most reviewers of *Damned* make the obvious connection between this novel and Dante's *Inferno*. Although these reviewers mention the apparent influence of *The Inferno* upon *Damned*, they do not explore in any depth the literary implications of Palahniuk's parody of Dante. In "Chuck Palahniuk's Latest An Empowering Inferno," Claude Peck reports Madison Spencer, the thirteen-year-old narrator who has died of a marijuana overdose and finds herself in hell, will appear in two future Palahniuk novels, *Doomed*, which will follow her journey through purgatory, and *Delivered*, describing her eventual trip to paradise, clearly tracing Dante's progression in *The Divine Comedy*. Peck mentions Palahniuk researched Dante as well as Sartre's *No Exit* to create his pack of teenage stereotypes (geek, jock, punk, cheerleader, etc.) reminiscent of the 1985 movie *The Breakfast Club*. In an interview with Adam Weinstein, Palahniuk confirms plans to write this Dante-inspired trilogy. Weinstein portrays Madison as "Our Virgil" who leads readers through what the 2011 book jacket describes as "the *Inferno* by way of *The Breakfast Club*." Janet Maslin notes in particular Palahniuk's domestication of hell. She claims that he "appreciates that hell has great visual potential. And he exploits the idea a girl raised by a movie star (her mother) and a producer (her father) with bankrupt show-business values would actually find hell kind of homey." Darren Richard Carlaw posits, "Mr. Palahniuk is one of literature's great agitators.... And sadly, the easily offended will miss out on reading a humorous thought provoking novel." In her study of narrative, Alice Bennett comments that *Damned* is comparable to other works that deal with the afterlife: "As well as establishing references to each other, the popular fictions ... show a logic for using the dead narrator which goes beyond the experimental, and into an exploration of how literary genres develop out of the eccentric or aberrant experiment. Like the afterlife, genre fictions make the singular into the serial, and emphasize repetition, parody and return" (116).

By drawing on Dante's *Inferno* as his template for hell, Palahniuk assumes most readers are familiar with the basic framework of this setting. Different from *Pygmy* and *Tell-All*, Palahniuk can count on his audience having more common knowledge about hell than he could take for granted concerning 1970s karate films or 1940s–1950s gossip journalism. The audience's ability to make the connection between *Damned* and *The Inferno* serves as Palahniuk's first layer of parody, but through an additional layer of simulation, one that imitates Judy Blume's famous young-adult work *Are You There God? It's Me, Margaret*, Palahniuk moves into more complex parodic territory. Not every reader, let alone the typical Palahniuk fan, might be familiar with Blume's text. Moreover, not many readers would probably ever consider making the connection between these two vastly different works. The mashing together of these two disparate referents is Palahniuk at his creative best, and the yoking of these two major texts (both are respected as seminal works in their genres) allows him to have parodic literary fun with two socially serious topics, puberty and damnation. Through this duality, he can be flagrantly vulgar and obscene describing hell yet maintain a G or PG-type rating because of the adolescent point of view. For instance, he can gross out his audience with landmarks such as lakes full of human ejaculate, excrement, and blood, but Madison has a limited vocabulary (even though she balks at the inference she is too naïve to know such language) in how she can term genitalia, calling such body parts "woo-woos" and "hoo-hoos" (103). In effect, by imitating Dante's elaborately mapped out literary geography of hell and taking content from Blume's depictions of the hellish experiences associated with the feminine rite of passage into adolescence, Palahniuk offers a postmodern parody that merges high culture and popular culture. In an interview posted on *The Cult: The Official Chuck Palahniuk Website*, Palahniuk explains his intentions for *Damned*: "My next novel, the one for 2011 ... [is] about an eleven-year-old girl who finds herself in Hell and learns how to manipulate the corrupt system of demons and bodily fluids. Imagine if *The Shawshank Redemption* had a baby by *The Lovely Bones* and it was raised by Judy Blume, and you have my next project. It's so frustrating when this girl, Madison, realizes that she'll never grow up and become an adult" ("Doubleday's").[1] Considering Linda Hutcheon's theory of parody as illustrating similarity but emphasizing difference, readers can see how Palahniuk imitates Dante's classic *The Inferno*, accentuates this with an imitation of Blume's young adult novel, and consequently produces something wonderfully different and thoroughly innovative through his transgressive fiction.

Palahniuk predicted *Damned* would be the first book in a trilogy following Madison through hell, purgatory, and paradise (the three-part structure of *The Divine Comedy*), and the publication of *Doomed* confirms Palahniuk is moving Madison out of hell and back onto Earth in his next novel—and Palahniuk progresses into technoculture as Madison uses Twitter as the vehicle to begin her posts in that narrative. Through his parody of *The Inferno*, Palahniuk deals with the nature of sin, the consequences of moral decisions, and the issues related to divine justice and Christian mercy, although he does so by poking a finger at American consumerism and secular capitalism. He treats the extremely religious, sacred, and catholic subject of damnation through his characteristically sarcastic, irreverent, and satirical style. As Palahniuk claims in *Stranger Than Fiction*, a dominant

Six. Damned *as Parody of Dante's* Inferno

theme in his writing is an individual trying to become a part of a community (xv). In the tradition of the bildungsroman, *Damned* essentially traces Madison's journey toward self-empowerment, a process that evolves during her adventures with a small, cohesive group of friends. Through the course of this coming of age story, Madison transforms from a self-conscious nerd into an assertive leader, and thereafter, she becomes a respected and revered member of the underworld community. Madison blooms (pardon the pun on "Blume") during her stay in hell, and her newfound confidence is fostered by the trust that others have in her decisions. Not only does she make friends with whom she would never socialize if she were alive, but she becomes the number one telemarketer for the hellish soul-seeking corporation, going so far as recruiting those close to death to commit sins so they will spend eternity with Satan. Combining the two referent texts, Palahniuk produces an ironic subversion that emphasizes how incredibly difficult both hell and puberty can be, especially taken together.

Scaffolding his hell based on the architecture presented in *The Inferno*, Palahniuk emulates Dante's ingenious system of checks and balances. Dante strategically creates a punishment to equal the nature of a sin, and Palahniuk also offers just as appropriate imaginative retribution. By contemporizing Dante's hell for a twenty-first-century audience, Palahniuk is able to blend different kinds of figures and subjects—just as Dante did for his medieval audience—to make various statements about punitive payback and divine authority. Palahniuk's significations, however, suggest spirituality is now tied to popular culture, and the divine or overreaching power is not necessarily related to a supreme being as much as it is to widespread media exploitation and to those who influence media production. In Madison's hell, influenced by her parents' projections, Satan is likely to be Ann Coulter, Styrofoam, Big Tobacco, or Japanese fishing nets (18), yet, in the end, Satan portrays himself as a Hollywood-wannabe chauffeur peddling a screenplay. Hellish currency is brand-named candy bars, one punishment is the constant broadcast of *The English Patient* or *The Piano*, and the two available jobs are Internet pornography and telephone solicitation, definitely not what Dante would have ever envisioned for a future hell, but, of course, Dante's ideology was firmly grounded in religion. The beginning of each chapter is obviously an allusion to Blume's novel, but Palahniuk's book is definitely not intended for young readers, yet neither was Dante's. Whereas Dante's scenes promote traditional Christian doctrine, Palahniuk's display his usual skepticism of anything sacred. As he mentions in an interview with C. P. Farley, Palahniuk takes ideas related to common, ordinary, typical human experience and reproduces them through his brand of transgressive fiction. Palahniuk's parody of *The Inferno* by way of *Are You There God? It's Me, Margaret* is an excellent example, maybe the best one, of Palahniuk putting Hutcheon's theory of parody into practice. The similarities between the referents and Palahniuk's novel are clear, but Palahniuk's recasting of those works for contemporary American readers allows him to create a text that is distinctly his own. As Chris Barton comments, "When it comes to drawing up a vision of hell, there are few American writers better suited to the job than Chuck Palahniuk." Perhaps better than anyone else, Palahniuk captures the twenty-first-century idiosyncratically American version of hell.

To accomplish this, Palahniuk condenses Dante's nine circles and ancillary ledges for one broad terrain of punishment that closely resembles the layout of an amusement park. Instead of creating Dante's hierarchy of sins from Limbo, Lust, Gluttony, Greed, Anger, Heresy, Violence, Fraud, and Treachery, descending from least to most abhorrent to God, Palahniuk offers rows of perpendicular cells for sinners surrounded by delineated areas that are constructed from human by-products as well as contrived from Satan's lively imagination. This enables Palahniuk to offer a landscape comprised of locations such as Vomit Pond, River of Hot Saliva, Dandruff Desert, Great Plains of Broken Glass, Mountain of Toenail Clippings, in addition to the more disgusting Steaming Dog Pile Mountains, Swamp of Rancid Perspiration, and Great Ocean of Wasted Sperm. Palahniuk's Sea of Insects corresponds in texture to Dante's "infernal hurricane" (5.31) of lustful shades prohibited from human touch, and Shit Lake imitates the "filth / That out of human privies seemed to flow" (18.114–15) set in Dante's bolgia (or stony ditch) dedicated to the Flatterers. Madison remarks that her hell—with its *"oceans of scalding-hot barf"* (7), "poop-scented air" (29), and "fat, black houseflies" (29)—resembles in all of it grossness more popular culture than high culture:

> Probably any grown-up would pee herself silly, seeing the flying vampire bats and majestic, cascading waterfalls of smelling poop. No doubt the fault is entirely my own, because if I'd ever imagined Hell it was as a fiery version of that classic Hollywood masterpiece *The Breakfast Club*, populated, let's remember, by a hypersocial, pretty cheerleader, a rebel stoner type, a dumb football jock, a brainy geek, and a misanthropic psycho, all locked together in their high school library doing detention on an otherwise ordinary Saturday [7].

In each of Dante's circles, the sin is typically defined, the punishment is described, and then exemplary sinners are tortured, and Dante is extremely creative in how these sinners are gruesomely punished. Examples of these circles include the Sluggish who are forced beneath slime (Canto

VII); the Suicides who, assuming forms of trees, have their limbs broken by half-bird, half-female Harpies (Canto XIII); the Violent against God and the Violent against Nature who crawl on a desert of burning sand where flames fall as rain showers (Canto XIV); and the Hypocrites forced to wear gilded, heavy, lead-lined coats (Canto XXIII). Furthermore, there are the hideous images of shackled giants (Canto XXXI) and a frozen Lucifer at the bottom of hell (Canto XXXIV).[2] Dante surveys a broad range of deities from mythology in his hell, and through Leonard's nerdy knowledge of demons, Palahniuk makes his hell equally international, including ones such as Ahriman (25), Benoth (49), Dagon (50), among many others.[3] Considering all of this, Madison comments that Dante did not accurately fictionalize hell: "Other people, like famous Italian poet Dante Alighieri, I'm sorry to say, simply hoisted a generous helping of campy make-believe on the readers" (8). More important, this statement reveals that Madison is familiar with *The Inferno*, and this increases her credibility since she recognizes Dante as another *homo viator* on a spiritual journey.

A couple of comparisons between Dante's and Palahniuk's depictions of hell support Madison's comment. The two writers certainly present their hells in two contrasting fashions. Granted, Dante's mathematical poetic style is vastly different from Palahniuk's minimalist prose sentences in terms of technique, but this does not deflect from their similar purposes in presenting hell as the quintessential venue to torment sinners. After he meets his guide Virgil, Dante is warned about what he will see during his journey, in essence provided with an overview of the inferno, purgatory, and paradise structure of the three sections of *The Divine Comedy*. In one of the most famous parts of *The Inferno*, Virgil states,

> Therefore I think and judge it for the best
> Thou follow me, and I will be thy guide,
> And lead thee hence through the eternal place,
> Where thou shalt hear the desperate lamentations,
> Shalt see the ancient spirits disconsolate,
> Who cry out each one for the second death;
> And thou shalt see those who contented are
> Within the fire, because they hope to come,
> Whene'er it may be, to the blessed people;
> To whom, then, if thou wishest to ascend,
> A soul shall be for that than I more worthy;
> With her at my departure I will leave thee [1.112–23].

Although Madison's comment about Dante is not altogether true, she has a point in that Dante insinuates horrible acts but does not necessarily flush them out with the same rich descriptions that she gives to her hell.

In Canto XXI, for instance, the level devoted to disloyal lawyers, black devils run along an arch with sinners over their shoulders, and these poor souls are eventually thrown into boiling black pitch. These devils are the stereotypical pitch-fork wielding demons presented throughout popular culture. Dante reports,

> Who, while he looks, delays not his departure;
> And I beheld behind us a black devil,
> Running along upon the crag, approach.
> Ah, how ferocious was he in his aspect!
> And how he seemed to me in action ruthless,
> With open wings and light upon his feet!
> His shoulders, which sharp-pointed were and high,
> A sinner did encumber with both haunches,
> And he held clutched the sinews of the feet [28–36].

A few lines later, Dante states, "They seized him then with more than a hundred rakes; / They said: 'It here behooves thee to dance covered, / That, if thou canst, thou secretly mayest pilfer'" (52–54). This scene concludes, "They lowered their rakes, and [said] 'Wilt though have me hit him,' / They said to one another, 'On the rump?' / And answered: 'Yes; see that thou nick him with it'" (100–03). Just like Dante, Madison is communicating her vision of hell to her audience, and readers are left to trust her instinct when it comes to accurate portrayals of what happens to sinners. In Dante's version, hell must be so unattractive that it will subsequently discourage readers to commit sins, hence the purpose of horrific scenes should be to warn and deter, and readers should fear eternal punishment by fiery demons, such as those described. In Palahniuk's version, Madison is more objective and referential. Although her descriptions might be more graphically unappealing, they are neither didactic nor pedagogic. In other words, Dante's aim is to persuade people not to sin, whereas Palahniuk's goal is to cover all of the distasteful and disgusting nuances of hell.

In terms of vividness, the edge goes to Palahniuk rather than to Dante. In Canto XXIV, on the seventh bolgia in the eighth circle, thieves are ripped apart by serpents only to recover and be tortured again. This is comparable to what occurs to Patterson when Madison first meets him. Regardless which is more shocking, Dante's description is still powerful. Dante begins, "And I beheld therein a terrible throng / Of serpents, and of a monstrous kind, / That the remembrance still congeals my blood" (82–84). He then describes,

> Among this cruel and most dismal throng
> People were running naked and affrighted,
> Without the hope of hole or heliotrope.

> They had their hands with serpents bound behind them;
>   These riveted upon their reins the tail
>   And head, and were in front of them entwined.
> And lo! At one who was upon our side
>   There darted forth a serpent, which transfixed him
>   There where the neck is knotted to the shoulders,
> Nor 'O' so quickly e'er, nor 'I' was written,
>   As he took fire, burned; and ashes wholly
>   Behoved it that in falling he became.
> And when he on the ground was destroyed,
>   The ashes drew together, and of themselves
>   Into himself they instantly returned [91–105].

Palahniuk's depiction is a bit more gruesome. Madison begins with Patterson's tormentor: "The horned figure stops beside a cage wherein a mortal man cowers and screams wearing the frayed, sullied uniform of some football team. With jagged eagle talons instead of hands, the horned figure flips the lock on the man's cage, reaches in and snatches about in the small space while the screaming football man dodges and evades being caught" (25). She then describes the ghastly ripping apart of the body: "Their combined wails sound hoarse and broken from effort. In the same manner you'd dismember a steamed crab, the horned figure grasps one of the football man's legs and twists it around and around, the hip socket popping and tendons snapping, until the leg pulls free from the torso. Repeating the process, the figure removes each of the man's limbs, lifting each to his own mouth of jagged shark's teeth and biting the meaty, hypertrophied flesh from the man's bones" (26). Both accounts emphasize physical hellish punishment, but Palahniuk's is less cautionary and more matter of fact—demons rip apart inhabitants in hell not for remediation but apparently for recreation, just for the fun of inflicting torture.

Another comparable scene in both works relates to severed heads. In Canto XXVIII devoted to the Sowers of Discord, the most grotesque images in this circle relate to Bertram de Born, who carries his decapitated head in his hands. Dante begins, "I truly saw, and still I seem to see it, / A trunk without a head walk in like manner / As walked the others of the mournful herd" (118–20). He then continues,

> And by the hair it held the head dissevered,
>   Hung from the hand in fashion of a lantern,
>   And that upon us gazed and said: 'O me!'
> It of itself made to itself a lamp,
>   And they were two in one, and one in two;
>   How that can be, He knows who so ordains it.
> When it was come close to the bridge's foot,

> It lifted high its arm with all the head,
>   To bring more closely unto us its words,
> Which were: 'Behold now the sore penalty,
>   Thou, who dost breathing to the dead beholding;
> Behold if any be as great as this.
> And so that thou may carry news of me,
>   Know that Bertram de Born am I, the same
> Who gave to the Young King the evil comfort [121–35].

This relates to Archer's decapitation, although Palahniuk has a much different use for the detached head. In the most sexually humorous situation in the novel, one that rivals probably the strangest situations in any of his books, Palahniuk places Archer's decapitated head in front of Pszepolnica's clitoris. Madison states, "In the open air, slick with the juices of female passion and drooling wildly, Archer gasps a breath. His eyes dilated and crossed with pleasure, he shouts. His lips webbed with the noxious fluids inherent in adult sexual congress. Archer shouts, 'I AM THE LIZARD KING…!' At that, I stuff his head back to do hidden oral battle with the stiffening engorged clitoral tissues" (77). Even though Palahniuk's version is much more graphic than Dante's, there is basically similarity in structure. This is not to suggest, however, Dante is not equally grotesque. Dante's other descriptions concerning the Sowers of Discord are brutally intense. The Prophet Mahomet is sliced open from his head to his hips, "Rent from the chin to where one breaketh wind / Between his legs were hanging down his entrails; / His heart was visible, and the dismal sack / That maketh excrement of what is eaten" (28.22–27), and there are ghastly images, such as "I saw two sitting leaned against each other, / As leans in heating platter against platter, / From head to foot bespotted o'er with scabs…. And every one was plying fast the bite / Of nails upon himself, for the great rage / Of itching which no other succor had" (29.73–81). He is just as shocking in his depiction in Canto XXXIII of Ugolino della Gherardesca gnawing the skull of his former collaborator Archbishop Ruggieri. Ugolino wipes the gore from his mouth on the back of Ruggieri's head. Just as ghastly are the depictions in Canto XIX when the flaming legs of the Fraudulent protrude from holes in the ground and in Canto XX where the soothsayers or sorcerers have their heads turned around their bodies, only to weep on their buttocks. Dante is simply more suggestive and less direct than Palahniuk in his selection of descriptions, and Dante's portrayals in English obviously depend on translation. Furthermore, romantic insinuation might be more horrifying—the power of the imagination can magnify and amplify hell into anyone's absolute worst nightmare. Ultimately, Dante might win the description battle if illustrations are considered. In terms of imagery,

Six. Damned *as Parody of Dante's* Inferno

Gustave Doré's renditions of Dante's verse likely trump, at least in stark engravings of human anguish, everything Palahniuk lays out on his pages.

Palahniuk's blending of Dante and Blume provides an almost diabolical version of the proverbial tween/teenage wasteland full of angst, antipathy, and self-pity. This is obvious through Madison's and Margaret's meditative dialogues beginning each chapter, and Palahniuk relies upon these to emphasize the intertextuality. In these initial contemplative prayers, both Margaret and Madison are apprehensive. Margaret states, for instance, *"Are you there God? It's me, Margaret. We're moving today. I'm so scared God. I've never lived anywhere but here. Suppose I hate my new school? Suppose everyone hates me? Please help me God. Don't let New Jersey be too horrible. Thank you"* (1). Madison's tone is more sarcastic yet also suggests insecurity: *"Are you there, Satan? It's me, Madison. I'm just now arrived here, in Hell, but it's not my fault except for maybe dying from an overdose of marijuana. Maybe I'm in Hell because I'm fat—a Real Porker. If you can go to Hell for having low self-esteem, that's why I'm here. I wish I could lie and tell you I'm bone-thin with blond hair and big ta-tas. But, trust me, I'm fat for a really good reason"* (1). As the stories progress, the introductions demonstrate how the two characters gain experience and acquire knowledge, consequently mature, and ultimately transition into adulthood. Even though both ask their deities for assistance, they actually become increasingly self-reliant and self-assured without any visible evidence of divine intervention. Their gestures are more invocative than practical. For example, after she gets her Gro-Bra (41) and completes her infamous "I must—I must—I must increase my bust" (46) calisthenics, Margaret reports, *"Are you there God? It's me, Margaret. I just did an exercise to help me grow. Have you thought about it God? About my growing, I mean. I've got a bra now. It would be nice if I had something to put in it. Of course, if you don't think I'm ready I'll understand. I'm having a test in school tomorrow. Please let me get a good grade on it God. I want you to be proud of me. Thank you"* (50). This is a particularly famous passage about breast exercises: "That night I really worked hard. I read the first two chapters in my social studies book four times. Then I sat on my bedroom floor and did my exercise. 'I must—I must—I must increase my bust!' I did it thirty-five times and climbed into bed" (50). In other sections, Margaret offers information about boys, school, and religion.[4] Madison is much less reverent and is definitely more assertive: *"Are you there, Satan? It's me, Madison. After a somewhat rocky start, I'm having simply the best time. I continue to meet new people, and I'm sorry about the mix-up.... Just imagine: me mistaking just some ordinary, nobody-special demon for you. I'm learning something new and interesting all the time from Leonard. On top of that, I've concocted a way-brilliant idea for how to overcome my insidious addiction to hope"* (30).[5] Concerning attitude, Margaret asks for direct intervention from God to assist her, but Madison assumes an indirect approach toward Satan, wanting his help but not appearing overly desperate, posturing as less needy and less passive.

Palahniuk's portrayal of Madison's sexual development is another inversion of what Blume's Margaret experiences. Margaret's female nemesis is Laura Danker, who has the potential because of her breasts to be the next Hillary Brite (71), *Playboy* playmate, and who supposedly kisses Moose and the other boys whom Margaret and her group of Pre-Teen Sensations (33) name in their Boy Books (46–47).[6] The comparable passage in *Damned* exposes obvious intertextuality for the sake of satire as well as sarcasm. In her diatribe toward Babette, Madison responds:

> It's my experience that girls tend to be terrifically smart until they grow breasts. You may dismiss this observation as my personal prejudice, based on my own tender age, but thirteen years seems to be when human beings reach their fullest flower of intelligence, personality, and pluck. Both girls and boys. Not to boast, but I believe a person is her most truly exceptional at the age of thirteen—look at Pippi Longstocking, Pollyanna, Tom Sawyer, and Dennis the Menace—before she finds herself conflicted and steered by hormones and crushing gender expectations. Let girls get their menstruation or boys have their first wet dream, and they instantly forget their own brilliance and talent [12–13].[7]

Margaret is constantly comparing herself to stereotypical standards for feminine attractiveness—worth noting is the patriarchy behind *Playboy* setting the bar for female physicality—and Madison is no different in how she perceives her body image, craves male acceptance, and even desires male objectification. The extremely graphic sexual scene in which Madison manipulates the demon Psezpolnica's genitalia to save Archer (53–60) demonstrates that Madison understands sexuality (and this is also confirmed by her accounts of how her parents promoted sexual freedom), and this polemic about "girls and boys" illustrates how Madison is obviously not as naïve as Margaret. In other words, Madison understands boys much better than her fictional counterpart. During this scene, Madison loses one of her practical Bass Weejuns (59), and later she sheds them entirely for gaudy high heels (112), and this switch in shoes is reminiscent of Margaret's own dilemma whether or not to go sockless while wearing her loafers (13). Palahniuk stays true to Blume when he addresses Madison physically and emotionally maturing, but the manner in which he portrays these changes is very different. As Madison's quick decision to shed the loafers but Margaret's decision to keep hers indicates, Madison is simply ahead of Margaret in terms of overall maturity, and this could be because of the two-year difference in ages as well as the forty year variance in sexual attitudes.

Palahniuk's portrayal of hope emphasizes the irony concerning both comparisons to Dante and Blume. Whereas Dante defines hell primarily through its hopelessness, Palahniuk's hell is one in which hope is definitely a possibility, going so far as to allow sinners to challenge their divine placement through a salvation test (182). Dante's famous cautionary inscription at the entrance to hell reads, "All hope abandon, ye who enter in!" (3.9), and Virgil emphasizes that the inhabitants in hell, even those in Limbo, are doomed to suffer because of this hopelessness. Margaret waits impatiently to become a woman, and through her frame of reference, this move is sanctioned by growing breasts and beginning menstruation—both happen at the end of the book—but she also grapples with the decision to claim either Judaism or Christianity. Madison does not agonize over her ideological affiliation, but she recognizes that since she is in hell she is not supposed to hope, and her apparent hopefulness paradoxically causes her distress. She first tries to fit in with the other hopeless sinners, an attempt at conformity typical of a thirteen-year-old, yet this fails, and her progression toward asserting her hope is precisely how, and this is the crucial point concerning his application of postmodern parody, Palahniuk subverts Dante's *Inferno*. To Madison, hell conversely becomes associated with optimism, not the realm of pessimism perpetuated by Dante. In fact, Palahniuk's hell is the happening place where the hip souls spend eternity. And, more important, viewed as such, hell is not the horrible place (paramount in Dante's vision) to fear but the cool location to desire, where one rubs elbows with the fun-loving celebrity dead. Madison comments, "My biggest gripe is still hope. In Hell, hope is a really, really bad habit, like smoking cigarettes or fingernail biting. Hope is something really tough and tenacious you have to give up. It's an addiction to break" (20–21).[8] She later states, "My name is Madison ... and I'm a hope-aholic" (36).[9] In one section, Madison sees herself as Satan's accomplice:

> There they both are: the H-word [Hope] and the G-word [God], proof of my tenacious addiction to all things upbeat and optimistic. To be honest, all my effort thus far to remain spotless, mind my posture, present myself as perky, affect a cheerful smile, is calculated to endear myself to Satan. In my best-case scenario I see myself assuming a kind of sidekick or comic-relief role.... So ingrained is my spunky nature that I can't even allow the Prince of Darkness to indulge in the doldrums. I truly am a sort of flesh-and-blood form of Zoloft [38–39].

Viewed in this context, Madison's strangulation by Hello Kitty condoms (and who but Palahniuk would devise such a way to die) is the catalyst for her spiritual revelation and consequently her newly developed self-identity. If she had continued to live as a mortal, she would not have had this opportunity to learn how to gain self-confidence. Strangely, of all places for this to occur, it happens in hell. By the second half of the novel, Madison seems to have lost interest in breasts and menstruation as avenues to become a woman, and she no longer is jealous of Babette's *Playboy* playmate style of feminine attractiveness.

This transformation unquestionably leads to Madison's self-empowerment. Away from the control of her parents, she actually thrives in the underworld. Her discovery how she died may be the turning point in her self-perception: "However, in the light of the truth: that I did not die of a marijuana overdose ... nor did Goran reveal himself as my romantic ideal ... my schemes have brought nothing except heartache to my family.... Thus, it would follow that I am not so smart. And with that, my entire concept of self is undermined" (177). This momentary self-esteem letdown precipitates her inevitable confidence buildup. Flexing her muscles, she defeats, among other contemporary archetypes of pure evil and satanic ingenuity, Hitler (192), Countess Bathory (192), Catherine de Medicis (193), Caligula (195), Vlad the Impaler (196), King Ethelred (197), Thug Behram (197), Bluebeard (197), Hannibal (199), Genghis Khan (199), and Idi Amin (234). Put simply, Madison loves being in hell, and she frankly flourishes in her new role as hellish revolutionary. In fact, she beats up many of the most notoriously bad people in history, and to apply a sports adage, she is at the top of her game. If these figures had lived before Dante, they would have surely found their places in *The Inferno*. In terms of the marketing of hell, these would serve as Dante's primary spokespeople to represent the Catholic cardinal sins, the most atrocious crimes, and worst vices known to humanity. Defiantly, she asserts, "Behold, my name is Madison Spencer, child of Antonio and Camille Spencer, citizen of Hell, and my army is as numberless as the stars. As is the wealth of my candy. I bid all the demons and devils of Hades immediately to open their stout fortress unto me" (199). Palahniuk completely turns around the purpose of Dante's hell by allowing Madison, as a remake of Blume's Margaret, to reinvent herself in the one place readers, who are probably familiar with *The Inferno*, would definitely not expect this to happen. An allegiance to her own self-will is stressed in Madison's declaration: "I am free to review my story, to reinvent myself, my world, at any given moment.... No more am I a passive damsel who waits for circumstance to decide her fate; now have I become the scalawag, the swashbuckler, the Heathcliff of my dreams bent on rescuing myself.... No longer am I limited" (201). Unlike Margaret, Madison has ultimately become a feminist. She appears unstoppable, and her defiance toward patriarchy is representative in her reaction toward

Satan, perhaps the embodiment of patriarchal reign, seemingly controlling her actions.

In a sense, Madison is the personification of third-wave feminism, particularly as pronounced by renowned feminist advocate Naomi Wolf in *Fire with Fire: The New Female Power and How It Will Change the 21st Century*. Explaining how women conform in a male-dominated society, Wolf explains that as females mature they repress the "bad girl" in favor of the "good girl." The feminine "inner child" basically conforms to societal expectations of how a female should act and provides attitudes and behaviors to meet those established gender preconceptions. As she mentions, the inner child is good and is associated with compassion (318). Wolf adds that this inner child has another side, one that is a "mischievous, boisterous, unregenerate twin, the inner *bad girl* lurking in the female psyche" (318). Wolf describes the bad girl in this manner: "Every molecule of the child seeks every pleasure. She is sensuous, grasping, self-absorbed, fierce, greedy, megalomaniacal, and utterly certain that she is entitled to have her ego, her power, and her way. For the few years between her first consciousness and the curtailment of all her badness, her dreams are more vivid and her world more saturated with passion and apparitions and ecstasy than it will ever be again. She has no manners. She is a very naughty girl" (319). Wolf claims this bad girl is sacrificed for the good girl, and to become empowered, the bad girl must be acknowledged. Wolf instructs her female audience:

> Now imagine that you can reach her when you need to. Imagine that you can lay claim to the force of her desire, to her sky-high self-regard, when you are fighting for your rights, negotiating about sex or housework, or putting a price on your labors. Amplify her wishes to adult scope: the respect she wanted on the playground, and in her fantasies of recognition, you want from Capitol Hill. Do not call it "masculine," that will to power in yourself, that desire to transform the world and be *seen*. That is *in* us. It always has been. Use it to walk through this historic door [320].

Wolf's description is almost a template for Madison's transformation, and Madison clearly moves from the "good girl" at the beginning of the novel—just like Margaret, one who conforms to her parents and the wishes of other agencies—to the "bad girl" who is willing to satisfy her appetites. Madison learns how to rebel.

This change probably began before Madison died, perhaps when she lied to her parents so she could stay at the boarding school over Christmas break. In bad-girl mode, she rejects decorum, convention, everything connected to authority. Walking naked outside the dormitory, thinking about campus security, and enjoying the falling ice crystals, Madison exclaims in bad-girl vocabulary, "All of me felt the thrill of being touched at that same instant. You see, I wanted to be discovered. I wanted to be seen at the very height of my prepubescent power, my tits-out, bare-fanny, legally off-limits kiddie-porn Lolita power" (67). In hell, as she gains control, Madison replaces her desire to just fit in, which was what she initially wanted, with much more authority: "Yes, now it's power I want. Not affection. I don't want that kind of pointless, impotent power, as earlier discussed. Mark my words: Being dead isn't all sitting around in remorseful reflection and bitter self-recrimination. Death, like life, is what you make of it" (195). In short, Madison has tapped into her inner bad girl. Rising to the peak of her power, Madison offers a pontific declaration when she claims, "Behold, my name is Madison Spencer" (199). This is reminiscent of Achilles or Odysseus in Homer's ancient hero epics or details from one of Dante's characters exhibiting unmistakable personal hubris, pride serving as a reason for landing in hell. Basically, Madison assimilates qualities of the bad girl feminist persona, and thus she embodies the powerful woman whom Wolf envisions. Palahniuk responds to third-wave feminism in his most recent novel, *Beautiful You*, presenting a dilemma that corresponds to the one faced by directly by Madison:

> The truth was, Penelope Anne Harrigan was still being a good daughter—obedient, bright, dutiful—who did as she was told. She'd always deferred to the advice of other, older people. Yet she yearned for something beyond earning the approval of her parents and surrogate parents. With apologies to Simone de Beauvoir, Penny didn't want to be a third-wave *anything*. No offense to Bella Abzug, but neither did she want to be a post-*anything*. She didn't want to replicate the victories of Susan B. Anthony and Helen Gurley Brown. She wanted a choice beyond: Housewife versus lawyer. Madonna versus whore. An option not mired in the lingering detritus of some Victorian era dream. Penny wanted something beyond feminism itself [5].

Regardless, Madison is essentially the personification of Girl Power, and her self-image does not depend, as with Margaret, on boys or boobs or any other societal dictates concerning gender. Whereas Margaret is the good girl, her actions still influenced by patriarchal prescriptions for what is proper feminine behavior, Madison has definitely connected with her inner bad girl. She does not qualify any of her victories over major patriarchal villains (and some matriarchal) by relating herself to Anthony, Brown, or other notable feminists. Madison is only Madison, and, as simply an assertive individual, she is similar to Penny in how her determination transcends formal gender distinctions, not manifested as "post-*anything*."

In *Beautiful You*, Palahniuk addresses several issues related to feminism, particularly how women such as Madison create their own destinies. The narrator comments about twenty-five-year-old Penny, "She hadn't found her dream as a well-behaved daughter. Nor had she found it by regurgitating the hidebound ideology of her professors. It comforted her to think that every girl of her generation was facing the same crisis. They'd all inherited a legacy of freedom, and they owed it to the future to forge a new frontier for the next generation of young women. To break new ground" (6). Palahniuk then emphasizes how Penny only wants to promote her own ideology, not one affiliated with others: "She'd never trusted her own natural impulses and instincts. Among her greatest fears was the possibility that she might never discover and develop her deepest talents and intuitions. Her *special gifts*. Her life would be wasted in pursuing the goals set for her by other people. Instead, she wanted to reclaim a power and authority—a primitive, irresistible force—that transcended gender roles. She dreamed of wielding a raw magic that predated civilization itself" (6). Palahniuk raises many questions concerning feminism in this novel about a multibillionaire who markets products for female masturbatory pleasure. Significantly, Madison foreshadows Penny, even though Madison returns as an empowered young woman in *Doomed* and is definitely not as mature as Penny. In a way, Penny is almost what Madison might have been or could have been if she had lived. The two vary in terms of socioeconomic backgrounds, but they share similar attitudes nonetheless.

Known for his surprise endings, Palahniuk calls this power into question when Madison raises the philosophical question whether Satan has written a screenplay that is actually the entire story of her life, with Madison consequently only a character within a divine fiction. Essentially, Madison wonders if she has determined her own destiny. Palahniuk strives for plot twists when the unexpected occurs, an ironic conclusion representative of existential reality or absurdist expectation when the outlandish and the far-fetched are perfectly plausible. He accomplishes this in *Damned*. Madison herself comments, *"Are you there, Satan? It's me, Madison, and I'm not your Jane Eyre. I'm nobody's Catherine Earnshaw. And you? You're certainly no writer. You're not the boss of me; you're just messing with my head. If anybody wrote me it would be Judy Blume or Barbara Cartland. I have confidence and determination and free will—at least, I guess I do…"* (236). Palahniuk refers to Blume's *Forever Amber* (107), and he directly provides a typical Blume storyline "moment" before Madison and Goran smoke pot and Madison is strangled: "For a Judy Blume instant, our fingers touched" (152). Within this text, which is mainly her journal, Madison refers to Emily Bronte (62), Alice Walker (74), Jane Austen (140), Mary Shelley (142), and Margaret Mitchell (143), often comparing herself to renowned literary heroines. During the scene with Pszpolnica, Palahniuk borrows closely from the famous Brobdingnagian section in Swift's *Gulliver's Travels* in which Gulliver must sexually please beautiful ladies of court (72–78). Palahniuk pokes fun at himself in this sexually graphic section in the novel. Madison summarizes the section about Gulliver with an accolade: "Overwhelmed with sickness and horror, exhausted, our enslaved Gulliver is forced to labor until the giant women are satisfied [sexually]. In all of English literature, few passages can match this one of Swift's for its descriptive bluntness and unwelcome, masculine crudity" (73). Evidently, Madison has not read Palahniuk's story "Guts" in *Haunted*. Palahniuk provides a Swiftian description of Madison clinging to body hair, navigating through skin folds, and reacting to female genitalia. Significantly, through the act of writing, Madison expresses herself into self-empowerment comparable to how Margaret does in Blume's book. Madison is capable of contextualizing her experience by relating it through the filter of this literary work, the narrative she is creating, which is evident in her references indirectly to Dante and directly to Blume. In other words, she makes sense of those experiences through that literary relationship and the act of writing. Reciprocally, readers interpret Madison through those prior textualizations that she lists as well as through Dante and Blume. Readers interpret Madison through those intertextualities. In this way, Madison acquires credibility through those associations with her literary counterparts; she is reinforced, is supported, and is fortified by her connection with her fictional predecessors. This also raises the question about authorship and master narratives since Palahniuk is inferring (maybe promoting) Satan is the master author, perhaps one who has the divine license to create canonical literary masterworks. This is not a surprise considering the underlying binary working in the novel. To many readers, great books are the products of divine inspiration, but most would consider these inspired by God not Satan. Palahniuk turns this around by possibly giving divine creative authority to Satan.

    This irony is what makes *Damned* such a great illustration of Hutcheon's theory of postmodern parody. Palahniuk draws from Dante and Blume to make thoroughly postmodern points about sin, punishment, and redemption, not to mention puberty and adolescence. And, he accomplishes this through his distinctively transgressive style. At the end of the novel, Madison offers this response to the idea she is only Satan's creation: *"As the child outlives the father, so must the character bury the author. If you are, in fact, my continuing author, then killing you will end my existence as well. Small loss. Such a life, as your puppet, is not worth living. But if I destroy you and your dreck script, and I still exist ... then my existence will be glorious, for I will become my own master. When I return to Hell, prepare to die by my hand.*

Or be ready to kill me" (242). This declaration puts the exclamation point on Madison's coming of age. Paradoxically, a similar rebellious outburst occasioned Satan's banishment from heaven, but in this context, Madison's defiance will set up her exodus from this hellish location and her move toward heaven. Considering the function of postmodern parody to reflect the similarity but to emphasize the difference, Madison's hell does not include all that much punishment for sin (at least not after she and the others reach the city), and her description of burgeoning womanhood is quite mature. Madison even relates hell to a rehab or a detox facility (46) and to a marginalized neighborhood (215), and along these lines, Palahniuk could be inferring hell may not be a creation born out of religion but a terrestrial location already present in readers' lives. Palahniuk's version also does not have the religious or moral purpose of the other texts related to the subject, and this is why reading *Damned* is so much fun, just like watching *Your Pretty Face Is Going to Hell* or any other program that does not take itself too seriously and does not try to force home any kind of spiritual or ethical agenda. Through her narrative, Madison displays a self-reflexive irreverence toward religion and all it entails, and this amplifies her newly developed confidence, courage, and determination. Unlike Dante who almost constantly bewails the fate of those he recognizes in hell, Madison assertively assumes her role in this divine master plan. While Virgil constantly reminds Dante that the souls are in hell for quite valid reasons, Madison's helpers remind her that there are loopholes about placement into this demonic region, and she can indeed ask for a "do over" in what is fundamentally Dante's divinely correct hell.

The constant presence of Blume's influence calls attention to Madison's narrative as a metacommentary. Through Madison's imitation of Margaret's writing, Palahniuk consistently focuses on writing a means to stimulate change. Margaret addresses God, but she is also formulating her impressions of the situations that directly affect her, such as when she hashes out her feelings about family, puberty, and, probably most significant, religion. Madison mimics this strategy to make sense of why she ends up in hell, and a running question throughout the story is how she arrived at this location, with the presumed answer a marijuana overdose. Readers know that no one really dies of this cause. Marijuana might be a remote or an immediate cause, but not many fatalities result just from the smoking of marijuana, at least these accidents do not receive substantial media attention. Madison takes advantage of writing as an approach to understand her world, and readers sometimes notice her writing about her own writing with a tinge of sarcasm, particularly when she is self-conscious about assuming an informal or chatty tone in her statements directed toward Satan. As the narrative progresses, Madison is much less self-reflexive and more referential toward the content. She focuses more on the incidents and less on her own feelings. Technically, this entire novel is Madison writing herself out of hell. Just as readers see Margaret achieving closure at the end of her narrative by reaching conclusions, which displays to young adults (specifically pre-adolescent females) how they will also get through the ordeal being at this stage in their lives, Madison places attention squarely on writing as understanding. The references to famous writers and Madison's defiance toward Satan as an author both point toward the textualization of Madison's entire life experience. In other words, Palahniuk shows Madison realizing that her life is essentially a text, and her anxiety is warranted because she is not certain who is indeed writing that text. Just like Margaret, Madison has assumed she has had the power to textualize her own life through the chapters, and she is reasonably alarmed to find out Satan might be author of the script that basically defines her very existence. Madison rebels against Satan's claim of authority, but Palahniuk is still nebulous concerning who has true authorship.

Palahniuk never truly solves this problem of textuality, intentionally leaving this ambiguous. At the end of *Damned*, Madison finds out the true identities of her friends and discovers their Halloween costumes actually depict who they were. She then realizes kids will wear Hello Kitty condoms around their necks as a "cheap parody" of herself (224–27). Palahniuk is obviously offering a figurative attempt to point a self-deprecating finger toward his own book. As Hutcheon comments, parody allows a writer to respond to a previous text from within a current one (*Poetics* 35), and Palahniuk certainly goes inside Blume's and Dante's texts to respond to the hellishness of adolescent agitation and uncomfortableness in *Damned*. Furthermore, his postmodern parody certainly goes well beyond cheap imitation. Palahniuk makes hell both a terrifying yet appealing location for Madison's rite of passage. In ancient epics, heroes learned their destinies through their travels in the underworld, as certainly was the case with Odysseus in *The Odyssey* and Aeneas in *The Aeneid*. Palahniuk continues this literary tradition, and Madison may be the contemporary reincarnation of the ancient epic hero, in this case a thoroughly feminist version. Madison continues to mature as the main character in Palahniuk's next novel, *Doomed*, and readers must wait to see conclusively through the third novel in the series how Palahniuk answers the question concerning whether Madison has the free will to write her own life story and to determine her destiny or if she is a prefabricated characterization who will travel a predestined path according to Satan's already composed master narrative. Regardless, just as Dante experiences a transformation moving from hell into purgatory, Madison will inevitably face major changes when she progresses toward her own next level, one that certainly will provide her with additional opportunities for even greater self-actualization.

Seven

The Elephant Man in *Invisible Monsters Remix*

In "The Wish Book: A Reintroduction to *Invisible Monsters*," Chuck Palahniuk reveals that as a child he enjoyed browsing back and forth through pages in the Sears catalogue, or what was called the "wish book" (vi). Palahniuk also mentions how he liked leafing through *Vogue* and other magazines during visits to the local laundromat (vii). He states that the catalogue and the magazines gave him the idea for a recursive arrangement strategy in a novel: "Trying to read a story was like trying to navigate through a Las Vegas casino. It was designed to entice and seduce you. It was designed to trap you. I got lost. I loved it. I told myself, *Why can't a novel do this?*" (vii). Palahniuk wanted to publish *Invisible Monsters* in this recursive format, but Norton editors requested a linear plot sequence. Palahniuk supplied what was wanted: "So I hammered the story into a nice, smooth, straight line. I threw out the magic" (viii-ix).

Palahniuk published his story as intended in *Invisible Monsters Remix*. Critical commentary related to this novel is mixed. For instance, a critic for *Kirkus Reviews* comments, "In matter of substance, there is not much of a 'remix' to be had here, just a 'Now, please jump to chapter Forty,' Choose-Your-Own-Adventure style that doesn't so much reorder the book as augment the disjointed, whiplash atmosphere its author intended. The book that *Kirkus* drubbed 'Too clever by half' in 1999 [when *Invisible Monsters* was published] is still here in its ghoulish entirety" ("Palahniuk, Chuck"). On the other hand, Suzanne Lindgren writes, "Each chapter is a piece of a puzzle created by Palahniuk, assembled by the reader, who is paging frantically from back to front, trying to keep track of each piece until some of it starts to fit together. It's terrific fun" (80).[1] Besides the narrative going back and forth, literally moving from one chapter in the beginning to another chapter at the end, there are additional chapters that serve

Seven. The Elephant Man in Invisible Monsters Remix

as commentary for the main narrative. One of these extra sections is Chapter 18 in which Palahniuk describes Daisy St. Patience's reworking of David Lynch's *The Elephant Man*. Daisy stages an opening scene with a gyrating Joseph Merrick as a male stripper slavered in baby oil wearing oversized mirrored sunglasses and a small swimsuit. Unlike the movie character or his counterpart in the play, this Elephant Man works his audience into a sexual frenzy: "No, the way Daisy told the story, he didn't just stand there like an object for physicians to stare at. Nobody screamed. Nobody wept quietly into their handkerchiefs, or barfed" (117). Unmistakably, Daisy's Elephant Man viewers are there for the sex show. In typical Palahniuk style, the stripper Elephant Man works his crowd: "His skeleton might have been tortured, but his capped teeth looked perfect, blazing white in the spotlight. Delivering it home, hot, to those whale-boned mamas.... Working his mutilations with the arrogance of a *Playgirl* centerfold, Merrick executed perfect backflips. He did handstands and shook his junk in everyone's cookie-cutter Victorian face" (116). This version is definitely not the one most people picture in their minds when they see the nomenclature "Elephant Man."

Readers begin to ascribe meaning to Shannon based upon their recollections of the previous Merrick in film and play and the present Merrick in Chapter 18. The movie *The Elephant Man* is probably a more familiar intertextual referent than the play, so that is the work readers most likely consider while they read Chapter 18, even though the play precedes the film. The play debuted in 1979, and the film was released in 1980. Lynch's version is supposedly not based on Bernard Pomerance's play. Pomerance writes in his play's introductory notes,

> *The Elephant Man* was suggested by the life of John Merrick, known as The Elephant Man. It is recounted by Sir Frederick Treves in *The Elephant Man and Other Reminiscences*, Cassell and Co. Ltd., 1923. This account is reprinted in *The Elephant Man, A Study in Human Dignity*, by Ashley Montagu, Ballantine Books, 1973, to whom much credit is due for reviving contemporary interest in the story. My own knowledge of it came via my brother Michael, who told me the story, provided me with Treve's memoirs until I came on my own copy, and sent me the Montagu book [v].

Both the play and the movie include Merrick building a model cathedral as a primary metaphor. The movie version of Joseph Merrick's life left an indelible impression in American popular culture concerning persons with physical challenges, and this film as well as *Mask* became the standards concerning how people with facial abnormalities are still portrayed, in both positive and negative ways (Seth MacFarlane has parodied both in his cartoon comedies).

Chapter 18 provides an interesting subtext through which to interpret *Invisible Monsters Remix*. Through parody, Palahniuk retells the story of the Elephant Man to provide a referent to interpret Shannon McFarland's motivation. The male dancer Merrick is obviously different from the movie version; nevertheless, after Palahniuk introduces this comparison, readers subsequently begin to recall the pathetic, grotesque Merrick, recast him as the eye-candy stripper Merrick, and apply this reading to Shannon and her situation as a half-faced (reference to the movie/play Merrick) former model (reference to the stripper Merrick). Chapter 18 promotes a different interpretation of Shannon from Palahniuk's first version, *Invisible Monsters*. Initially, the references to the film *The Elephant Man* call attention to Shannon's self-loathing in the guise of sarcasm and sacrifice, but the end of *Invisible Monsters Remix* suggests a different reading of this character. The "jump to" lead-ins are frequent markers to indicate a moving forward toward the future, Shannon's shedding the psychologically damaging and emotionally crippling baggage from the past. Conversely, Shannon is stuck in her past and often seems incapable of moving ahead. As the movie-version Elephant Man moves forward in his life through the assistance of his friends, Shannon remains entrenched in her past and subsequently firmly planted in her own private pity party. At the conclusion of the back-and-forth rotation, smack in the middle of the book, Shannon sacrifices her identity, essentially herself, to her brother. Palahniuk's arrangement actually imitates Shannon's process toward selflessly bestowing what is basically all she has left to Shane, her individuality. As she states on the last few pages, "This is all my identification, my birth certificate, my everything. You can be Shannon McFarland from now on. My career. The ninety-degree attention. It's yours. All of it. Everyone. I hope it's enough for you. It's everything I have left" (130).

Without the reference to *The Elephant Man*, readers would look at Shannon differently, viewing her with sympathy but with less admiration. Shannon's family is certainly dysfunctional, perhaps not as badly as she thinks, yet there is no question that she harbors deeply rooted resentments toward her parents. Compared to the background of Merrick, whose mother's mysterious encounter with an elephant at the beginning of the film is the mystical reason for his deformity, Shannon's upbringing was functional, even overly nurturing and protective.[2] Juxtaposed against the hardships endured by Merrick, Shannon's decision to shoot herself in the face, to willingly disfigure herself to such an extreme, is an unbelievable act of self-indulgence. The only incident in which she could empathize with Merrick's plight is when people glare at her in the supermarket when she steals the frozen turkey, as employees are too astonished, a combination of fascination and repulsion, to charge her for the bird (276–78). The child's scream that a monster is stealing food (278) is comparable to how surprised Victorians respond to the degree of Merrick's deformity. At the beginning of the novel, Shannon appears to have an egotistical misconception concerning her place in the world, much in the same way Joe from *Fight Club* cultivates his own self-deception by attending self-help meetings, pretending to have horrendous diseases, while he seems to enjoy the perks of living a middle-class American life. Instead of creating an alter ego with whom to wage psychological warfare and starting a fight club, Shannon chooses self-mutilation and an awkward relationship with her brother. She cannot find adequate meaning of self-worth through her social notoriety or her physical beauty, so she covets her brother's seemingly successful ability to reinvent himself. In a sense, *Fight Club* and *Invisible Monsters Remix* both portray main characters dealing with selfish indignation, just from different genders. Both Joe and Shannon are full of self-pity and struggle with self-identity.[3] Significantly, Chapter 18 allows readers to assess more fully the intensity of Shannon's own identity crisis.

The non-linear organization promotes this reading of Shannon. The straightforward arrangement of *Invisible Monsters* causes readers to feel more compassion for Shannon because her problems occur one after another, a steady stream as a reader moves from chapter to chapter. The back-and-forth arrangement in *Invisible Monsters Remix* allows readers to lose interest, if only momentarily, in her plight. Palahniuk understands how diversions affect readers' abilities to cleanly process information, and the extra chapters provide distractions from Shannon's situation. Instead of readers moving linearly through Shannon's hardships, they get the details about her family in Chapter 7 and then see "Now, Please, Jump to Chapter Thirty-Four," which begins, "Jump to around midnight to Evie's house, where I catch Seth Thomas trying to kill me" (219). The time to thumb through the pages is not long, only seconds, but there is the opportunity for readers to minimize details in a way they would not if they were just turning one page after another. As sad as this may sound, readers may just lose interest in Shannon's predicament while they traverse from the front to the back of the book. In fact, Shannon mimics this behavior while she surfs the hospital television and comes across her and Evie's Num-Num Snack Factory commercial. She first comes across a talk show comparable to any one of the sensational shock-talks broadcast each afternoon, and there is a person who evidently drank human blood, one who lived with his deceased mother, and one who ate her baby (44). She changes channels three times to a similar program. In this one, the participants include a woman who is a prostitute, a man who was raped in prison, and a man who slept with his father (44). As Shannon channel surfs, she becomes desensitized to the obvious dysfunction that is broadcast, and readers share this same disinterest as they navigate the novel's chapters. Instead of the sustained presentation of Shannon's dysfunctional life, readers see blips and segments, and the lag time between these allow them to feel more apathetic toward Shannon's problems.

The McFarlands try, no matter how awkwardly, to rectify their past actions toward Shannon's brother Shane. In "Bullets and Blades: Narcissism and Violence in *Invisible Monsters*," Andy Johnson contends, "Shannon and her brother Shane reveal layers of narcissism and a hunger for attention throughout the novel deeply rooted in a childhood of abuse and neglect. As children, they vied for their parents' attention" (65).[4] The Thanksgiving dinner is an exercise in gay semantics, and the parents are obsessed with politically correct significations. As the father comments, while grabbing a turkey leg: "With this gay stuff you have to be so careful since everything means something in secret code. I mean, we didn't want to give people the wrong idea" (243). The conversation is sparked by Shannon's compliment about the new tablecloth, which she learns was originally intended to be an AIDS memorial quilt. The conversation thereafter is hilarious in a Palahniuk transgressively uncomfortable way. During the passing of olives, cranberries, and other dishes, the father describes what various colors signify (i.e., brown refers to rimming, red to fisting, and yellow to watersports) (244). Shannon's resentment toward her brother by being blamed for his death is apparent, and at the height of this scene, when she thinks, "All this sick horrible sex talk over Thanksgiving, I can't take this" (245), there is miscommunication over "felching." The question is posed what this means, and Shannon reacts with a no-nonsense definition related to anal sex and the transmission of fluids (246). The father then comments the mistaken word was "fletching," cutting turkey into thin slices. The reader is then directed to another chapter and has a chance to consider this new scene. Between processing the content in this section and then thumbing to the next one, a reader has the opportunity to evaluate Shannon as a victim of dysfunction or as a spoiled daughter insensitive to her parents' concerns. During Christmas, when Shannon confronts her parents for being overly zealous, her father responds with rote political correctness: "Don't marginalize our oppression" (59). This statement seethes with irony. As Johnson comments, "Palahniuk uses Shane to play with the ways sexuality disturbs middle class suburbia. Like David Lynch's films [such as

Seven. The Elephant Man in Invisible Monsters Remix 115

The Elephant Man], Palahniuk urges readers to look beyond the patina of normalcy to see the rolling confusion beneath—not in an effort to criticize traditional family life, but to reveal the truth behind it" (69).

Shannon's statements unquestionably influence reader reaction to her self-deception. She eventually realizes her hatred of Evie is driven by their being so much alike, and readers discover Evie is extremely spoiled. Evie receives frequent gifts of ten million dollars, and after Evan (her birth name) begged at sixteen to become a female (147), her family paid for various surgeries that led to her super-model career as a private stock, Evelyn Cottrell, Inc. (228). Thinking about Evie, Shannon admits, "But what I hate most is how she's just like me. What I really hate is me, so I hate pretty much everybody" (145). While she and Evie are on a photoshoot in a junkyard, Evie admits, "I just thought being a woman would be … not such a disappointment" (72). Shannon is wondering the same about her life, and her refrain of "Give me" (286–92) masks her nervous sarcasm that inadvertently exposes her deep insecurities.[5] As she interrupts Manus's murder plot, she sees herself as gorgeous, as "so sex furniture" (220). Shannon's romantic remembrance of attractiveness in the Espre cotton sundress displays her desire for super-model stardom: "You'd walk onto a patio, it was a great feeling, a million spotlights picking you out of the crowd, or walk into a restaurant when outside it was ninety degrees, and everyone would turn and look as if you'd just been awarded some major distinguished award for a major lifetime achievement" (260). For emphasis, she concludes, "That's how I felt. I can remember this kind of attention. It always felt ninety degrees hot" (260). Moreover, she repeats how embarrassed and humiliated she felt while photographed at the hospital wearing only the "little patch up front" (260) for underwear, but her tone betrays itself in that she almost anticipates the attention.[6] She ultimately concludes, "Jump to the truth. I was the stupid one" (134), and this leads to her admitting she loved being the focus of everyone's gaze because of physical attractiveness: "The truth is I was addicted to being beautiful, and that's not something you just walk away from. Being addicted to all that attention, I had to stop cold turkey" (135). Unfortunately, sections revealing Shannon's egotism equal the number of those reflecting her insecurity, and there is almost always an underlying tone of self-loathing in statements related to herself. The duality of self-love and self-hatred is at the heart of this novel.

Her rationale for self-mutilation is to stop being the center of attention. As Shannon confesses, "I wanted the everyday reassurance of being mutilated. The way a crippled deformed birth-defected disfigured girl can drive her car with the windows open and not care how the wind makes her hair look, that's the kind of freedom I was after" (135–36). Shannon begins this passage by coveting deformity: "You know how you look at ugly hunchback girls, and they are so lucky. Nobody drags them out at night so they can't finish their doctoral thesis papers. They don't get yelled at by fashion photographers if they get infected ingrown bikini hairs. You look at burn victims and think how much time they save not looking in mirrors to check their skin for sun damage" (135). In his article about *Invisible Monsters*, Johnson offers an insightful approach to viewing Shannon in this situation: "Her eventual desire to mutilate her face signals her intense longing for growth—not merely change. Shannon knows that her ego rests on her need for approval, so a trifling change will not suffice to enact the transition she wants. As a model she has learned that real change must be beyond skin deep. She needs to reformulate how she thinks about herself, and that requires a drastic, permanent alteration of her beauty" (68). The statement that lends itself to the title reveals the paradox associated with seeking approval through mutilation, someone at once acknowledged and avoided because of abnormality: "I'm an invisible monster, and I'm incapable of loving anybody" (192). She states this after she lists the horrible things that have been done to her by others thus far in the novel. The urban industrial images in *The Elephant Man* and the images of the meat freezer, the junk yard, and the Num-Num by-product grinder both reflect sterility and detachment associated with Joseph Merrick and Shannon McFarland. This is contrasted, however, when Shannon thinks about her death, after Seth's botched murder attempt in Evie's home, and she lapses into self-pity: "My dad, he'd go to my funeral and talk to everybody about how I was always about to go back to college and finish my personal fitness training degree and then no doubt go on to medical school. Dad, Dad, Dad, Daddy, I couldn't get past the fetal pig in Biology 101. Now I'm the cadaver. Sorry, Mom. Sorry, God" (211). Readers are left to decide if Shannon deserves their sympathy or their derision, and dialogue such as this displays Shannon's tendency to rehearse expectations about the future in her mind. The warmth she may feel in her heart is contrasted by the coldness of the outside world, and this is complicated by Shannon and Brandy believing in the impartiality of cause/effect outcomes: if they take one action, a predictable reaction will follow. Case in point, Shannon reasons that shooting herself in the face will make her less attractive and therefore more invisible, and this is certainly not what occurs. Both characters struggle with the difference between appearance and reality, and, as a result, they make illogical decisions. Shane's struggle with gender identity illustrates this point.

Seven. The Elephant Man in Invisible Monsters Remix

Gender perception is a major motif in this novel, and any discussion of Chapter 18 must acknowledge its relevance. In *Gender Trouble: Feminisms and the Subversion of Identity*, Judith Butler addresses gender as performance, proposing that gender is not determined by static male and female markers, codes, or labels, but is rather governed by dynamic performances that are scripted, rehearsed, and staged. Butler writes, "Gender ought not to be construed as a stable identity or locus of agency from which various acts follow; rather, gender is an identity tenuously constituted in time, instituted in an exterior space through a *stylized repetition of acts*. The effect of gender is produced through the stylization of the body and, hence, must be understood as the mundane way in which bodily gestures, movements, and styles of various kinds constitute the illusion of an abiding gendered self" (140).[7] Butler considers female impersonation a form of "gender parody," and, as she states, "as much as drag creates a unified picture of 'woman' (what its critics often oppose), it also reveals the distinctness of those aspects of gendered experience which are falsely naturalized as a unity through the regulatory fiction of heterosexual coherence. *In imitating gender, drag implicitly reveals the imitative structure of gender itself—as well as its contingency*" (137). Butler points out that this parody does not have a fixed referent:

> The notion of gender parody defended here does not assume that there is an original which such parodic identities imitate. Indeed, the parody is of the very notion of an original; just as the psychoanalytic notion of gender identification is constituted by a fantasy of a fantasy, the transfiguration of an Other who is always already a "figure" in that double sense, so gender parody reveals that the original identity after which gender fashions itself is an imitation without an origin. To be more precise, it is a production which, in effect—that is, in its effect—postures as an imitation [138].[8]

Shane performs as Brandy Alexander, and he imitates all of the mannerisms related to his perception of femininity. The Rhea sisters embrace Shane's desire for drag and facilitate his performance, paying for his breast implants and subsidizing other means for Shane to continue his role as Brandy Alexander. As a male stripper, Palahniuk's Elephant Man is also performing as a sexual commodity that can be objectified by those who watch him on the stage. This Elephant Man has made the decision to exploit himself sexually for an audience, to become physically attractive through tooth capping and to execute physical feats such as backflips to give his viewers the man-hunk show for which they paid. The strip club is comparable to a Victorian geek show in that both promote performers who rely on their physical anomalies for profit. Shane as disfigured person (through the hairspray can explosion) and then as Brandy Alexander and

Merrick as Elephant Man and then as male stripper allow for the subversion and reversal of their "normal" or "original" identities, both questioned by Butler as being static entities. Shane as heterosexual male becomes identified as bisexual male and finally as Brandy Alexander. According to historical accounts as well as versions of these in the movie and in the play, Merrick was exploited first as a side-show oddity and then as a London social attraction. Considering Butler's theory, Merrick as a stripper serves as an appropriate compliment to Shane's performance as Brandy Alexander. In this novel, Shane and Merrick may apply various masks and assume multiple personas, inventing (and potentially reinventing) different versions of themselves, depending upon the contexts or the situations.

Palahniuk's selection of the name Brandy Alexander reinforces this significance. As demonstrated by the references to the adult film industry in *Snuff*, Palahniuk knows his pornography, and he undoubtedly knew that Brandy Alexander, besides being a popular alcoholic beverage, was a popular porn actress (although her name is correctly spelled "Alexandre") from the mid–1980s to the mid–1990s. According to the *Internet Adult Film Database*, this naturally blond actress with measurements of 34C–24–35 is credited with eighty-four film performances ("Brandy"). Alexandre is reported to be an outspoken advocate of strict confidentiality concerning the distribution of former adult performer information, especially the releasing of actual names and current addresses, and she has a reputation for outspoken comments and a sometimes abrasive personality.[9] Not many readers will probably make the connection between the two, but considering how this is a novel that addresses gender performance, Shane's transgender identity may indeed be predicated upon either his or the Rhea sisters' interpretation of the porn starlet. If Brandy Alexander is based on Brandy Alexandre, then the signification of whom Shane is modeled lends itself to associations related to porn performers and all the sexual connotations related to that profession. Furthermore, this makes the description of Merrick as a stripper a bit more intriguing. Just as the Rhea sisters have prospered financially through their Katty Kathy doll mimicking stereotypical feminine cattiness through sarcastic comments (198), Shane reaps the benefits psychologically and physically from the sexual porn icon whom he may emulate. Palahniuk does not masquerade the obvious exploitation of the female body and the commodification of femininity in this novel, especially when he displays Shannon and Evie posing in skimpy outfits in the stereotypically masculine contexts of a slaughterhouse and a junkyard, and the transfiguration of Shane as not only a voluptuous drag queen but a sensuous porn-star impersonator indicates that Shane wants to be someone desired for appearance and surface rather than personality and substance. If a reader recognizes the allusion to Brandy Alexandre, this is undoubtedly the image he or she will attach to Brandy Alexander. Incidentally, Palahniuk plays with this type of image-making when he portrays a transvestite as the porn star Cassie Wright during an online interview, with Palahniuk himself serving as the interviewer, and he deconstructs feminine Cassie through this clearly masculine replica. Applying Butler's theory, Palahniuk addresses gender performance in *Snuff* as well as in this novel.

A closer look at Palahniuk's references to the Elephant Man in Chapter 18 confirms these points about gender performance. When Palahniuk introduces this scene, he makes sure to highlight that readers should already be familiar with the topic: "We all know the scene in the classic movie *The Elephant Man*, the David Lynch masterpiece, but Daisy's version is better" (114). Shannon is really Daisy; therefore, she is one who is creating this version of Merrick. During their initial meeting, Brandy bestows upon Shannon the personality Daisy St. Patience, one of many names Brandy gives to her (200). Brandy even comments, "Posing girl, you are *so* godawful ugly. Did you let an elephant sit on your face or what?" (279). Daisy's depiction of the Elephant Man certainly takes biographical liberties: "History tells us the Elephant Man didn't sport sexy Speedo tan lines—those sexy runway lines that point the shortcut to some sexy Elephant Man groin, groin, groin. Rumor has it he didn't shave his legs or wax his chest, not even while he was touring the European Continent. Again, history records that he was twenty-one, twenty-two years old. Who's to say Joseph Merrick didn't get his elephant ears pierced for some hot saddle plugs?" (115). In Daisy's account, Merrick pumps his thighs to Donna Summer and Lady Gaga as a definite object of desire. At the end of the chapter, Daisy concludes, "And if that's not *exactly* how it actually happened … well, that's the way it should've" (118). The irony is Brandy and Shannon's collaboration of the content, assuming this section is a joint effort, points toward the physical objectification and media exploitation Shannon is supposedly rebelling against, and more important, is the reason behind her disfigurement. If reinvention is at the heart of this novel, remaking Joseph Merrick in this manner ultimately calls into question Shannon's motivation. In effect, this only emphasizes her own vanity, especially when she constantly seems to wrestle with her resentments toward the fashion industry, which is consistently lampooned through the Rhea sisters' Katty Kathy doll with outrageous 46–16–26 measurements (198) and Brandy's worship of gossip columnist Rona Barrett (26). Likewise, one only needs to consider Brandy's catalogues displaying different grades and variations of products available for vaginoplasty. One passage demonstrates this effectively: "Picture-perfect, state-of-the-art vaginas lengthened using sections of colon, self-cleaning and lubricated with its own mucosa. Sensate clitorises made by cropping and rerouting bits of glans penis. The Cadillac of vaginoplasty. Some of these Cadillacs turn out so successful the flood of colon mucosa means wearing a maxi-pad every day" (99). Toward the beginning of the novel, Shannon mentions how Brandy passes around photos of perfect clitorises and vaginas, ones "better than the real thing" (21), almost as if they are accessories to costumes. Imitation body parts hold as much cultural caché as designer suits, jewelry, or handbags. These scenes are contrasted by the extremely realistic descriptions of skin dermabrasion and skin grafting (82–90), operations that Shannon is reluctant to discuss. On the one hand, Shannon believes physical attractiveness provides empowerment; on the other, she despises everything associated with that form of empowerment. Just as significant are the black and white pictures Shannon views during her face reconstruction (82) contrasted by the color pictures Brandy peruses considering her plastic surgery (99). Shane comments, however: "A sexual reassignment surgery is a miracle for some people, but if you don't want one, it's the ultimate form of self-mutilation" (111). There is an opposition between utility (a necessary operation for function) and cosmetic (an extravagant operation for vanity). Simply put, Shannon is a mess of contradictions, and because of this, readers have difficulty interpreting the "real" Shannon through the totality of all her performances.

The Joseph Merrick character in *The Elephant Man* was virtually a model of humility. At the beginning of the film, he is introduced as an animal, controlled by a master, unable to communicate, something to be put on display at a geek show as well as a medical meeting. As the movie progresses, Merrick is humanized into an innocent victim who is exploited not only by Mr. Bytes but also by Dr. Treves. The movie obviously plays upon viewer emotion by showing Merrick against the backdrop of Victorian social hypocrisy and dehumanizing industrialization. One particularly pathetic scene shows Mrs. Treves breaking down emotionally after Merrick admits he has tried to be a "good boy" so his mother would, if ever located, accept him. Just like Shannon, Merrick becomes a celebrity, but he does not take advantage of this stardom. In other words, as someone exploited most of his life, he does not in turn exploit his newfound power. When Merrick dies, and "Adagio for Strings" is played to evoke additional sympathy, his spirituality is emphasized by the beautiful model church, with meticulously detailed brickwork and perfectly angled cathedral towers. Lynch basically canonizes Merrick at the end of his film. In popular culture, the most famous scene in the film is when a hooded Merrick is cornered by a mob in a public bathroom and he pronounces, "I am not an animal. I am not an animal. I am a human being. I am a man." Perhaps the greatest line should be the one when Merrick tells Treves, after the doctor appears to feel sorry for Merrick, "I am happy every hour of the day." Considering the difficulty in getting at a "true" Shannon, Palahniuk may provide the intertextual reference to *The Elephant Man* to expose how one character has humility in the face of hardship and how another gives into self-centeredness during a time of boredom.

This is not the case. A comparison to the movie/play version of Merrick reveals a tremendous spiritual deficiency in Shannon, but Palahniuk's version of Merrick as the stripper Elephant Man contradicts this interpretation. Palahniuk's Elephant Man is clearly exploiting his own sexuality, and this appears, in the context of the novel, perfectly fine. The vehicle for Shannon's redemption appears to be her own self-exploitation by redefining her own self-identity as something to be given away, commodified as something of value to be transferred from her to her brother. Shannon's gift is a supreme gesture of contrition and of retribution. This is also a way for Shannon to promote her brother's gender performance. Yet, Shannon cannot really give away something she does not possess, and readers could question whether she has learned anything by the end of the novel, but this supreme act demonstrates Shannon's literal self-sacrifice (actually the sacrificing of her own self). Readers discover Shane put the hairspray can in the fire, and he admits his sex-change operation is more punitive than beneficial: "I'm only doing this because it's the biggest mistake I can think to make. It's stupid and destructive, and anybody you ask will tell you I'm wrong. That is why I have to go through with it.... The bigger the mistake looks, the better chance I'll have to break out and live a real life" (110). There may be optimism on the final page, however, when Shannon cuts her veils and appears ready to address life: "The Truth. My Future. Just regular reality ... completely and totally, permanently and without hope, forever and ever I love Brandy Alexander. And that's enough" (133). This might indicate a love that is one of humility and not of vanity, and Shannon's epiphany at that moment might be the spiritual message of acceptance in the entire novel. Shannon's wound is indeed the catalyst that reunites her with her brother. And, when one thinks about self-sacrifice, Shane's contraction of gonorrhea was the result of his wanting to save his father from being arrested for child abuse (157–58), the Rhea sisters take care of Shane, and Brandy Alexander certainly looks out for Shannon. As Johnson mentions, "The challenge for the McFarlands, then, is to break through their narcissism to feel a connection with each other and the world at large ... the time spent on the road with her brother [has] helped heal the pain and resentment from [Shannon's] childhood. She no longer needs the adulation of an audience to find self-worth" (71). Johnson also comments that for Shannon and Shane "self-directed violence provides the pathway to transcendence" (66). In terms of performance, both Shannon and Shane have almost always had to "act" to appease others, whether these actions were for their parents, the Rhea sisters, talent agents, or anyone who tried to understand who they essentially are. At the end of the novel, they find personas, brother and sister, that satisfy deep needs in themselves. Shannon and Shane seem constantly to look forward toward the next performance occasion instead of appreciating the immediate moment. At the conclusion, they are able to situate themselves firmly in the present.

In terms of Butler's performance theory, Shannon is giving her role to her brother. Throughout the narrative, she has revealed that she is someone extremely uncomfortable with the part she plays in the performance that is her life. In several sections, Shannon's story is not that different from student creative writers who attempt to express their feelings in innovative and insightful ways, and they write fiction that is basically creative non-fiction about their lives, not that far from what many of the authors compose in the writers' commune in *Haunted*. These writers will describe horrible events that occurred in their lives, they will discuss addictions or psychoses, and they will explain disastrously dysfunctional relationships. Instructors new to this kind of course will "ohhh" and "ahhh" over what is at its core self-pity spread out all over the pages. Shannon wears this kind of authorial persona in many places of her narrative, although she takes it off and replaces it with something different when she travels with Brandy Alexander, partially because she must assume the role of Brandy's caretaker, forced to forget her own problems by caring for someone else. Shannon performs another role when she gives Shannon her identity, and gender is crucial in this switching of places. Shannon appears strongest when she is capable of giving up the culturally and socially constructed feminine identity that she has tried to assume as a model. After she relinquishes this, she is free to become whomever she decides, and being partially faceless serves as a metaphor for her lack of any permanent or existing self. Her veil is literally as well as figuratively her mask. Most likely, she will no longer go back to the role of Shannon, Daisy, or any of the other titles previously attributed to her. She will be totally free to recreate herself into anything except the self-proclaimed invisible monster. At the end of this book, she no longer views herself in this role.

And, at the end, Shannon just wants to be normal, and she has experienced the vast change from being a fashion model (visually attractive) to a frightening monster (visually unattractive). Now she, like the Elephant Man, just wants to be like everyone else, existing comfortably within her own skin according to her own standards of gender and sexuality. As Chapter 18 suggests, Shannon and Merrick can turn their unattractiveness into attractiveness through performance. In the movie, Merrick commits suicide by lying prostrate, imitating how everyone normally sleeps. Referring to Palahniuk's comments about *Invisible Monsters Remix*, this might the magic that Palahniuk maybe left out of *Invisible Monsters*. The addition of Chapter 18 provides a greater opportunity to define the invisible monster as the insecurity that manifests itself as resentment in each one of us. Every character in *Invisible Monsters Remix* seems to be trying to understand his or her true identity, and each one learns, to use the old adage, "beauty is only skin deep." There is no doubt the stripper Elephant Man understands how to move his audience toward admiring rather than abhorring his physicality. Each character is to some extent self-deceived, and through the forfeiting of the self and the ego, as Shannon ultimately succeeds in accomplishing, there is hope for optimism. Shannon learns that the seeming contradiction is true: the more one gives away, the more one receives in return. She also finally understands that true beauty is the expression of the compassionate soul.

Eight

Empowerment

Much of Chuck Palahniuk's writing, not just the novels addressed in the previous chapters, could be considered Marxist. Palahniuk addresses traditional class conflict and the division between the bourgeoisie and the proletariat by depicting how those who consider themselves blue-collar fight—literally as well as figuratively—for inclusion into the community full of those enjoying what is perceived as white-collar prosperity. The problem in the twenty-first century is that the traditional line, the nostalgic ideal of visible separation, between the bourgeoisie and proletariat is not so easily demarcated by the color of a shirt collar. Many people who hold jobs requiring college degrees earn low wages, and everyone knows having a college degree does not always guarantee a "good" job but fundamentally makes a person more attractive for service positions (or the military). Holding a University of Oregon degree, Palahniuk aligns himself with the working-class, and he portrays himself as the muscular truck mechanic as often as he postures as the nerdy creative artist. Palahniuk's fan base is equally chameleon, representing a widespread and diverse international population. Palahniuk frequently attacks the American Dream, undermining all the patriotic aphorisms perpetuated through nationalistic texts such as Benjamin Franklin's *Poor Richard's Almanack*: hard work leads to success, honesty is always the best policy, and nothing worth having is easily obtained. Palahniuk's characters understand that social Darwinism remains the true operating principle, and survival of the fittest depends upon how well they can adapt in what is still very much a naturalistic universe.

In each of the novels treated in the previous chapters, marginalization and disenfranchisement have been the overriding themes, and this is logical considering the transgressive fictional genre, as transgressive writing reacts against prescribed cultural and social norms—or in many circumstances blasts into generally-accepted religious, philosophical, and ethical totalizing systems. Within this framework, Palahniuk's characters demand empowerment, and they gain it any way they can, regardless of traditional ethical or moral principles. In *Haunted*, the participants compete for the dubious honor of being rescued so they can sell their stories to the highest bidders. Their literary masterpieces turn out to be the sensational stories that they hope will launch them into the media spotlight. In *Pygmy*, the outsider, immediately labeled with a pejorative nickname, relinquishes his previous ideology, assimilates into Americana, and achieves iconic status as the community hero. In *Snuff*, Cassie Wright attains record-book immortality through sexual intercourse with 600 men, but only after mounting the erection of the comatose last performer. In *Tell-All*, Hazie Coogan sabotages the life of her stardom surrogate Katherine Kenton, finally murdering her for Hollywood notoriety. In *Damned*, Madison Spencer overcomes adolescent insecurities ultimately to defeat historically famous villains and become Miss Popularity in hell. And lastly, in *Invisible Monsters Remix*, Shannon McFarland bestows an identity that she thinks still has media currency upon her brother Shane, and Shannon, once the epitome of American feminine attractiveness, seems okay with remaining along the social periphery, sacrificing her spot in the center for a place in the shadows.

These characters do not represent the traditional American marginalized or disenfranchised, at least not the ones promoted through the cultural diversity classifications disseminated throughout American media. In *Haunted*, Lady Baglady was a wealthy socialite who wore the homeless-vagabond persona for recreation, Mother Nature was a homeopathic therapist who moonlighted as a high-priced foot prostitute, and Director Denial held an administrative supervisory position as a social worker in a police station. In *Pygmy*, the Cedar family is presumably the typical middle-class American family, although Donald Cedar works at a secret government lab and Mrs. Cedar peddles cordless sex vibrators. In *Snuff*, Cassie is a matriarch in the porn industry, obviously not exploited or manipulated (at least not according to her background) as many adult actresses are at the other end of the porn star spectrum. In *Tell-All*, Hazie clearly has control of Kenton's already famous life well before the end of the novel, and she is certainly not abused, ignored, or unappreciated in her job position, even when she balks at wearing a formal maid uniform. In *Damned*, Madison's mother is a star and her father is a billionaire, and with houses all over the world, never-ending professional accolades, and always-following paparazzi, Madison has literally grown up with a silver spoon in her mouth. In *Invisible Monsters Remix*, Shannon has enjoyed media attention and has relished public fame, with her face adorning the covers of the best women's magazines, living a life coveted by both men and women. Palahniuk demonstrates, however, that in America these types of people can indeed occupy the same marginalized positions on the cusp of cultural or social power alongside traditionally disadvantaged groups. Granted, his female characters can already claim their places as can Shane McFarland as a LGBT representative and Whittier as someone diseased, and, of course, Pygmy must begin on the border because he is not a citizen, but all of the others would, by traditionally accepted dictates, ostensibly have a stake in the American power core. Palahniuk provides the much needed literary illustrations of how everybody in twenty-first-century America may claim this distinction, which explains why so many readers identify with the dysfunctional situations in his novels. Palahniuk shows how anyone may declare cultural powerlessness, no matter race, sexuality, religion, economics, or other bureaucratic markers that differentiate the American haves from the have nots. This salient quality to represent a widespread audience is precisely what makes Palahniuk a major literary voice in contemporary American culture.

Palahniuk began all of this in his first novel, *Fight Club*, and although many readers might not consider this book a working-class text, it fits the standard definition for this genre.[1] In "Why Working-Class Literature Matters," Sherry Linkon lists the criteria theorists agree classify a text "working class": "a focus on work, accurate representation of the material and social conditions of working-class life, validation of working-class culture, resistance to existing power structures, [and] rejection or critique of the standard middle-class narrative of upward mobility." In "Six Points on Class," Michael Zweig writes that the working class have "relatively little power at work" as well as "little personal control over the pace or content of their work [or] supervisory control over the work lives of others" (116). Within his definition of working class, Zweig subdivides various "collars," white collar referring to office and service workers, blue collar to manual laborers, and pink collar to female service workers (116). Chuck Palahniuk's *Fight Club* may be considered a working-class text based upon Linkon's and Zweig's definitions. The novel addresses Marxism's concern with class, power, and marginalization, and it presents the basic dichotomies between the proletariat and the bourgeoisie, the privileged and the deserving, and the haves and the have nots. The work's central conflict is unquestionably between those who traditionally control power and those who desire to control it. Palahniuk admits in his "Afterword" that many working-class readers express a strong affinity with the main characters, and several grassroots fight clubs have started based solely upon his book (209–12). In

"Toward a Theory of Working Class Literature," Renny Christopher and Carolyn Whitson claim working-class literature "calls for action by the reader, calls for change in the conditions detailed in the literature" (72). Although most of the criticism concerning *Fight Club* addresses gender, the novel's vast appeal is more likely related to its relevance as working-class literature. *Fight Club* advocates social change, but not through the violence that is typically associated with the story and perpetuated by the popular film. Instead, *Fight Club* calls for more moderate action toward class inequity, action that falls somewhere between Tyler's radicalism and Joe's subservience.

Palahniuk's depiction of the white-collar working class makes *Fight Club* unique compared to most working-class literature. In *The White Collar Working Class*, Richard Sobel supports the argument that the traditional distinction between the white-collar employee being a social stratum higher than the blue-collar worker is fading, and the two levels are increasingly difficult to differentiate. Sobel points out white-collar labor is comprised of "a diversity of professional, managerial, clerical, and sales occupations that have traditionally involved status distinctions from the rest of the labor force" (1). Now those distinctions are harder to separate. Although white collar is not the same as middle class, particular white-collar jobs (e.g., lawyers and managers) are associated with the middle class. Today, many of these white-collar jobs are labor positions, and according to Sobel, are working class. These people are defined by the value of the work they produce, they have little representation in administrative issues, and they do not necessarily earn a middle-class living. As Sobel comments, "In essence, white collar and blue collar do not represent 'horizontal' class differences; instead 'vertical' class distinctions divide white collar and blue collar occupations" (2). This is a crucial concept concerning how the various characters in the preceding chapters view themselves. Even though many of the characters in *Haunted* are privileged, they are not satisfied with what they have. Cassie is partially participating in the gang bang for financial reasons. Shannon undoubtedly is not poor, probably situated in the middle class, but she still is unfulfilled, as is Madison concerning her family. At the end of *Tell-All*, Hazie has achieved wealth, but readers predict this will not make her happy. Pygmy scoffs at American capitalist excess and waste. *Fight Club* is the first Palahniuk novel to treat what Sobel discusses, the marginalization and disenfranchisement of those who twenty years or certainly thirty years ago would certainly not be included in these categories, the middle class who supposedly enjoy American prosperity.

The narrator, Joe, affords the luxury of buying into what he considers to be this wonderful middle-class lifestyle, and he makes a point of branding all of the commodities attached to this social level. In his prestigious high-rise apartment that closely resembles a thickly walled "filing cabinet" (41), he has a Njurunda coffee table, Alle cutlery, a Vild hall clock, Hemlig hat boxes, a Mommala quilt-cover set, and a Klipsk shelving unit. Joe comments, "The people I know who used to sit in the bathroom with pornography, now they sit in the bathroom with their IKEA furniture catalogue" (43), and he confesses that his obsession to consume according to socially determined values of prestige have taken over his life. When Tyler and Joe threaten to blackmail the projectionist union president and the hotel manager (a point in the novel when the narrator clearly hints Tyler and Joe are the same entity), they accept physical abuse because of the unfair class advantage. Realizing the union boss will not kill him, Tyler says, "You have too much to lose. I have nothing. You have everything" (114–15). As a result, Joe relies upon his body for exchange value. The hotel manager has his social position as leverage—he has authority over Joe—so Joe sacrifices his body in retaliation against the power inequality. Joe also gains power via the support groups, where people who have genuinely lost or are in the process of losing all physical control over their bodies attempt to reestablish it through community. This is also perpetuated through Tyler's formation of Project Mayhem. Tyler informs the Assault Committee, "What we have to do … is remind these guys what kind of power they still have" (120). When Joe is taken on his birthday ride, the mechanic screams out the car window, "As long as you're at fight club, you're not how much money you've got in the bank. You're not your job. You're not your family, and you're not who you tell yourself" (143). The mechanic later comments, "I see the strongest and the smartest men who have ever lived … and these men are pumping gas and waiting tables" (149). Fight Club allows these men who feel the same social frustration as Joe to gain a sense of control through physical exertion. Through the famous list of rules, they, not some administrative entity, are able to impose their own restrictions and to establish, at least during the hours of Fight Club, an environment in which physicality, not social class, is power. Instead of allowing administrators to dictate their actions, the men of Fight Club decide how to exert their own physical power, and this opportunity is emancipating.

Ultimately, Fight Club serves the means for Joe and those like him to become empowered. In the "Afterword," which was added to the 2005 edition of the 1996 novel, Palahniuk explains that his story, written to "kill a slow afternoon at work" (213), was originally only seven pages and based upon real life events. He said the inspiration was a Bill Moyer television program about street gangs populated by young men with absent fathers, and he was particularly interested in the rules imposed upon the young men as a form of rehabilitation: "the bookstores were full of books like *The Joy Luck Club* and *The Divine Secrets of the Ya-Ya Sisterhood* and *How to Make an American Quilt*. These were all novels that presented a social model for women to be together. To sit together and tell their stories. To share their lives. But there was no novel that presented a new social model for men to share their lives" (214). His response, the story version of "Fight Club," was planned to be "something nonthreatening" (214). Palahniuk admits a friend worried that readers might copycat some of the events in *Fight Club*, and Palahniuk replies that he and his friends "were just blue-collar nobodies living in Oregon with public school educations. There was nothing [he] could imagine that a million people weren't already doing" (215). Palahniuk vastly underrated the power of *Fight Club*. Palahniuk summarizes in the "Afterword" several of the popular culture references to his novel, from the Office Depot sample label with the 420 Paper Street address to the *Saturday Night Live* spoof "Fight-Like-A-Girl Club" to people in Texas wearing "Save Marla Singer" t-shirts (211–12). One reason why readers have bestowed cult-bible status to the literal words in the novel is that they recognize them as a call to action. *Fight Club* is undoubtedly subversive, but is so in a more innocuous way than may be apparent. Palahniuk is not calling for the workers to rise in rebellion and destroy Wall Street; he is simply asking readers to be self-reflective and begin their own self-empowerment. In other words, change comes from within, not from without.

This is precisely what Palahniuk is advocating in the novels addressed in the previous chapters. Even though Palahniuk's characters do not always end up in what would be generally assumed morally or ethically exemplary places, they seem to finish in better positions than when they began. Granted, dismemberment, cannibalism, and death are not attractive final options for most of those in *Haunted*. Cassie Wright and Branch Bacardi having their genitalia melted together does not appear positive. Jawless Shannon McFarland bestowing her identity on a hospitalized brother Shane could be an act of sacrifice or compassion but could also be viewed as eschewing personal responsibility. Hazie Coogan getting away with all of her lies, let alone a major crime, just does not seem fair. Pygmy is the town hero, but then there is the school shooting leading to mass murder that precedes his receiving this honor. Madison will be released from hell, yet she remains dead, at least this is where readers are left at the conclusion of *Damned*. True, these characters might not appear to be left with positive situations or bright futures. The point is, however, that all of these major Palahniuk characters took action toward something better. Every one of them, even those who did not survive Whittier's writing retreat, made the decision to act. They took initiative to react against the forces that marginalized and disenfranchised them, even though they understood, and this is a crucial point, success would not be measured by the standards promoted through American media propaganda and capitalist commercialism.

This establishes the importance of Palahniuk's parody. Looking at each of the major characters remaining at the end of the six novels, one can see how the fight is what provides redeeming hope, and this hope is what sets them apart. In all honesty, readers can guess before cracking the first page of a Palahniuk novel that someone will either die or become physically mangled. Needless to say, readers most likely begin a Palahniuk story with the assumption something bad will happen to someone in an unordinary manner. Readers can also assume characters will be disadvantaged in some unusual, unique, unorthodox or counterculture way. Hence, readers truly appreciate how these characters rise, react, respond, and even retaliate against whatever forces attempt to keep them down. These characters discover a semblance of hope, not in the religious deity sense of hope but in the twelve-step Higher Power version, and they find the energy to either exploit themselves or to exploit their own situations to move ahead, at least upward farther than where they began. In the six novels, the main characters eventually latch onto a thread of optimism, the feeling that things can indeed get better, and this leads to their taking action, albeit sometimes in self-destructive ways.

By referring to previous texts through parody, Palahniuk places his own characters' striving for individual power within the same parameters as others with whom readers can identify and understand. In this way, readers are at a common starting place with their assumptions, and Palahniuk subsequently takes those prejudices into entirely unexpected and unpredicted directions. A reason why Palahniuk has such an extensive following is, for better or worse, readers identify with his characters' plights. Going back to the cult popularity of *Fight Club*, everyone is capable of claiming powerlessness against forces he or she might not identify—a person may just feel "outside," and he or she may suspect, true or false, that others are on the "inside." Palahniuk's presentation of people taking stands against their current predicaments in extremely transgressive ways is what twenty-first-century readers want to see. They want to feel attached to a raw, gritty, and belligerent movement against established authority, whether it is affiliated with the church, the school, the government, or any other gigantic seemingly omnipotent bureaucracy that usurps or undermines power from each person. Palahniuk will continue to be the voice of the individual alone in the universe who may not want to be heard as much as want to take a punch at what keeps that person stifled, muffled, or silent. Cassie was not willing to let Branch deprive her of achieving number sex act 600, Shannon was not willing to let her brother continue without her name, and Madison was not willing to allow Satan to control her destiny. These three were, on the contrary, willing to take action to accomplish their goals. Readers can only conjecture what will happen beyond the temporal borders of the narratives, but at least they know the characters were willing to fight for what they believed by the end of each novel.

Taken all together, readers can appreciate what Palahniuk is attempting through his fiction when they understand how he applies previous forms and genres, relies on intertextuality and hyperreality, and responds to literary theory and criticism. In her review of Palahniuk's most recent novel *Beautiful You*, Paula Bomer writes, "Palahniuk is a novelist of ideas, I suppose, but that doesn't necessarily mean they're good ones." She adds, after questioning the initial premise that a man could achieve world domination via a line of sex toys, "And while the novel delivers moments of awkward humor and some nominally feminist plot twists, the language and the ridiculousness of this particular concept remain hard to digest." Loyal Palahniuk readers realize that Bomer is looking at *Beautiful You* all wrong. First, she probably does not even believe someone could rule the world by marketing a new line of sexual vibrators and related products. Second, she probably expects traditional romance in a novel claiming to be about sexuality. Third, she is probably being polite when she mentions Palahniuk's "awkward humor." A Palahniuk fan will just grin after looking at this review because he or she neither questions the plausibility of the initial premise nor is surprised by the execution of that premise within the narrative. Through *Beautiful You*, for instance, Palahniuk supplies his audience with hope they too could come up with a similar scheme to get them more money, more prestige, more fame, more of everything that those in the American power center appear to have. Or, on the other side, they could cheer for the underdog Penny Harrigan in her fight against the corruption of mega-wealthy and super-powerful C. Linus Maxwell in a clearly defined good versus evil battle. Readers who understand how the Palahniuk universe operates are immune against such knee-jerk conservative reactions against this style of transgressive fiction.

In "The Fringe Is the Future," Palahniuk addresses why he writes about the marginalized and disenfranchised. Palahniuk states, "People ask me why I write about characters who seem to live on the margins of society, and my answer is always that the fringe is the future. Outside the mainstream, people are engaged in constant small experiments, testing new social models, new hierarchies, new personal identities. The most successful of those experiments—what begin as cults, fads, crazes, or manias—the ones that serve people best grow to become the next mainstream" (9). Palahniuk concludes, "The fringe is the future" (9). Although some people would vehemently disagree, there is an implosion currently happening in the power circle: those on the border of this circle have staked deep claims in the space on the inside, and they are acquiring that to which they firmly believe they are entitled. People traditionally in the center have been pushed to the outside. Or, to be honest, there really have not been any people in that location for some time. Now there are political, corporate, bureaucratic entities occupying that middle space, and those social anathemas are being assualted from all sides. A struggle is occurring to move them off of the center apex. Anyone today may claim some quality that makes him or her diverse—anyone with ADHD, who is a heroin addict, who has depression, who is overweight, who is underweight, who is from a divorced family, who is from a single-parent family, who is past fifty years of age, who is under eighteen years of age, who is from a certain region of the United States, who has any other quality outside of the power circle—and each person has the right to express dissatisfaction withnot having his or her rightful portion of power. As Palahniuk claims in this essay, there is an ebb and flow in how people react to power: one group will close off a street through an act of civil disobedience (7–8), but more than likely a later group, perhaps from another generation, will want that same street opened and will threaten their own brand of civil protest (11).

Palahniuk also refers to twelve-step meetings (as well as fight clubs and other alternative venues) as replacing the church for the traditional gathering place, the communal location frequented by those with similar ideologies (10). Through his job of chauffeuring the sick to recovery meetings, Palahniuk learned about various support communities and the twelve steps toward recovery. The particulars about the twelve steps are in the "big book" of *Alcoholics Anonymous*, the "How It Works" section. Pertinent steps related to this reading are the following:

2. Came to believe that a Power greater than ourselves could restore us to sanity.
3. Made a decision to turn our will and our lives over to the care of God *as we understood Him.*

4. Made a searching and fearless and moral inventory of ourselves.
5. Admitted to God, to ourselves, and to another human being the exact nature of our wrongs.
8. Made a list of all persons we had harmed, and became willing to make amends to them all.
9. Made direct amends to such people wherever possible, except when to do so would injure them or others [59].

In *Fight Club*, during recovery meetings, Joe meets Marla, initially his nemesis but later his girlfriend, who like him is a faker who frequents the gatherings to fill some psychological or spiritual vacuum within her soul. Joe competes with Marla for attention, and after mentioning that Chloe, the "genuine article" (36) of the afflicted, has succumbed to brain disease, he states, "No, she wants it all. The cancers, the parasites ... she never dreamed she could feel so 'smarvelous. She actually felt alive. Her skin was clearing up. All her life, she never saw a dead person. There was no real sense of life because she had nothing to contrast it with. Oh, but now there was dying and death and loss and grief. Weeping and shuddering, terror and remorse. Now that she knows where we're all going, Marla feels every moment of her life" (38). In many ways, the characters in the five novels are similar to people at twelve-step meetings. Joe says about his first such gathering, "there were introductions: this is Alice, this is Brenda, this is Dover. Everyone smiles with that invisible gun to their head" (19). In this capacity, the group in *Haunted* serves as a support community, continuing Joe's sentences with "this is Reverend Godless ... and I dress in drag and allow people to hit me for money to blow up churches," or "this is Sister Vigilante ... and I use a bowling ball to hurt people," and the list could continue with the stories functioning as testimonials from the participants. Furthermore, *Tell-All* is Hazie's long recovery fourth-step personal inventory of her actions, although she might not take responsibility for all that she should, and the descriptions in *Invisible Monsters Remix* allow Shannon to think about those whom she has harmed and subsequently to make amends to them through eighth and ninth steps, as Shannon's final act is definitely an amends toward Shane.

In the same way, Cassie makes amends with her daughter Sheila, as Cassie admits she has known all along that she is her porn-baby (176). In fact, *Damned* is entirely about personal inventory and making amends, and Madison's narrative is comparable to the twelve-step meeting confessional, which could have the alternative for each chapter beginning, "My name is Madison, and I am a hope-aholic." If nothing else, at the end of the novel,

Archer seems to make amends for his little brother's death (238–41). Introspectively, Pymgy looks closely at his own actions both in America and previously during his indoctrination in his homeland, and he has a revelation when he decides to defect. Significantly, readers are participants during these fictional support meetings, figuratively listening to these speakers' confessions, words they need to express to an audience to achieve community and hence empowerment. This is not exactly the same epiphany that Chloe has when she announced "the only good news she had" (35), that she was prepared to die, but it is still a life-changing epiphany. All of Palahniuk's characters engage in something like twelve-step programs toward personal empowerment, and they have their own concepts of the Higher Power according to who or what they believe it to be. Joe may believe these meeting are without hope, but they are actually full, although perhaps not what one would normally or typically term hope, yet this is Palahniuk's entire point: this is hope that is along the fringe. Joe states about hugging Big Bob dying of testicular cancer, "This should be my favorite part, being held and crying with Big Bob without hope. We all work so hard all the time. This is the only place I ever really relax and give up" (18). In reality, Palahniuk once held a job driving terminally ill people to exactly these types of meetings, and he intentionally portrays Joe's self-deception in this section. Just like the others, Joe yearns for the support community that will help him to change his life.

Through this twelve-step empowerment, Palahniuk's characters represent those who are beginning to stake their claims on the inside. They might not be very deep into this territory, but that is fine with them. Palahniuk does not present a world that is comparable to the one in "Harrison Bergeron" in which Kurt Vonnegut satirizes the concept of total social equality by putting weights on ballerinas and forcing critical thinkers to wear earplugs with distracting sounds, but he presents characters who have comparable psychological burdens and cultural restraints breaking free as the two dancers in the final scene in that story. In comparison, the movement of combatants during a fight club displays a different dance from the ones in Vonnegut's story. Sometimes Palahniuk's characters achieve what they desire for about as long as those two, who free themselves from the constraining shackles designed ironically to make them equal. His characters meet the same metaphorical fate as Vonnegut's two characters, who are shot by the Handicapper General after they take just a few strides toward spiritual enlightenment and personal empowerment. Vonnegut shows how state-enforced equality leads to more of a dystopian rather than a utopian society, and Palahniuk similarly presents how total equality is not something that can be aggressively enforced in American culture. Instead, action must spread from the grassroots level, and productive change may be sporadic and subtle. Palahniuk's characters make the effort for that momentary euphoria or fleeting serenity by confronting their problems while at the same time realizing there may not be much they can really do to solve them, maybe the same paradox associated with the Nightmare Box, a vision of clarity that is sublime, awesome, and frightening, all at the same time.

If Palahniuk is calling for action through his novels, rhetorically manipulating readers to take ownership of their own lives instead of allowing other agencies to take that ability away from them, the question is how do readers apply Palahniuk? The next chapter will address this to some degree. Palahniuk readers know to be wary of any totalizing system advertising enlightenment, whether it is capitalism (or any other –ism) or any ideology that has "the" avenue toward prosperity. The referent texts that Palahniuk parodies are all in one sense propagating one of these abstract doctrines that recruit allegiance. Boccaccio and Dante have Christianity as their foundations, obviously more so Dante as *The Divine Comedy* is essentially a theological discourse. Underlying *Snuff* is the principle of the hard work ethic, as Cassie has risen above her Hollywood and porn counterparts to achieve lasting stardom, and her story, comparable to Pygmy's is about endurance, stamina, and skill. Both Cassie and Pygmy understand the importance of patience and humility. *Tell-All* also promotes these qualities, but from the other side, as Hazie patiently waits in her service job eventually to succeed at the expense of others, and the Hollywood in this novel varies little from the one (Hollywood politics as well as porn politics) portrayed in *Snuff* or, for that matter, the stereotypical glamor industry in which Shannon McFarland works. Readers identify the parodies through Palahniuk's inversion of what they imitate, and they all lead the same direction: self-empowerment. Readers see people in almost unbelievable situations, and they watch them aspire for something better. To many readers, this should be the goal of most fiction. What readers would not want something greater than what they already have? If Palahniuk is correct, even those who seem to have it all still believe they should have more. Perception is everything, and at least most of Palahniuk's characters look at their worlds with clear vision. It would be a stretch to say Palahniuk's readers emulate what they see in the stories, and it would be pretentious to assume these readers dig deep into the moral and ethical depths of his fiction to mine spiritual or philosophical gems of wisdom that will enrich their lives. No, that would not be an accurate assessment. Most of the time, however, readers receive an honest coverage unadulterated with the fluff and the façade incorporated into the fiction of other, more mainstream authors. Palahniuk's readers appreciate this, and they can bounce the ideas presented in *Haunted*, *Snuff*, *Pygmy*, *Tell-All*, *Damned*, and *Invisible Monsters Remix* off of the values, beliefs, and attitudes that govern their own lives. This is how readers apply Palahniuk's fiction, definitely not as models set forth to imitate, but as scenarios laid out to contemplate. Most Palahniuk readers would never really think about participating in fight clubs, but those same people have felt the same frustration as the characters in that novel and have thought about similar types of rebellion.

Ideally, almost all of Palahniuk's writing is a parody of Stephen Crane's poem from *War Is Kind*,

> A man said to the universe:
> "Sir, I exist!"
> "However," replied the universe,
> "The fact has not created in me
> A sense of obligation."

Palahniuk's characters demonstrate this fortitude, and readers respect and admire how they express through their actions the declaration "I exist!" Unfortunately, these characters often receive a similar cosmic riposte. This reply might be the message transmitted through the Nightmare Box, the reality that their place in the world is—no matter how they want to perceive it—as it should be, this and nothing more. Even in the face of this, most of the Palahniuk characters maintain a sense of hope and are still willing to fight for whatever they feel entitled, and that may not be very much, but at least it is something, and with that something they exist, emphasized with an exclamation point.

NINE

The Rhetorical Situation

In the previous sections of this book, an introductory chapter offered a definition of postmodern parody, several chapters applied this literary device to six of Chuck Palahniuk's novels, and one chapter provided a rationale for Palahniuk's application of this literary feature. This chapter will focus primarily on the effectiveness of Palahniuk's use of postmodern parody in those six novels. Instead of systematically referring to data such as the specific number of copies these six novels sold or polling readers to determine how well they understood Palahniuk's ideas, a more appropriate approach for this study is to assess these texts within a rhetorical framework, actually to analyze how effectively Palahniuk's novels function as rhetorical texts, essentially to treat *Haunted*, *Snuff*, *Pygmy*, *Tell-All*, *Damned*, and *Invisible Monsters Remix* as rhetorical discourse. In his seminal essay "The Rhetorical Situation," Lloyd Bitzer provides the critical apparatus through which Palahniuk's novels may be assessed as rhetorical fiction. A summary of critical theories that define postmodern parody, an application of these theories to Palahniuk's six novels, and a justification of Palahniuk's use of postmodern parody have been presented in the preceding chapters. This section will draw upon that previous information to demonstrate that Palahniuk's novels succeed as rhetorical texts. Palahniuk not only responds appropriately to the rhetorical situations outside of his novels, but he creates narrators who react effectively to the rhetorical situations inside their own fictional settings.

Before addressing the particular novels, attention must be directed toward literature as persuasion, the basis of rhetorical fiction. In *The Rhetoric of Fiction*, Wayne Booth explains the various literary techniques authors employ to manipulate audiences while maintaining positions outside of the texts.[1] In his introduction, Booth states that his study will investigate whether "rhetoric is compatible with art" (xiv), and he clarifies how he perceives the relationship between rhetoric and literature: "In writing about the rhetoric of fiction, I am not primarily interested in didactic fiction, fiction used for propaganda or instruction. My subject is the technique of non-didactic fiction, viewed as the art of communicating with readers—the rhetorical resources available to the writer of epic, novel, or short story as he tries, consciously or unconsciously, to impose his fictional world upon the reader" (xiii).[2] Thus, Booth analyzes "the author's means of controlling his reader" (xiii) by creating realistic characters who live within the boundaries of their fictional worlds. In the third chapter entitled "All Authors Should Be Objective," Booth explains that the best method for writers to create believable, lifelike personas is for them to remain consciously divorced from their fiction. In other words, authors might characterize voices in their texts that reflect their social and political philosophies, but these voices should also independently interact within the contexts of the works. They should not obviously function as mouthpieces espousing the authors' ideologies. Granted, as an expressive form, any text will reflect some aspect of its creator, but when a character appears to articulate only an author's words, the writer corrupts the text, making the fiction less imaginative and more instructive. Booth scolds Hardy for sententiousness in *The Mayor of Casterbridge* (27), and he praises Fielding, Swift, Thackeray, and Joyce for artistically persuading their audiences to believe that their characters are completely free from any authorial intrusion outside of the contexts of their literature (75).

To create these realistic voices, and in turn to neutralize the narrators, Booth recommends that writers invent "implied authors." He points out, "The 'implied author' chooses, consciously or unconsciously, what we read; we infer as an ideal, literary, created version of the real man [the author]; he is the sum of all his choices" (*Rhetoric* 75). Booth further explains that when a writer creates an implied author, he generates "not simply an ideal, impersonal 'man in general' but an implied version of 'himself' that is different from the implied authors that we meet in other men's works.... Whether we call this implied author an 'official scribe,' or adapt the term recently revived by Kathleen Tillotson [in *The Tale and the Teller*]—the author's 'second self'—it is clear that the picture the reader gets of this presence is one of the author's most important effects" (*Rhetoric* 70–71). Hence, the artist creates a character whose persona serves as a surrogate author within a text. Instead of writers obtrusively telling their audiences what they want them to think or to feel as they read, their characters should independently show through their words and through their actions the messages underlying the fictions. Booth argues that D. H. Lawrence failed, for instance, to maintain an appropriate stance in *Lady Chatterley's Lover*. Just as he criticized Hardy, Booth reprimands Lawrence for undisguisedly forcing his voice into the language of his characters, and he blames Lawrence for imposing on his audience unconvincing characters speaking in dubious situations (*Rhetoric* 79). Although Booth concedes that several scholars praise Lawrence as a brilliant novelist, he comments that these critics cannot discuss Lawrence without "spending most of their energies on the preachments" (*Rhetoric* 80). To Booth, Lawrence is an excellent example of an author who subverts the integrity of his fiction by imposing his ideology on his readers.

In an essay entitled "The Rhetorical Stance," targeted toward instructors of rhetoric more than critics of literature, Booth describes the balance an author should maintain in a text, fiction or non-fiction. Addressing mostly teachers, he offers pragmatic advice to instructors concerning the nature of a writing situation. In this regard, he defines the optimal position a writer must assume toward an audience and a topic: a stance "depends on discovering and maintaining in any writing situation a proper balance among the three elements that are at work in any communicative effort: the available arguments about the subject itself, the interests and peculiarities of the audience, and the voice, the implied character, of the speaker" (111).[3] Booth further names two corruptions that affect these three variables, "unbalanced stances often assumed by people who think they are practicing the arts of persuasion": the "pedant's stance" and the "advertiser's stance" (111). When authors assume the pedant's stance, they are "ignoring or underplaying the personal relationship of speaker and audience and depending entirely on statements about a subject—that is, the notion of a job done for a particular audience is left out" (111). As Booth mentions, this discourse "appears more for bibliographies than for readers" (111). The second rhetorical position, the advertiser's stance, "comes from *under*valuing the subject and overvaluing pure effect: how to win friends and influence people" (114). The writer manipulates, caring less about informing the readers than winning their attention and support. In relation to his *Rhetoric of Fiction*, Booth believes that a writer should present a subject through a voice that draws the reader into the prose without necessarily appearing overtly manipulative or persuasive. In his opinion, Lawrence failed to do this through the gamekeeper in his novel: the gamekeeper Oliver Mellors is unabashedly Lawrence's spokesperson to promote his doctrine of sexuality, especially relating to blood consciousness and phallic consciousness. Palahniuk's stance in his six novels can be evaluated likewise using Booth's theory of rhetorical balance, especially his ideas pertaining to voice.

The primary tool, however, to judge Palahniuk's authorial positioning is Bitzer's "rhetorical situation." Bitzer's framework for defining rhetorical situation provides an excellent vehicle through which to assess a writer's ability to maintain this balance in any text. In "The Rhetorical Situation," Bitzer states, "Rhetoric is situational.... Rhetorical works belong to the class of things which obtain their character from the circumstances of the historical context in which they occur" (3). He continues, "a work of rhetoric is pragmatic; it comes into existence for the sake of something beyond itself; it functions ultimately to produce action or change in the world; it performs some task" (3–4). Bitzer then cites three constituents within a rhetorical situation: exigence, audience, and constraints. Exigence is defined as "an imperfection marked by urgency; it is a defect, an obstacle, something waiting to be done, a thing which is other than it should be" (6). Exigence demands change. There may be many exigencies in a situation, but if an exigence, such as "winter," cannot be modified, it is not rhetorical (6): "An exigence is rhetorical when it is capable of positive modification" (7). Bitzer further explains that "in any rhetorical situation there will be at least one controlling exigence which functions as the organizing principle; it specifies the audience to be addressed and the change to be effected" (7). The second constituent is audience, which determines the focus of the rhetoric. A rhetorical discourse "produces change by influencing the decision and action of persons who function as mediators of change" (7), and these persons differ from general readers in that they are directly affected by the exigence. As an illustration, Bitzer states that scientists and poets write to audiences, but their audiences are not rhetorical. Scientific readers observe data and poetic readers experience poetry, yet they are not necessarily influenced to initiate change while they are reading. Bitzer clarifies, "But the rhetorical audience must be capable of serving as mediator of the change which the discourse functions to produce" (8). The third constituent is made up of constraints. Bitzer defines these as "persons, events, objects, and relations which are parts of the situation because they have the power to constrain decision and action needed to modify the exigence" (8). Bitzer offers several instances of this term, such as attitudes, beliefs, and traditions, but he also mentions that "when the orator enters the situation, his discourse not only harnesses constraints given by the situation but provides additional constraints—for example his personal character, his logical proofs, and his style" (8). Bitzer also includes the Aristotelian proofs in this category: the "artistic proofs," the constraints controlled by the rhetor and his method, influence decision and action, as do the "inartistic proofs," the constraints controlled by the situation itself (8).

Bitzer differentiates between a rhetorical situation and a fictive situation, clarifying that an action within a novel is only applicable within the fictional setting. He also mentions that "we should note, however, that the fictive rhetorical discourse within a play or novel may become genuinely rhetorical outside fictive context—if there is a real situation for which the discourse is a rhetorical response. Also, of course, the play or novel itself may be understood as a rhetorical response having poetic form" (10). By this definition, the novels addressed thus far are Palahniuk's fictive rhetorical responses to the real social situations of marginalization and disenfranchisement that he witnesses in contemporary America. Through the various narrators and main characters, Palahniuk assumes rhetorical masks through which he can effectively express and promote his ideology. Seen this way, each of the six novels provides Palahniuk with an opportunity to manipulate readers toward assuming certain perspectives. In other words, through his literary creations, Palahniuk persuades his audience toward particular ideological positions and thus serves as the facilitator coercing his readers toward taking action that will lead to productive change. The question might be what constitutes these perspectives and positions, but this has been partially answered in the previous chapters. Palahniuk addresses a broad range of readers, many of whom believe themselves to be marginalized and disenfranchised, and through his fiction, he persuades them to take action to change their current situations. Without a doubt, Palahniuk strongly advocates action—the kind that is rebellious, subversive, and forceful—and he attempts to sway his audience toward becoming their own mediators of change leading to their own personal self-empowerments, the ultimate goal. Moreover, through his writing, Palahniuk motivates readers to assert themselves against socioeconomic, political, and cultural entities that are seemingly omnipotent and constitute the power center. He continues to inspire a grassroots effort to push each of his readers toward individual self-actualization. *Fight Club* spawned a cult movement in which people began asserting their rights toward their personal entitlements, and Palahniuk's subsequent novels continue—although not near as radically or violently—the tradition initiated by that book. Palahniuk rhetorically initiated audience change through *Fight Club*, but that text was also his rhetorical response to a social exigence that initiated its creation.

Rhetoric originates from occasion; there must be a situation in which change can be established through discourse. According to Bitzer's theory, the exigence is the call that prompts the response, and Palahniuk is known for responding to stimuli from the media. He is sensitive to major issues, but what makes him unique is that he stays receptive toward peripherally significant debates, those that are on the outside of the mainstream. An illustration of the Palahniuk creative process might be helpful, and the following is just a scenario to demonstrate possible Palahniuk protocol—he has not admitted to considering this as a subject for one of his novels. Recently, there has been debate in the media concerning the University of Alabama's Alpha Phi Sorority 2015 fall recruitment video. One might contend it is presumptuous to declare Palahniuk would target such an area, but predicting possibilities based on Palahniuk's creative *modus operandi*, this conjecture might be right on the mark. The sorority has deleted the video from its website, but the clip has gone viral on the Internet and is available through *YouTube* (the address is on the works cited page). The recruitment video is innocuous, as there is nothing offensive, obscene, vulgar, or profane. The video is definitely not pornographic. There are media reports, however, that criticize the piece for displaying a homogenous group of blond, slim, tanned, physically beautiful Caucasian women bouncing around their sorority house, at the University of Alabama football stadium, and on a dock surrounded by water. These apparently happy and healthy young women wear short skirts, daisy dukes, and swim suits. The young women dance in formations of lines and circles, blow silver glitter as well as flirty kisses, and smile with mouths full of perfect teeth. Several sisters hit each other with long inflatable swim floats, and one Alpha Phi co-ed sucks innocently on a popsicle. The recruiting video has been compared to current *Playboy* playmate videos shot outside the Playboy mansion and the now defunct *Girls Gone Wild* videos that often exploited college-age women.[4] Reactions have ranged from the video promoting stereotypes associated with sexy, vapid sorority girls to discriminating against women of other body types and racial ethnicities. The clip has been called demeaning by objectifying the female body and undermining feminism, even though defenders contend it promotes third-wave feminism and celebrates womanhood. Thus, frame of reference determines interpretation: the video could be full of sensuous nymphs adorned in white gowns prancing around phallic totems, or it could simply present the Alpha Phi Beta Mu's rich heritage of recruiting attractive females who are interested in a common ideological community. These young women appear to be in the power center, privileged and comfortable, but Palahniuk hunts for this type of media image, knowing full well that what is on the surface often betrays itself. Many of the women in the video may feel marginalized or disenfranchised.

This issue relates to various heavy subjects, very controversial and extremely volatile, including racism and sexism, but the overall social or

Nine. The Rhetorical Situation

cultural impact of the content is not all that influential in the big picture. In short, a sorority's recruitment video is not going to affect most peoples' lives directly. This is probably a public interest story to place at the end of television news broadcasts (where it has appeared on major networks), on daytime talk shows, and on cable news programs, but it is certainly not lead-story material. Yet, this is the kind of subject Palahniuk would address, and he could look at this issue from all sides depending on whom he chooses as his narrator. He could select one of the sorority women and look at recruitment from her point of view. He could choose to treat the topic from a first-year female recruit's vision of the initiation process. He could opt for a parent's stance, a boyfriend's stance, a girlfriend's stance, a professor's stance, whatever perspective would provide the most advantageous position to advance his rhetorical agenda. In addition to deciding upon narration, Palahniuk would complete his characteristic research of trivial and esoteric information related to the subject, and he would also draw on commentators to enhance this presentation. In some ways, Camille Paglia is a female version of Chuck Palahniuk, and one could see him borrow from her commentary concerning sorority interpersonal relationships, particularly ones dealing with dating and partying. For instance, Paglia's statement in "It's a Jungle Out There" could find its place in Palahniuk's story: "College men are at their hormonal peak. They have just left their mothers and are questing for their male identity. In groups, they are dangerous. A woman going to a fraternity party is walking into Testosterone Flats, full of prickly cacti and blazing guns. If she goes, she should be armed with resolute alertness.... A girl who gets drunk at a fraternity party is a fool. A girl who goes upstairs alone with a brother at a fraternity party is an idiot" (539). Palahniuk would counter this of course with arguments from the other side, perhaps from Peggy Reeves Sanday's *Fraternity Gang Rape* or other sources that look at sorority date rape from the opposite stance, and he would also fill out these descriptions with informative, referential, objective content. Here is where he would include many of his characteristic factoids.

Now is when Palahniuk would see the opportunity for parody, and perhaps the best approach might be a remake of Tom Wolfe's 2004 novel about college life entitled *I Am Charlotte Simmons*. Similar to how Palahniuk adapted *Are You There God? It's Me, Margaret* in *Damned*, Palahniuk could alter the story of college co-ed Charlotte's quest for social status and peer popularity by having her pledge her allegiance to a sorority. Palahniuk could model his school from Wolfe's Dupont University, and assuming the story's perspective would be from his main character's point of view as Charlotte's story is told from hers, he could have his narrator navigate through the nuances of the panhellenic community as Wolfe has Charlotte traverse within the major cliques on the Dupont campus. Palahniuk's female could deal with comparable Charlotte Simmons problems such as roommate conflicts, class boredom, relationship anxieties, as well as getting drunk for the first time, essentially getting date raped at a fraternity social, and then facing all of the resulting frustrations that inevitably come afterward. Palahniuk could display the apparent similarities between his 2015 story and Wolfe's 2004 plot, but he would scatter within these clear differences, probably affiliated with the transgressive. There is no telling what the Palahniuk imagination would invent in terms of this transgression, but chances are there would be a lot more sexuality in Palahniuk's novel than in Wolfe's, even though Wolfe's novel provides stereotypical, hyperbolic, and exaggerated instances of sexuality. One could foresee Palahniuk having a bit of fun with males and females in unisex bathrooms and showers, and he would likely include a vibrator somewhere in the sequence of his female character's daily routine or nightly ritual. He might have confused yet interesting sexual trysts between his character and ones like Adam Gellin and Beverly Amory, and he would certainly depict complexities concerning gender. Palahniuk would also perhaps include someone's self-mutilation, self-disfigurement, or self-dismemberment, with a chance for violence and brutality thrown in among these. Someone is bound to die an unlikely, uncommon, or unforeseen death—maybe someone like Jojo Johanssen would die during a basketball game or someone like Hoyt Thorpe would have an accident while watching ESPN (maybe even *SportsCenter* as Saint Rey frat brothers watch in Wolfe's novel), Internet porn, or, to perpetuate parody and promote metacommentary, a movie about the college experience, something along the lines of *Animal House*, *St. Elmo's Fire*, *Legally Blonde*, *Revenge of the Nerds*, or any other film that would accentuate the intertextuality. Sooner or later, however, Palahniuk would offer an ironic twist, stressing the difference between his story and Wolfe's, and this ironic signaling would emphasize the purpose of the postmodern parody. This would connect to the initial impetus, the Alpha Phi Sorority video, but would subvert the obvious or dominant reading of it in some way. If all of this sounds farfetched, remember that Palahniuk refers to Penny Harrigan as an undisclosed sorority co-ed in *Beautiful You* and makes references to Sigma Chi fraternity dances (28), dates (42), and erections (70). In fact, Penny's account of sexual assault with a "beer-saturated Zeta Delt" is reminiscent of Charlotte's incident with Hoyt (474–90): "It was during a high-spirited Pledge Week mixer. In retrospect, she recognized that she might've promised the young man more than she was willing to deliver. Frustrated, he had thrown her to the ground and straddled her, a knee planted on either side of her struggling torso. His muscular hands began the savage task of shredding her brightly flowered afternoon frock. He fumbled with the zipper of his chinos, producing an angry red erection" (28). The opinions of Paglia, Sanday, and others would be applicable here. Penny is saved by the mysterious CIA-like men in black who protect her. These last few paragraphs could take the shape of a prospectus for a future Palahniuk novel. Again, assuming Palahniuk would write about sorority recruitment propaganda might seem audacious, but this video controversy lends itself to Palahniuk-type transgressive satire, ridicule, and farce.

Palahniuk's exigence, what inspires or stimulates him, is typically an issue that affects the general public, but the issue may be one that is specifically targeted toward the counterculture or related to the fringe population. Anyone who reads a Palahniuk novel may identify with what happens in the narrative and sympathize with the characters' dilemmas, but those who are already a little on the outside will empathize with the characters' plights much more quickly. Undeniably, Palahniuk addresses currently controversial social and cultural issues, but he does this from the periphery, from the borders, the corners, and the outer orbits. This observation point gives him an objective survey of all the aspects defining the issues, and then he can decide the best directions from which to attack them subjectively with his transgressive guns blazing. Claiming Palahniuk writes to a general audience is a safe designation for his overall readership because this includes both academic and non-academic followers of his fiction. Although many academics, pseudo-intellectuals, or nerdy book enthusiasts would deny reading a Palahniuk novel, the truth is that Palahniuk caters to this population as well as to the ordinary Barnes and Noble Bookstore pedestrian shopper who might run across one of his appealing novel covers and decide to read a Palahniuk story just for entertainment or to kill time. Avid readers with broad ranges of literary tastes buy Palahniuk books, as do recreational readers who rarely purchase any novels. Palahniuk transcends socioeconomic, educational, and political reader boundaries, and anyone could be a potential Palahniuk bookworm. That is, if he or she is ready for the transgressive bent that this writer follows. In the preceding chapters, if anything else, the broad range of Palahniuk subjects are surveyed—delving into content, *Haunted* is a much different book from *Tell-All*, which is a much different text from *Snuff*, and although the literary feature of parody links these works, they are not the same as *Lullaby*, *Rant*, *Survivor*, or *Diary*. Concerning his repertoire, Palahniuk is known most widely for *Fight Club*, yet that book is much different from the other fiction he creates.

As mentioned in previous chapters, Palahniuk claims that he responds to the call for community. He admits that many of his characters are searching for inclusion, affinity, or belonging. Granted, this is a universal theme incorporated into countless pieces of literature, although it is more frequently affiliated with the desire for greater humanity, the opposite of disconnectedness and isolation, a need for attachment and closeness. Palahniuk may say he is aiming for this goal, but in reality, this might be more of a suggestion than a given. Most of the major characters addressed thus far in this study have conflicting feelings about community. Although the characters in *Haunted* joined a commune, they are isolated according to their former life experiences and ideas related to privilege within the group. Each character actually seems ready to accomplish individually as much as he or she can within the confines of the theater, and there appears to be competition for which character will be most attractive for celebrity stardom when the group is rescued and the intensity of their deprivations are revealed. The same is the case for *Snuff* and *Pygmy* in that Cassie Wright and Pygmy both have personal agendas that must be accomplished, and participating in a community is basically par for the course: Cassie must have sex to achieve the gang-bang record, and Pygmy must coerce others if he will successfully infiltrate the town. In *Tell-All*, Hazie Coogan must gain the trust of Katherine Kenton, Webster Carlton Westward III, and others if she wants celebrity notoriety—she must bide her time in Hollywood until her situation is just right for her to move Katherine and Webster out of her way toward stardom. In *Invisible Monsters Remix*, Shannon relishes her individuality until she travels with Brandy Alexander, bonding with her brother only after she has exhausted other possibilities for friendship with Evie Cottrell and Manus Kelly or bonding with her parents. In *Damned*, Madison is at the mercy of Satan's decision (or whatever divine authoritarian bureaucracy determines whether she was misplaced into hell), and her connection with others is fostered aptly enough with references to *The Breakfast Club*, her cohort of peers also being punished by appointments into hell. Palahniuk succeeds in demonstrating how these diverse characters are accepted into communities, but the adhesiveness of these bonds is not as strong or as definitive as they might be if fictionalized by other authors. Palahniuk is subtle in his presentation of community, and considering many of his readers may also be outsiders looking toward the middle, this is a realistic and practical portrayal of how people weary of wholesale integration quickly into a social group (thrust into one as Madison is) would handle such a process. Although, this does not classify Palahniuk readers as predominantly introverts rather than extroverts. Madison's scouting of Babette's idiosyncrasies is an example of this paradoxical wanting to be recognized as "a part" while holding on to the comfort of remaining "apart." Madison interprets Babette's shoes, clothes, accessories, and mannerisms before she is willing to exert the effort to form an alliance, and, in reality, this is probably the same way most people form similar friendships.

The various exigencies calling Palahniuk's novels into creation (contemporary issues related to marginalization and disenfranchisement) and the diversity of Palahniuk's audience (a widespread readership dominated by those who claim degrees of powerlessness) influence Palahniuk's rhetorical stance and his choice of rhetorical constraints. As has been shown, critics (mostly reviewers and not necessarily scholars) have argued Palahniuk frequently assumes the advertiser's stance concerning his subjects, stressing effect rather than substance. This includes all of the commentary related to Palahniuk's penchant to shock readers. "Guts" is a prime example of the advertiser's stance with all of the grotesque description, and the back-and-forth flow of *Invisible Monsters Remix* illustrates the reliance on structure over practical presentation of material (worth noting is Palahniuk's justification for this format in the first paragraph of that chapter). Incidents related to the pedant's stance are all of the sections Palahniuk devotes to the plethora of factoid trivia or the informative minutiae of peculiar details. The particular references to porn celebrities, to Messalina, or to vibrators in *Snuff* serve as instances, but these do not compare to all of the household cleaning tips Palahniuk offers in *Survivor* (an incredible amount of household hints) or to the physiological precision he gives to describing female anatomy, arousal, and orgasm in *Beautiful You*. Concededly, one must admit Palahniuk sometimes takes the pedant's stance when he gets bogged down in substantial tidbits about this subject. All in all, however, Palahniuk maintains an effective balance concerning content and arrangement in the six novels discussed in the preceding chapters. He creates a suitable tone, which reflects an appropriate attitude toward the subject as well as establishes a proper distance between the speaker and the audience, and his coverage of the subject is the product of his research. This background work enables Palahniuk to take advantage of parody to respond to past texts and to move forward toward an ironic subversion of them. In this regard, Palahniuk selects exactly the right narrator to express his ideology and to articulate his ideas to his audience. No other selection of voice could have communicated to readers more effectively than Joe does in *Fight Club*, and this voice stands out over any particular identification (technically Joe has no name and is only "Joe" because of the narrator's self-references). There is an optimal amount of detail related to twelve-step meetings, home furnishings, soap-making skills, the service industry, and insurance claims adjusting. Furthermore, the impact of the short sentences, brief chapters, and idiomatic punctuation choreographed the action in the novel at an optimal pace and suitable cadence. Also worth mentioning is the paucity of emotional, melodramatic exposition; Palahniuk makes fun of this type of writing through Hazie's *Love Slave*. Related to Booth's theory of rhetorical stance, Palahniuk assumes an appropriate balance, and even though he may be blamed for diverging into the associated problem areas, those digressions could easily be justified if supported by Palahniuk's purposes. As has been discussed previously, the addition of Chapter 18 in *Invisible Monsters Remix* adds a significant layer of meaning to Shannon McFarland's story, all of those seemingly random descriptions of past and present porn stars in *Snuff* reinforce intertextuality, and the boldfacing of various celebrity names in *Tell-All* promotes semiotic word play and signification.

This leads to the importance of Palahniuk utilizing parody as the primary constraint to communicate his ideas and to address his audience. Palahniuk's planting his stories firmly into transgressive bedrock is also a device to influence his readers' opinions concerning the content. Of course, blunt, colloquial, and raw descriptions of violence and sexuality move the discourse in the direction of low culture rather than high culture, and they expose the content to obvious moral and ethical opposition from conservative viewpoints, let alone calling into question Palahniuk's decisions related to taste and decorum, but that is the nature of transgressive fiction. Palahniuk's writing is stuck deeply into that transgressive terrain. In a way, Palahniuk's application of parody as a literary device adds ethical appeal to the rhetoric of his fiction, enabling him to establish the authorial distance that Booth criticized Lawrence for not maintaining. By relating his content to previous presentations, Palahniuk constructs instant credibility. In terms of ancient rhetoric, he is metaphorically standing on the shoulders of literary giants such as Dante and Boccaccio, and if their approaches to their subjects have been revered and applauded, then his application is at least starting off in the right direction. Moreover, Palahniuk is assuming his readers will bring previous knowledge of karate films and gossip journalism to *Pygmy* and *Tell-All*, so he erects his stories on platforms that already have substantial literary and cultural undergirding. Parody is an excellent technique for Palahniuk to respond to the exigencies through a straightforward and uncomplicated strategy. Previous writers have addressed the same problems that Palahniuk confronts related to the human condition, so he only needs to update and contemporize these approaches, and since readers are already aware of these previous texts, they begin Palahniuk's stories with a sense of both expectation and familiarity. Palahniuk is building on what has been tested and proven to work for past readers, and in many cases, this offers him the freedom to take more liberties with format and with content, to play with characterization and to take chances with plot, and to experiment with traditional conventions of the novel as genre. In fact, parody is the vehicle that enables Palahniuk to become more imaginative, innovative, and interesting concerning transgressive fiction. Even though the assumption might be that parody is restrictive because it sets up preexisting textual boundaries, parody actually gives Palahniuk the flexibility to experiment in his writing by letting him move those boundaries in various directions. For decades (centuries if one goes all the way back in American culture to the *New England Primer*), American students learned how to write rhetorical sentences by imitating the writing of notable authors. In American schools, the Schoolroom Poets and American and British nineteenth-century essayists were sources for copying, as were the diverse sentences of John Steinbeck, Ernest Hemingway, and William Faulkner. One learned how to write effectively by mimicking writing deemed effective. Palahniuk's reliance on parody works on the same premise: a writer starts with something time-tested as acceptable and then develops his or her own creation from that base.

Even though Palahniuk draws from personal experience in his writing, he keeps a distance between himself and his characters. There may be similarities between him and his narrative personas, but he is not his fictional personalities in the same way as Mellors is ostensibly Lawrence's philosophical representative. Readers should not fall into the trap of committing New Criticism's intentional fallacy by equating a character's statements with the intentions of Palahniuk. Although some statements from Palahniuk's interviews and commentaries might filter through to his characters, there is not a one-to-one correlation between his words and a character's words (although he is not immune from inserting words of others into his characters' dialogues). None of the novels thus far addressed in his study are semi-autobiographical. Palahniuk is not Hazie, Pygmy, Madison, or any other of the major characters, and this is probably extremely fortunate for Palahniuk. There is nothing obvious or apparent to indicate that what occurs in Palahniuk's novels are manifestations of the author's deep-rooted psychological neuroses or unresolved psychoanalytical childhood traumas, although Palahniuk reports in many interviews that his writing is frequently influenced by what he might be doing during the time of its composition.

This said, when Palahniuk reads his works in front of audiences—and there are many clips of these events available online through *YouTube*—Palahniuk transforms himself into the voices he reads, wearing the rhetorical masks of his literary characters. This ability to distance himself from his creations is vital so that each individual is distinct for the fictional environment he or she inhabits, and along these lines, each of his characters addresses a discrete rhetorical situation within the stories he or she narrates. The nameless narrator of *Haunted* addresses his or her situation, as do the various speakers in *Snuff*, as does Pygmy in *Pygmy*, Hazie in *Tell-All*, Madison in *Damned*, and Shannon in *Invisible Monsters Remix*. Palahniuk's choice of parody is the constraint that serves as his first wave to communicate his ideas to his audience. His selection of narrators as constraints is his second wave, and within each novel, a narrator confronts his or her own version of the rhetorical situation. Palahniuk's application of parody and his choice of narrative voice are his two major rhetorical strategies within each of the six novels addressed in this study.

In *Haunted*, the nameless narrator's role is to tie together the numerous poems and stories and to guide readers chronologically through what is at its core a tragedy. Essentially, he or she (no indication of gender) serves as the editor and compiler of the collection. Whereas Boccaccio corrupts *The Decameron* by obviously intruding into the text—there is little effort to place him as a participant into the events, and clearly he is the "author" in his introduction and his conclusion—Palahniuk stays out of his setting by creating a narrator inside the action with no omniscience into the minds of the other characters. The narrator provides the audience with insight into what is happening in the theater, and this speaker uses "we" to emphasize his or her inclusion within what is occurring. This narrative voice provides the background information about the flyer posted in an Oregon café about the retreat, writes what are basically the author introductions via the poems preceding the stories (thus revealing characters' histories), and provides closure to the entire ordeal at the end of the text by citing what Brandon Whittier and the other characters say before the steel door is again closed. The audience does not know if this narrator survived. All that remains is what is written on the last page: the ones remaining have decided to wait out their suffering for the potential lucrative fame of being discovered by the media. This narrator is neither granted a poem nor a story, and although he or she does not provide stream of consciousness access to the other characters' thoughts and feelings, he or she is privy to information about who sabotages the water, electric, and heating utilities and who destroys the various dehydrated food supplies. This speaker appears to be level-headed and logical, but since Edgar Allan Poe was an influence on Palahniuk, one must remember many of Poe's narrators (such as ones in "The Black Cat," "The Tell-Tale Heart," or "William Wilson") are deceptively sane and they increasingly become insane—as they appear the most sane, they are at their most insane. This narrator never strays into what might be lunacy, and he or she definitely does not appear psychopathic or psychotic. There really is no reason to question this narrator's reliability. Among all of the participants, this character is a stabilizing force, and instead of relying on a clear-cut framing edifice of one section in the beginning to set up the historical context for the stories and then one section at the end to tie together the document as almost an apologia, as Boccaccio does rhetorically to defend his decisions in *The Decameron*, Palahniuk allows this nameless narrator simply to provide the narrative adhesive to keep his pastiche of texts together as a unit. In this way, Palahniuk provides a more seamless strategy for literary unity than his medieval counterpart.

This narrator's exigence is the urgency to transmit to readers the ultimate product of the retreat: the culmination of the *magnum opus* pieces the participants set out to create, the collection that becomes *Haunted*. Ironically, the individual writers did not realize that they in fact accomplished their goals by having their works read by a broad audience, readers of *Haunted*. This narrator compiles the document that consequently gives these writers the voices that they wanted to articulate. Palahniuk gauged this effect perfectly. Concerning *The Decameron*, readers do not know if the participants eventually succumbed to the Black Death, and, in the scheme of things, this point does not seem important. At the conclusion of *Haunted*, readers probably should not spend time wondering what happened after the last page to Whittier and the other survivors. Roland Barthes's message in his famous essay "The Death of the Author" may be relevant here. As Barthes points out, "As soon as a fact is *narrated* no longer with a view to acting directly on reality but intransitively, that is to say, finally outside of any function other than that of the very practice of the symbol itself, this disconnection [between the identity of the speaker and the content of the speech] occurs, the voice loses its origin, the author enters into his own death, writing begins" (142). In this regard, these texts stand on their own regardless of the nameless narrator's efforts to arrange or to edit them; the stories' exclusive meaning is privileged and has priority over their literary caretaker's linguistic meddling. To be honest, most readers of *Haunted* do not necessarily question who is telling this story or what the face looks like behind that narrative voice. Readers construct meaning in spite of the narrative voice, regardless of any authorial intervention to direct attention toward any metacommentary. As was mentioned in the chapter devoted to *Haunted*, some reviewers believe the stories could function on their own, exclusively as twenty-three separate tales, but this reaffirms the premise each writer is marginalized and disenfranchised even though each person is supposedly a participant within a commune, the writers' collective, a unified community of authors moving ahead together toward the same goal of writing lasting literature. These authors failed in an attempt to express a collective voice, but the narrator took what they produced and broadcast their individual submissions through this anthology. In a contemporary world in which every reader has been touched by some form of disease—everyone probably knows someone affected by cancer or another horrible form of illness—the narrator has essentially taken the dis-ease, the internal uneasiness, of these writers and published stories that could function in a sense as obituaries. Readers certainly understand these participants through the narrator's introductions, the poems, and the stories, but they know them more intimately through the additional information the narrator offers concerning how these personalities interact among the group. This narrator understood the urgency of getting these testimonies out to the audience.

The constraints the narrator applies are editorial. This is only what readers may surmise from what is included in the collective text that becomes *Haunted*. The placement of Saint Gut-Free's story so far in the beginning almost sets the precedent for the remaining texts. Much attention has been devoted to "Guts" for its graphic depiction of gross physicality, as the number of those who pass out or get sick during Palahniuk's public readings of this narrative continue to rise. Actually, this story is not any more disturbing in a transgressive way compared to Director Denial's story that includes the placing of a razor inside the vagina of a plastic doll (and seeing colleagues with cut tongues after they have returned the borrowed object), Comrade Snarky's tale about what should be a nurturing community of women who attack and assault a transgendered person who seeks fellowship amidst the group, or Lady Baglady's chilling account of witnessing a kidnapping and discovering a severed ear after the assailants speed off with the victim. All of these stories are terribly unsettling. Some are, however, fairly tame, such the Duke of Vandals telling about fleeing an art mafia, Miss Sneezy reporting she has escaped from a government facility, and Miss America confessing she was disrespected before she performed in a commercial for her exercise wheel. The juxtaposition of the more shocking stories with those that are less shocking is an appropriate organization decision. Through this strategy, Palahniuk subverts Boccaccio's story sequencing by gender through arranging his narratives based on grotesqueness. Boccaccio does not allow the plague to intrude into the country estates that his tellers occupy, but Palahniuk provides a microcosm of dis-ease inside the theater to imitate the distress felt by his characters previously outside the doors. The Nightmare Box stories emphasize this point, and the placement of Tess Clark's references to this, in addition to her own personal story, is a thematic ploy to stress the plague-like situation inside the theater setting. By first introducing Tess Clark as Whittier's accomplice, almost as if she were his sidekick or henchperson, and then having her express her own story about perception—her repulsive reaction to seeing herself and her husband nude in a homemade porn film—the narrator (and in turn Palahniuk) gains the audience's trust. When Mrs. Clark tells the stories about her daughter Cassandra, readers already have a personal connection with her by possibly identifying with how she raised this child after her husband left her "post-production." The placement of Mrs. Clark's stories evoke in readers sympathy, if not empathy, for Mrs. Clark as a victim of circumstance. All of the characters could be eligible for this designation. Palahniuk relies on shock as the primary effect to provoke reaction to all of his stories, but his arrangement of them is a secondary tool that serves as a constraint also to influence reader response.

A didactic rhetorical aim of both *Haunted* and *The Decameron* is to warn readers against major sins. Although Palahniuk does not appear to have a religious agenda, the stories nevertheless function as deterrents against committing sin. As was noted in the chapter dedicated to *Haunted*, the names of the characters have symbolic relevance in relation to the Christian virtues and vices. Palahniuk is not overtly putting his characters' actions within a Christian context, and arguing that he even may be doing so is well beyond the scope of this discussion, but taken at face value, the problems that confront most of the characters certainly may be attributed to the cardinal sins. Mrs. Clark's dilemma is born out of lust and vanity. She and her husband undergo cosmetic surgeries and complete other measures to ensure they look their best while having sex on film, and when their expectations do not match the reality of what they see on the monitor, that reality is too much to bear. "Guts" is obviously about lust, Chef Assassin's story about killing food critics is about wrath, Agent Tattletale's tale about defrauding insurance companies is about dishonesty, the Earl of Slander is avaricious, and Miss America is arrogant. Pride is the sin that is ancillary to all of the others, perhaps serves as their basis, exhibited in the narratives. Seen as such, *Haunted* is almost a cautionary book with an edifying aim that disseminates the message "Do not sin." Readers are never told the problems associated with the narrator, but if Palahniuk is consistent, this speaker must have personal defects that attracted him or her to the writing commune. No one in *Haunted* is without sin, and each participant's culpability may lead to his or her demise. This is, of course, not the case in Boccaccio's story, as the introduction that describes the personal qualities of the characters never points toward apparent moral flaws, but the characters in the stories are often emblematic of major vices. Most readers probably do not look for allegorical symbolism related to morality in Palahniuk's stories, but they certainly are also not attracted toward imitating the lifestyles of any of those presented either. True, Palahniuk readers formed fight clubs after reading his novel, yet it is doubtful any writing communes were developed to mimic what occurs in *Haunted*, and one only hopes readers did not attempt some of the activities (such as masturbating on top of pool drains, having sexual intercourse with plastic dolls, or pretending to be indigent slum people) at home.

In *Snuff*, Palahniuk applies a different approach by offering several narrators, and this effectively deflects attention from Cassie Wright and redirects it toward Sheila, the porn baby mentioned throughout the novel. In the chapter about this book, attention was given to *Snuff* as an example of hyperreality through imitation and intertextuality. In terms of parody, thinking about this text in totality as an imitation of a previous work, the narrative strategy resembles William Faulkner's approach in *As I Lay Dying*, with various characters expressing themselves in chapters devoted to each speaker's frame of reference. In Faulkner's story, there are fifteen characters who articulate in over fifty chapters their thoughts and feelings as they transport Addie Bundren (alive in the beginning but dead throughout) to her burial place in Jefferson, Mississippi. Considering Linda Hutcheon's claim that postmodern parody illustrates similarity but emphasizes difference, Faulkner's novel focuses on the journey this group undergoes to move the dead body of Bundren to her final resting place, and Palahniuk's title suggests his narrative will be about the death of a porn actress attempting to achieve the dubious honor of gang-bang queen. Palahniuk's story is essentially not about death but Sheila coming to terms with her relationship with parents Cassie and Branch Bacardi. Granted, besides the commentaries about life and death among multiple speakers, there is not a lot that connects *Snuff* and *As I Lay Dying*, yet Faulkner and Palahniuk rely heavily upon several voices to offer different perspectives as a crucial narrative strategy in both texts.

The different points of view in *Snuff* enhance the intertextuality as well as postpone the inevitable realization that Sheila, not Mr. 72, is Cassie's

Nine. The Rhetorical Situation

daughter. The chapters are divided by speakers: Sheila (Zelda Zonk), Mr. 72 (Darin Johnson), Mr. 137 (Dan Banyan), and Mr. 600 (Branch Bacardi). Significantly, Cassie never has a section in which readers view the action from her perspective. In a sense, as Faulkner's characters traverse the country toward their destination, the major characters in *Snuff* theoretically move in an assembly line eventually to be summoned by wrangler Sheila to head upstairs to perform. The four major voices are vastly different (just as Faulkner's are dissimilar), and Addie is given a narrative voice whereas Cassie is not. Darin Johnson is adamant in his belief he is Cassie's long-lost male heir, and his dialogue reveals his tenacity to communicate with whom he believes to be his blood mother. Darin is new to this environment, and he seems, expectedly so, to be uneasy among the various actors from all walks of life who are waiting to have intercourse with his mother. Darin is really out of his element in this porn bullpen setting, and although his intentions are honorable (as his gift of roses and his reluctance actually to have intercourse with his mother suggests), he is clearly self-deceived and misguided. His testimonies, however, draw readers into believing that he is Cassie's child, and the references to his masturbating to his proposed mother's movies online and the details related to his caressing the plastic replicas of Cassie's body parts (even wearing out the plastic with extended use) call into question his motivation. One wonders why he would perchance cultivate incestuous fantasies about Cassie and would want to actualize them through this gang bang. Nonetheless, Palahniuk dupes readers into believing the line of reasoning that Cassie is his mother. Darin's impressions of veteran porn star Branch and popular television star Dan indicate his self-consciousness while also displaying the other two actors' insecurities. When readers discover Sheila is the true porn child, an appropriate consolation is that Darin tells Sheila his real name—he is no longer depersonalized by a number. There is an underlying optimism that this young man who has sacrificed everything for this gang-bang chance with his perceived mother will at least get a chance to form a relationship with the woman who might have been his sister, as dysfunctional as all of this may sound.

The two older men form an interesting duality. Whereas Darin is not a professional actor without any aspirations or ambitions toward celebrity stardom—he is solely driven by a potential reunion with his mother, albeit this would happen pre-intercourse—Branch and Dan are at the tail end of their thespian careers. Dan's falsifying names on his stuffed toy dog Mr. Toto reveals his need for attention. The names on the signature puppy range from Bette Midler, Carol Channing, Debbie Reynolds, Carole Baker,

Tina Turner (8) to Tina Louise, Elizabeth Taylor, Natalie Wood, Deborah Harry (65). Dan eventually bonds with Cassie and gets her signature, with her changing the HIV that Branch pugnaciously markered on his forehead to "How I love U" (144). There are obvious homosexual inferences in Dan's background. The most revealing is the gay porn in which he performed before his television detective job that he swears was for extra money. Although pretentious, Dan is self-conscious, and his descriptions of the actors' bronzing, eating, and socializing demonstrate his own feelings of inadequacy during this event. Only after he has bonded with Darin and antagonized Branch does Dan seem comfortable. His comments about Branch serve as counterarguments to questions related to his own masculinity, as the two men form two different versions of maleness. Branch holds onto the vision of himself as the youthful actor in the movies with Cassie that play continuously on the monitors, and Dan is the more sensitive and compassionate actor who appears to understand Darin's problems. Dan is the voice that refers to Branch and Cassie's fusion as romantically reminiscent of *Romeo and Juliet* (194). Branch's ragged edges, crassness, and gruffness are presented through his language, and his homophobia is clearly visible to every performer, as he refers to "faggot porn" (153) and frequently bullies Dan. Palahniuk is obviously blending various characteristics constituting the stereotypical male porn star personality.

Palahniuk's portrayal of Branch's masculinity is a binary to Cassie's femininity. In heterosexual porn, Cassie is the beautifully attractive female, so there should be a key performer in the novel who functions as her opposite, the handsome macho male. Seen another way, porn icon Cassie needs a suitable male porn performer, someone at her level of expertise, to be her complement, her sexual counterpart. The information about how Cassie got into the porn business through his deception and exploitation erodes Branch's ethical credibility. His doping Cassie in order to have sex with her on tape is by moral standards plainly despicable, although Branch claims this video was Cassie's idea (140). The two actors share a porn history, and this bond has sustained what appears a friendship. Branch's call to his male escort service, only to find out the sole gigolo available is a has-been sex jockey, is comically ironic—when his cell phone goes off, readers see Branch is this has-been—and when he realizes the old performer on the screen is actually himself, one may think about the movie *The Wrestler* in which Mickey Rourke portrays a washed-up, physically deteriorated, pseudo-athlete who may only have one more true match in him. When Branch ingests the potassium cyanide, he decides arrogantly to prohibit Cassie from earning her record. She cannot have sex with number 600 if he is dead. Palahniuk's imaginative ending with Cassie straddling Branch, with the locket that once held Sheila's baby picture dangling, is completely unexpected. The references to burned body parts smelling like cooked meat adds to the surrealism of the scene; the aroma is comparable to hamburger and meatloaf seasoned with sweat and ozone (196). This moment is the culmination of egocentric and self-centered dialogue from Darin, Dan, and Branch. To be honest, none of the men in this novel are representative of strong ethical fiber. Cassie has the best moral compass, and Palahniuk strategically gives her the least amount of dialogue. Significantly, readers learn about Cassie by eavesdropping on the thoughts, feelings, and impressions of the three male actors and Sheila, and readers also make assumptions about her in a similar manner as those in the basement holding room who are waiting to meet her. Throughout the book, readers await the call to meet this porn goddess.

This finally happens through Darin's performance. Readers get the opportunity to see how he reacts to Cassie's apology that he is not her love child—she intentionally deceived the media by saying the child was male when it was really female. Deception is a motif in this story. This turn away from Mr. 72 shifts the focus toward Sheila. The dialogue between the three males and Sheila could be compared to chatter. If a reader were a participant and listening to the conversations, or better yet, if a reader asked questions about the others while standing in line, Palahniuk's sections would be the result, eavesdropping on their impressions. The characters play off of each other. Darin will think about something Branch does, and then Dan will think about this as well—but he will offer an alternative version of the action from a different point of view. Readers almost get a panoramic view of the basement through the varying commentaries of the same events. Thus, the same event will be told from many perspectives. This chatter is a significant rhetorical device, and readers are able to draw their own conclusions based upon either the synthesis of the information or by privileging one testimony over another. Readers may trust Darin over Branch or Dan, for instance, and Palahniuk allows readers this option. Sheila is a stable voice throughout the novel. She has a close affinity with Cassie in her role as assistant, but she also appears educated, intelligent, and assertive. She tells Cassie about Valeria Messalina, and she also knows about Annabel Chong. By the time Sheila reports the burning together of Branch and Cassie at the end of the novel, readers probably trust her judgment better than they would any of the male characters, even Dan who also describes the surreal scene. Sheila is for the most part reliable. She is duplicitous in that she has connived to get into this position of authority, but she is still a very likeable personality. Sheila has known from the beginning of the book that she is the porn baby, and she undoubtedly notices Darin's misguided assumptions that he is Cassie's progeny, but she nevertheless maintains a firm stance, even taking bribes without granting favors, during the entire porn shooting. Palahniuk ends the story with Sheila's assessment of events, and this is appropriate because no one actually could handle this responsibility as well as she does. The last line in the novel is appropriately Sheila stating that someone may notice her, and she mentions the name given to her by her mother, now recognized totally as Cassie.

Palahniuk characterizes Cassie perfectly through the other voices. Cassie is none of the pejorative prejudices associated with women in similar porn-flick enterprises. She is not a "dumb peroxide blond," "a washed-up bimbo," or a porn star regrettably returning to the stereotypically exploitative sex business to pay bills because she has run out of other options. She is not along the line of celebrities refusing to lower their moral standards by posing in *Playboy* at the height of their careers but who become quite willing to receive a check from Hugh Hefner when their cultural currency is waning, when they are older and less popular, or when they need to resuscitate a celebrity career that is expiring, close to death. Cassie is smart while having common sense, as demonstrated through intelligent conversations reported by Sheila. Cassie has an astute knowledge of Hollywood institutional history, and she and Sheila undertake the gigantic job of orchestrating a gang bang that contains more participants than the number of students who attend many high schools. Cassie is physically still in shape, as illustrated by the references to her jogging and really putting in the pin-pointed athletic vaginal-strength training to complete sex acts with 600 men. And, Palahniuk makes sure he shows Cassie is perceptive and intuitive, as she reveals at the end of the novel that she has known since their first meeting that Sheila is indeed her daughter. In addition to this point, Cassie is generous by preparing in advance to transfer all she has to her heir and to give that person authorization to receive a lucrative insurance allowance. As was mentioned in the third chapter, Cassie resembles actual porn matriarchs who have maybe not been successful mainstream (although some have moderate success in commercial films) but who have definitely established themselves through other venues of the sex industry and have maintained positive notoriety in the media. On the contrary, Cassie is not like Jenna Jameson, Janine Lindemulder, and other porn actresses who have been porn superstars but have had some difficulties outside of the business. Palahniuk mentions Ron Jeremy's penis as a fabricated mass-produced plastic sex toy, and Ron Jeremy has had lasting success in American popular culture in and out of the porn industry. Even though there are references to her performing some less-than-mainstream sex videos even by porn standards, Cassie has a clean record that is unblemished by major controversies broadcast by the media. Cassie is almost the Rocky Balboa of porn, and her gang bang is her fight with Apollo Creed, complete with her not necessarily winning or losing at the end of her bout—she achieves sex act 600 but is fused with sex performer 600. No real porn star has had such a momentous comeback, not even Marilyn Chambers, known for the groundbreaking 1972 porn film *Behind the Green Door* while at the same time serving as the "Ivory soap girl" for Ivory Snow detergent's marketing campaign. She innocently held a baby on the front of the Ivory Snow soap box. Chambers did not enjoy anything similar to what Cassie experiences when she returned to porn productions after a hiatus.

Palahniuk could be criticized for assuming a pedant's stance in *Snuff* by having Cassie and Sheila (the two women, of course, and not the men), know a tremendous amount of Hollywood and porn trivia. To establish hyperreality—a simulation of a simulation of a simulation and so on—Palahniuk must offer this extra information. There is nothing extraneous in the content that could be considered fluffy or superfluous. A possibility could be actors wearing a blue condom within a pink condom, and if blue is visible during an anal sex scene, the condom has torn (19). In the context of Dan's past video experience, this information is appropriate. The same is true for the references to Kegel exercises and Ben Wa balls. Details concerning these are logical if Cassie is training for a physically challenging event such as this gang bang. Moreover, Palahniuk could have updated his porn information, particularly about dead porn stars and the actual record in 2008 for Cassie's porn accomplishment. Many of the references he uses are from the 1990s, and he omits actresses who have exceeded 600 in their gang bangs. One may question how Sheila would have known all of this information about porn, and her knowledge might be considered obsessively perverted, but if she has known her mother is a porn star, her understanding of the porn industry is plausible. Her not knowing the reference of Zelda Zonk is surprising, however, because if Sheila would know trivia such about Annabel Chong as well as Ariel Levy and third-wave feminism (24), one would expect her capable of conducting some basic—and very easy—research about Zelda Zonk. A simple *Google* search (even around 2008 when the novel was published) provides the answer Zelda Zonk was a pseudonym for Marilyn Monroe, and Sheila would undoubtedly be computer savvy. Dan knows Hollywood trivia, and there is the information

Cassie knows about largely unknown or forgotten stars James Murray, George Hill, Peg Entwistle, and Gowili Andre (151). To generate the various phases of simulation, Palahniuk had to provide these concrete factoids related to Hollywood and porn. Otherwise, readers would not see the distinct nuances between the shades of meanings. After introducing the replica plastic toys of star genitalia "cloned a zillion times" (41), Palahniuk has Dan reveal all the names on Mr. Toto are fake (43). Palahniuk must consistently offer the identities of real people, almost in a similar way to how he drops names in *Tell-All*, to emphasize the simulation inherent in porn production (and reproduction). By its nature, porn allows viewers voyeuristically to engage sexually with simulations of simulations, and through his novel, Palahniuk specifies the names attached to the various copies, concretely identifying the imitations of imitations. The very act of intimacy through porn is a simulation—a viewer engages with mass-produced fantasy. To the porn viewer, attention to detail is extremely important. Cameras focus on close-ups of sexual acts, and then there is the all-important "money shot" that serves as closure for these sexual events.

In *Pygmy*, Palahniuk is responding to ethnic discrimination and racial prejudice, two extremely controversial subjects in current American culture. He also clearly blasts American xenophobia and jingoism, while directing major satirical salvos toward American capitalism and education. His satire is undisguised, and the humor is dark. To approach areas so charged with public opinion, Palahniuk had to select a format that would get his points across without offending his audience. Not that Palahniuk really seems to be afraid of ruffling reader feathers, but he especially needed to be rhetorical concerning how he would treat such volatile subjects. Selecting Pygmy as a foreign insurgent was a brilliant choice, and crafting him as someone likeable who views American culture with honestly innocent and somewhat naïve vision provides a safe perspective through which to address his content. Not only this, to reinforce Pygmy as a nice terrorist, as oxymoronic as that sounds, Palahniuk refers to karate films with honorable heroes, but this also points toward traditional discrimination and prejudice of Asians. Placing "nice" Pygmy within this "discriminatory" genre is a means for Palahniuk to reduce the chance that he will be seen as perpetuating negative Asian stereotypes. By parodying 1970s karate films, Palahniuk hopes the finger pointing at discrimination and prejudice will be directed at those who produced and supported that genre. Moreover, by drawing on the kung-fu film as a referent, Palahniuk provides a reflexive self-deprecating finger pointed at himself. In other words, Palahniuk starts off with Pygmy as the 1970s karate film hero to establish common knowledge with his audience, in particular those who remember these movies, and then he uses satire to mock his own presentation and to move toward Pygmy as an American hero. Palahniuk can effectively criticize American social and cultural evils through Pygmy's distinct perspective, and he can successfully satirize American ideology through parody of Asian karate films.

Palahniuk's choice of narrative form allows readers to see the process Pygmy undergoes toward defection. As Pygmy reports through dispatches to his homeland essentially what it means to be American, he reveals problems in American society and points out disparities in American culture. Pygmy is attempting to understand American customs as he writes about them, and through this discursive process, he eventually makes a decision to abort Operation Havoc and to remain in the Midwest with the Cedars. Jonathan Swift used this same approach to criticize English culture, politics, and society in the Houyhnhnm section of his famous satire *Gulliver's Travels*. As Gulliver describes his homeland to his master, he unconsciously exposes corruptions, inequalities, inadequacies, and other problems, and as the story progresses, Gulliver begins to identify more with the ultra-rational Houyhnhnms, who falsely believe their rationality has led to their utopian perfect society, and less with the Yahoos, basically humans who are ruled by instinct and have the same social flaws as Gulliver's English peers. Swift effectively satirizes many facets of human nature through this story, and Palahniuk achieves similar success by allowing Pygmy to report problems that he witnesses. Just as Gulliver assimilates into Houyhnhnm culture, Pygmy integrates into American culture. This comparison is not to suggest Palahniuk is parodying *Gulliver's Travels*, but it does infer Palahniuk is drawing upon a similar rhetorical technique as Swift to respond to problems effectively. Swift's "A Modest Proposal" remains a staple prose model in chapters devoted to argumentation in first-year writing textbooks. Just like Swift, Palahniuk is not necessarily offering solutions to these problems; he is simply bringing them out in the open for his audience's scrutiny. Swift is unquestionably a master satirist (maybe the best) in the world literary canon, and Palahniuk is certainly one of the most effective satirists currently in American literature. Taken further, an interesting parodic comparison could be made between Pygmy as Gulliver, the Cedars as possibly the Houyhnhnms, and the other foreign insurgents, now disguised as his classmates, as Yahoos, with Pygmy renouncing loyalty to his initial community and assimilating into a culture that is flawed but more attractive than the one from which he traveled. Donald Cedar and some of his neighbors certainly believe, as the Houyhnhnms, that they live in a national utopia, although Mrs. Cedar's comment at the end of the novel indicates at least she notices problems in her region of American society. Pygmy certainly participates in social and cultural rituals in similar degrees to how Gulliver immerses himself into Houyhnhnm social and cultural ceremonies, and Pygmy appears to enjoy more latitude to take part in politics than Gulliver does. In Palahniuk's version, Pygmy has the opportunity to infiltrate his community completely. The bottomline for Gulliver is that he is simply not a horse and must return to England.

As was cited in the chapter devoted to this novel, some reviewers do not fully understand why Palahniuk choses to have Pygmy write in broken English. Technically, Pygmy would write in his native language, not in English, but this aside, by choosing to communicate in English, readers expect qualities affiliated with Pygmy's writing. As was discussed in detail previously, Palahniuk pays close attention to Pygmy's style, and what might particularly appear out of place or linguistically odd is Pygmy's application of onomatopoeia to reflect karate moves or special kung-fu actions. The "zaps," "pows," or other words mimicking physical movements would probably not be articulated in this way in a realistic situation (again, they probably would not be expressed in English), but Palahniuk needs these descriptions to promote the comparison to 1970s karate films. In a way, Pygmy's language makes him appear child-like, speaking as a young child would talk, but this style is deceptive because Pygmy writes about mature topics and serious ideas. Pygmy's discussions affiliated with Trevor provide ideological justifications for what he does to the bully. His treatment of Mrs. Cedar's vibrator indulgences, given she is obsessed with self-stimulation, are objective and emotionless. Pygmy's portrayal of the mock UN session shooting is passionless yet informatively vivid. His depictions of the Wal-Mart and the church are antiseptic, but they display the influence upon his anti-capitalist and anti–Christian teachers and his loyalty to the doctrines associated with his homeland. Descriptions of all of these might be transmitted through improper non-Standard American English, but the points within those passages are clear and precise.

Palahniuk is perhaps at his Swiftian best when he has Pygmy describe what he does not necessarily understand. Being a teenager, Pygmy has the same sexual urges as Pig Brother, but he has a matter of fact approach to conception, noting Magda is designated to be his mate, and he does not catch the sexism behind Pig Brother's nicknames for female breasts or references to what are standard teenage sexual rituals. When Pygmy essentially rapes Trevor, there is perhaps anger in his words, but he might be mocking Trevor's own pejorative language. Pygmy rapes Trevor because he was trained to do so. Pygmy does not seem to have any interest whatsoever in the vibrator Cat Sister makes. He thinks about having sexual intercourse with her, but this is kind of sterile, especially since he is a teenager with raging hormones. Granted, Pygmy probably would not get very emotional in a dispatch to his homeland as this would be improper, irreverent, or illogical, but he definitely appears insensitive to peer female's anatomy. Case in point, Pygmy's extraction of the dildo from Chicken Mother's legs is succinct and curt, and he does not appear willing to move beyond a technical reporting of what happens. Palahniuk does not give Pygmy more than this ability to stay true to what he would indeed be able to articulate; Pygmy might not just be capable of expression beyond what is provided. Pygmy's using Listerine as cologne, thinking dog is beef, or considering the toilet a washbowl portray his gullibility. Palahniuk does all of this to show Pygmy as inherently good, and when he saves America from a terrorist attack, Pygmy discloses true selflessness and genuine altruism. Conversely, most of his American peers are egotistical and care only for themselves. This is visible in how the students act during the mock UN session. Pygmy is child-like but not childish, and Palahniuk's selection of him as the stereotypical karate hero in this novel's setting is appropriate. Readers want to believe in Pygmy at the end of the novel, and in an America full of discrimination and prejudice, they applaud this outsider making his way to the inside. Pygmy is at first guided by his devotion to his homeland's national agenda for terrorism, and he innocently practices the instruction given by his master teacher, no matter how lunatic this person is (as evidenced by the pedagogical sessions scheduled for anal intercourse implemented in terrorist combat). Pygmy is then driven by his moral conscience, and this causes him to act honorably and courageously as a human, not affiliated with any nationality or ideology, and no longer identified with the kung-fu hero of 1970s Asian karate films.

Readers probably do not react in a similar way toward Hazie Coogan in *Tell-All*, but Palahniuk does not want them to side with her as they might Pygmy. Hazie literally "tells all" about her insecurities during this novel, and in this sense, the text is a lengthy projection of how she perceives herself. She is the playwright, director, and actor in the screenplay that is her life. Needless to say, Hazie is narcissistic and egocentric, and she treats her audience as if readers are confidantes who condone her actions. This solipsism is expressed in Hazie's tone and through her propensity to drop names. Palahniuk wants readers to identify this early in the novel, and he uses the gossip column profession to mirror what Hazie is doing through her testimony. Just as gossip columnists build up and then tear down celebrities to earn their money, Hazie drops all the names to increase her own self-worth, her credibility, and, in rhetorical terms, her ethical appeal. She wants to increase her own social currency by surrounding herself with names of celebrities, and she depends upon the cultural quality of these names, their signification or meaning, to increase her own personal value. Hazie is counting on readers decoding the names that she mentions and then transferring the meaning from those codes to her. In other words, she wants to be a celebrity by association. The problem is, of course, Hazie is only rattling off name after name after name, and any affiliation with these people is for the most part remote and superficial (just through Katherine), but this gives readers true insight into Hazie's character and her motivation for settling as Katherine Kenton's maid when she definitely had early aspirations to be as famous as the woman whom she serves. Palahniuk's parody of the gossip column industry is a perfect venue to situate Hazie's manipulation of Katherine. Technically, the gossip columnists feed off of celebrity and notoriety, and Hazie certainly enjoys almost a symbiotic relationship with Katherine. Without Katherine, Hazie would not be the same person. Ideally, Hazie's "telling" reveals her psychosis and self-delusion.

As with *Pygmy*, Palahniuk relies on his readers' background knowledge concerning the subject for the foundation of this story. In *Pygmy*, Palahniuk builds upon readers' familiarity with 1970s karate films, and he does something similar with 1940s–1950s gossip journalism in this novel. Readers are not required to understand karate films or gossip journalism to enjoy either story, but they can better appreciate the underlying themes in both if they are able to identify some of the parodic relationships. To get readers to see Hazie's delusion, Palahniuk persuades through comparison. As was addressed in the chapter devoted to *Tell-All*, Palahniuk uses Lillian Hellman to initiate the parody, to drop various names, and to increase the hyperbole. Throughout the novel, Hellman performs super-human feats while zealously promoting America and all for which it stands, exaggerating a fervent patriotism and embodying a rabid feminism. Palahniuk incorporates in her personality a rugged individualism, a hard-work ethic, and take-charge determination. Even at the end of her screenplay, Hazie still refers to Hellman as a positive Hollywood force, not giving in to any of the distractions or catering to the sycophants that litter the celebrity landscape. These qualities could be interpreted negatively, as Hazie comments that diners at Hellman affairs grow tired of listening to Hellman's self-aggrandizing. Granted, Palahniuk portrays her as a self-centered braggart, but he also elevates her status as a Hollywood icon who does not seem to buckle under bad publicity or who succumbs to gossip journalists' scare tactics. Hellman takes action and asks questions later, and she exhibits adventure figure status in several of the play scenarios. Hellman is who Hazie wants to become, and although she snaps at Hellman and makes derogatory comments about her ego, Hazie talks too much about Hellman in too many situations not to admire her greatly. When all is said and done, Hellman is a survivor whose reputation cannot be diminished by the tinsel town gossipmongers, and this is the status Hazie wants to attain. In this manner, Palahniuk actually uses another character, Hellman, as a constraint to accentuate how he wants his audience to perceive Hazie. Through the comparison of the two characters, Palahniuk allows readers to understand Hazie's motivation more completely than if they just had to rely on interpreting her actions in isolation. Palahniuk offers Hellman as Hazie's sounding board, even though Hazie does not have a close friendship with Hellman. Moreover, putting a real person into his novel as a major character provides a unique reference point by which to assess Hazie.

As was mentioned in the survey of reviews about *Tell-All*, many critics do not understand the rhetorical significance of Palahniuk's boldfacing celebrity names (as well as places and objects). Concerning parody, Palahniuk is following gossip column protocol by highlighting names of famous people. Besides this, Palahniuk boldfaces to emphasize the importance that Hazie bestows upon a name as a social or cultural commodity, something with genuine value as readers process the name through their critical thinking and consider all of the semiotic connotations in addition to the denotations that they are capable of attributing to it. The real value of a name is the amount of celebrity meaning attached to it. In terms of ethical appeal, a list of names with which readers can attach celebrity prominence in turn elevates the status of the person associated with those names. That person is granted credibility through the connection. Palahniuk understands this well, and he inserts names with which his audience may easily identify with names they might not instantly recognize, so there is a blend of high culture with low culture, a mixing of the common with the esoteric, the ordinary thrown in with the arcane. Palahniuk clearly shows that Hazie gets a sense of power through the act of naming, of juxtaposing and organizing the names in her screenplay as she deems their significance, and she in turn influences their meaning by their linguistic placements—how one name will play off the other name next to it, or above it, or below it in the paragraph or on the page. Furthermore, Hazie certainly relishes this privileging of information. As an illustration of writing as a way to assume power, Hazie also seems to enjoy versions of Webster's memoir, particularly elaborating upon the misogynistic sections in which Katherine praises his omnipotent phallus, in this case definitely a symbol of patriarchal power in addition to being an object of feminine infatuation and a scepter wielding control over female sensuality.

The act of writing is also relevant to Palahniuk's parody. Palahniuk is lampooning the business of defamation through the façade of journalism. He wants his audience to relate that purpose in writing (the kind still found in contemporary pulp publications) to the types of writing in *Tell-All*. Hazie constructs her own gossip document through the name dropping in her screenplay, but she also creates a memoir—inventing ways for Katherine to die in her various revisions of her fabrications—in addition to her own memoir that eventually becomes a best-selling book. There are layers of textualities in this book. Moreover, the act of lying is important. As a matter of course, the gossip columns are known for fabrications, and names of famous gossip columnists establish the tone of deception. Hellman generates revisions of history, while Hazie lies to Katherine about pets and other everyday events. Hazie writes fictions when she creates versions of *Love Slave*, and then *Paragon* is definitely full of untruths. Taken out further, the veracity of Hazie's own statements throughout this screenplay should be questioned. At the conclusion, when Hazie warns readers "NOT" to hold her accountable to the previous information, let alone make her responsible for the verity of what it contains, readers should be weary—just as they should be when they read gossip journalism from the 1940s, 1950s ... or 2015. Reliability is an issue throughout this entire book. Palahniuk has had his own negative experiences with the media, and he has responded (sometimes impulsively) to instances when he thought interviewers or reporters were delving too closely into his personal life.[5] The subversion of truth is at the heart of *Tell-All*, and Palahniuk effectively takes advantage of Hazie as author to demonstrate the malleability of information. As Palahniuk illustrates (and knows from his personal life), the truth can be stretched beyond its original shape and twisted into a new entity. Concerning form and speaker as rhetorical constraints, Hazie and boldface help Palahniuk to react to the problems associated with the packaging of truth in the media. As Hazie infers at the end, what is false may be taken as true if it is marketed in the proper way—gossip always has the potential to be transformed into what the audience believes to be fact.

Palahniuk's parody is more obvious in *Damned* than it is in *Pygmy* or *Tell-All*. The influences of Dante Alighieri's *Inferno* and Judy Blume's *Are You There God? It's Me, Margaret* are apparent in form as well as content. Palahniuk does not set out to address good versus evil or anything related to Christianity or any other religion, not that any reader would expect him to do so. This novel about hell is basically secular. Even though Satan is a character, and there are various devils, demons, and creatures taken from several myths and religions, there is little preaching, proselytizing, or evangelizing, and, again, not that any reader would expect Palahniuk to go in that direction. This is significant, however, since there are inherently reader expectations associated with any text proposing to be about heaven or hell, and the probability to offend is more possible with this kind of subject than attached to gossip journals, karate films, or writing communes. If readers begin *Snuff* already expecting content dealing with pornography (and gasp when they discover the book is really about a gang bang featuring one woman and 600 men), they might anticipate either an edifying or ameliorating book related to spirituality, which is probably not likely with Palahniuk, or a text that is irreverent, profane, and blasphemous, along the same lines as *Snuff*, which is probably much more the case. Readers will discover that *Damned* is not as low-culture, anti-religion, or anti-spirituality as they expected. If Palahniuk had decided to treat his dominant themes of marginalization and disenfranchisement only through a parody of Dante's *Inferno*, *Damned* would be a vastly different book. Palahniuk would have exerted his free will to blast, belittle, blaspheme, and bomb American society and culture. Instead, combining his parody of Dante's hell with a parody of Blume's young adult novel keeps Palahniuk more conservative in his content choices than he would have been otherwise. Moreover, selecting a teenage narrator helps to neutralize the transgression to something less provocative but more interesting. Palahniuk may still be criticized for profanity, vulgarity, and obscenity in this novel (Pszepolnica's orgasm section is a prime example), but he could have gone much farther into the transgressive if he did not rely on Madison's point of view.

Madison's stance in this text is crucial. Every chapter is addressed to Satan as Margaret's sections are targeted toward God. An important difference between the two is religion. Margaret struggles with pre-adolescent problems such as breasts, boys, and menstruation, but she also wrestles with her introduction into the practices of religions. Her father is Jewish and her mother is Christian, so she is confronted with the dilemma an interfaith marriage introduces, which is intensified by Jewish and Christian grandparents who want to claim her for their respective faiths. Margaret is plagued by jealousy toward Laura Danker because she is maturing more quickly, and even though she is rebellious toward her grandmother and spends "two minutes in the closet" with a boy, she is fairly obedient, courteous, and cooperative. At the end of Blume's novel, Margaret moves toward selecting one religion. On the other hand, Madison's father is a wealthy capitalist, her mother is a famous actress, and both parents are ultra-liberal, environmentally conscious neo-hippies, advocating nudity, drugs, and enlightenment. Madison has grown up in an atmosphere that should have been liberating and freeing, but as most readers know from experience, adolescence is rough going no matter the situation. Madison assumes she has died of a marijuana overdose, a detail that illustrates the disparity between Madison's and Margaret's lifestyles. Even though Madison is given carte blanche to experiment with drugs and in other areas, she is extremely level-headed with common sense and personal restraint, and her posts to Satan imitate in form and in content the posts Margaret writes to God, regardless of their two very different backgrounds. Readers might wonder if Palahniuk intended to update Blume's 1970 text for a 2011 audience, and if the setting were not hell, this might be the case. In a sense, compared to Dante's *Inferno*, *Damned* is almost like a *Candyland* children's board game version of hell. The references to name-brand candies as exchange currency and to almost a *Scooby-Doo* ensemble of participants—with Madison as a version of Velma, Babette as Daphne, and Patterson as Fred and Archer as a 2011 model of 1969–1970 Shaggy—lessens the intense religious weight of the subject. Most readers would agree going to hell is not an attractive option; this is a tremendously frightening possibility to many. Palahniuk literally candy-coats the notion of eternal damnation, and Madison undergoes adult problems through child-like sensibilities. Suffocation resulting from a string of Hello Kitty condoms is probably not a death one would associate with childhood growing pains. Palahniuk essentially undermines the afterlife as a serious subject by having Madison address Satan in a chit-chatty conversational manner and by creating a Willy Wonka–type landscape littered with candy. Palahniuk amplifies this by allowing Madison to beat up famously bad bullies. Compared to Dante's hell, Palahniuk provides a cartoon version where brutal punitive torture is replaced with forced capitalist labor.

Palahniuk's selection of this form is extremely effective. Each chapter heading directed toward Satan counterbalances the descriptions of the terrain in hell. Madison reports to Satan just as Margaret reports to God all that is occurring in her world, and readers view what are essentially confessionals to these deities. After her notes to Satan, which are obviously modeled after Margaret's notes in Blume's book, Madison provides more mature and subsequently more transgressive commentary, but this is still tempered with the early-adolescent point of view, so Madison is never allowed to provide any information that is too offensive. Her titles of places such as Ocean of Wasted Sperm and Shit Lake are simply proper nouns, and when she discusses her relationship with Goran, she never strays into improper or tasteless descriptions of her feelings toward him. Madison has manners, even in hell, and this is significant because readers might not think hell is typically the place for such a focus on etiquette. The actual civilizing of hell in this regard helps readers digest this content more easily. The audience will bring preconceptions about hell and associations with Satan to bear on this text, and Madison being a lot like Margaret restrains Palahniuk from going a bit too far in the direction of the transgressive. In other words, creating a Madison who is like the *Scooby-Doo* Velma serves the rhetorical purpose of alleviating or defusing reader anxiety possibly connected to a story about hell, but it also limits how far he can go concerning sexuality, violence, or profanity. As was mentioned in the chapter dedicated to *Damned*, Madison keeps the discussion in terms of decorum proper (considering just her reports) or a little edgy (thinking about the Pszepolnica scene and types of landmarks), but without her, Palahniuk could have easily strayed into pornographic territory. Through consistent sentences similar to "I am only telling you this, Satan," Madison shows that even though she is more mature than Margaret and a little older, she still faces similar problems, and this is pivotal concerning how readers perceive the purpose of the book. Madison curses, but this is the profanity of someone learning how to use this language. Madison would never become a "Vulgar McVulgarity," to imitate her style of neologisms.

If *Are You There God? It's Me, Margaret* is a traditional coming-of-age story for young women, *Damned* takes this one step further as a treatise about female empowerment in a post-feminist society. To make a temporal leap, a middle-aged Margaret might be likely to give a book such as *Damned* to her own grandchild. Margaret might be the hip grandmother who would allow her granddaughter to read Palahniuk, and if the parents raised a fuss, she would probably just point out her granddaughter could read (and see and listen to) a lot worse on the World Wide Web. In *Snuff*, Palahniuk pokes fun at Naomi Wolf and third-wave feminism's pretentiousness, but during her quest through hell, Margaret defeats some major icons of evil and asserts her will in a jurisdiction supposedly ruled by the Prince of Darkness. In this regard, Satan sanctions and even promotes Madison as third-wave feminist, if one believes Madison is a character in Satan's screenplay. Carrying this out, Satan allows a female to exert this power—not a male—in the underworld, and since this hell is fundamentally by most counts secular, Madison as the leader could be a rhetorical strategy to promote women's rights outside the boundaries of the text. In other words, through his novel *Damned*, Palahniuk is proclaiming a pro-woman stance. Furthermore, whereas Margaret is happy that she is immersed into womanhood through her first period, Madison is exhilarated through beating up hellish personalities and becoming a successful spokesperson for corporate (not corporeal) hell. Margaret finds fulfillment through traditional feminine rites of passage; Madison gains confidence through traditional masculine avenues of self-satisfaction. Rhetorically, Palahniuk is supporting cultural diversity through Madison, at least on the fringe—figuratively all the way on the margin in hell. This begs the question John Milton once mentioned in *Paradise Lost*, if it is better to rule in hell or to serve in heaven, and Madison seems content to select the former, at least until she finds out she is approved to leave. Ideally, Palahniuk is offering a parodic subversion of *Paradise Lost* by allowing Madison to rebel against Satan, and although she is not exiled from hell, she is cast out because of a bureaucratic foul-up. Madison is a parodic version of Milton's Satan, as Madison also sees her hell as almost a heaven but acknowledges true love rests with God. An entire chapter could be devoted to this connection with *Paradise Lost* in the context of the two other referent texts.

Of the six novels interpreted in the previous chapters, *Damned* probably provides the most fertile ground for literary analysis according to the traditional English-major methodology of interpreting metaphor, symbolism, and other literary features. A reader who wants to dive into such a reading of this novel could investigate the purposes of the particular demons whom Palahniuk takes from various mythologies and religions. Study could be applied to the historical personalities whom Palahniuk places into hell. They are the most notoriously evil figures from the past, but similar to *Tell-All* and the location of the boldfaced names, Palahniuk must have systematically situated these characters for various reasons. He also must have had a plan for the geographical features, where and why they are in their specific locales in their particular quadrants. Palahniuk certainly did not randomly create this hell; he undoubtedly had a rhetorical purpose for each decision how to build his underworld. The parody of Blume's novel is more static than the parody of Dante's *Inferno*, and given the nature of these to referent sources, one would expect as much. *The Inferno* is a treasure trove of symbols and metaphors, and some editions of this work actually devote a half of each page to footnotes explaining the literary features as well as the Biblical, historical, social, cultural, and literary allusions. As a rhetorical vehicle, parody of Blume's text shaped how readers perceive Madison and set up her transformation from a psychologically unsteady and unsure adolescent into an intellectually assertive and confident adult. As the novel progresses, readers discover that Madison is extremely well read, and her knowledge of Blume, Dante, Swift, and many British Romantic and

Victorian writers increases her credibility. This combined with her knowledge of popular culture enhances her reliability. Hell gives Madison the opportunity for growth and in turn success that she would not have been offered if she lived with her parents, and the irony of this is Madison had all of the socioeconomic advantages available while she was alive. She had to lose everything, including her life, to accomplish more than what Margaret did. Madison is an excellent example of someone not fitting the typical classifications for marginalization or disenfranchisement but feeling powerless nonetheless.

Shannon does not achieve personal empowerment as defiantly as Madison, but at the end of *Invisible Monsters Remix*, she experiences a significant change. As mentioned in the chapter devoted to the novel, reviewers both loved and hated Palahniuk's decision on a back-and-forth arrangement of chapters. Also in that section, attention was given to how readers may lose attention during the thumbing from one section in the front of the book to the back of the book and so forth. This was seen as both positive as well as negative. Considering the format as a rhetorical ploy, however, the recursive reading motion imitates Shannon's own struggle to understand her feelings. The organization of the novel reflects Shannon's disjointed emotions. Viewed in this way, Palahniuk chose an effective strategy outside of the pages to help readers identify with his character's internal psychological dilemma. In much of the book, Shannon appears conceited, unappreciative, and insensitive. The straight-forward arrangement of *Invisible Monsters* substantiates this interpretation of her personality. Although some critics may argue Palahniuk commits the mistake of assuming the advertiser's stance in *Invisible Monsters Remix*, recycling a previous story and reselling the product with a different packaging, Palahniuk had to make crucial decisions how to reorganize this work without undermining the integrity of the story and confusing general readers who just chose to purchase the book for an entertaining experience. There is a saying that the problem with some postmodern novels is that they are postmodern, and this points a finger at authors who experiment with content and form at the expense of the general reader who simply wants to follow a plot in the sequence of Freyteg's Triangle (based on Aristotle's ideas), a narrative with a beginning, a middle, and an end, plus other features that help the story to be more attractive to readers. Palahniuk successfully provides an innovative text while also not sacrificing readability for effect. Readers can follow Shannon's working through her emotional baggage, literally seeing the disconnectedness between her thoughts and her feelings, and as they get to the middle of the book, while the conclusion gets closer and the flipping of pages is tighter, they achieve closure as Shannon bestows her identity upon her brother Shane. Likewise, readers work from the margins toward the center as Shannon migrates from the emotional outside to the rational inside, when she makes what is the most important decision of her life. Readers literally follow Shannon's movement from marginalization.

Palahniuk's choice of injury for Shannon is definitely the perfect metaphor through which to display her psychological conflict. As a fashion model, Shannon earned a living through marketing her physically attractive self, and this outer surface-level Shannon did not accurately reflect the inner soul-level Shannon. Palahniuk's references to the Num-Num Snack Factory products display the level of self-degradation to which Shannon has fallen. These products are, to be honest, putrid and disgusting. The apparatus resembles a meat grinder that mixes up all of the unwanted carnal by-products, and after some turns of a crank, presto they morph into appealingly delicious spreads to put on crackers. Ultimately, Shannon is an infomercial piece of sex furniture, and the photoshoot locations also depict her as sexual eye candy in logically unattractive places, next to dead animal carcasses and abandoned automobile wrecks. Shannon's destruction of half of her face is the perfect metaphor to communicate how she no longer wants to be noticed just by her physiognomy. Her interaction with her parents during Thanksgiving clearly shows that she does not feel respected for her intellect as well as for what she believes, thinks, or feels; from her perspective, she is fundamentally Shane's sister, and her parents are catering to Shane's causes and not reaching out to the daughter who presently needs their attention. Covers of editions of *Invisible Monsters* and *Invisible Monsters Remix* have attempted to illustrate Shannon's face, and Palahniuk fans have posted online their numerous renditions of how they expect Shannon to look, but each individual reader's imaginative construction of her face is what matters—how each person visualizes Shannon in his or her mind is important. Palahniuk even promotes this imaginative experience by first presenting Shannon as a monster (the grocery store turkey scene is an example), but by the end of the novel, most readers have probably even forgotten Shannon is indeed missing half of her face. Rhetorically, Palahniuk develops Shannon's situation with Brandy Alexander so effectively that readers might forget the initial meeting between the two that precipitated the odyssey they take in the second half of the story. In this way, readers lose track of Shannon's disfiguration and concentrate on her internal feelings rather than her external features. When she gives Shane her identity at the end, a sister simply passes along a gift to her brother. Shannon's emotional attributes take priority over her physical appearance.

Palahniuk's additions of chapters to *Invisible Monsters* increase the rhetorical merit of the content as well as set up the opportunity for parody. Without Chapter 18, *Invisible Monsters Remix* might resemble previous texts such as Mary Shelley's *Frankenstein*, Dalton Trumbo's *Johnny Got His Gun*, or stories in which a disfigured character expresses himself or herself through stream of consciousness or first-person narration, but there is not any obvious resemblance between this novel in its entirety and referent sources. Palahniuk's remake of the Elephant Man's story calls direct attention to a parodic connection between Shannon and Joseph Merrick. Revitalizing Merrick as a stripper who works the crowd, knowing that eyes are watching him, portrays a figure often seen as pathetically disabled and relying solely on the assistance of others transformed into a person who is unafraid to shake what he has, to objectify his own body, and to exploit his notoriety for his own purposes. This Elephant Man is an independent person who is guided by his own choices, ones determined by his own agenda, and he is not passively subservient to anyone. This depiction of Merrick offers a touchstone by which to test Shannon, and through this perspective, she is first seen as self-indulgent but then viewed as, like the dancing Merrick, to paraphrase a line from William Ernest Henley's "Invictus," master of her own fate and captain of her own soul. Both she and this Merrick are unconquerable. Although this might sound trite, all of the major characters in the six novels studied thus far are invincible according to their own standards, and these standards are the only ones that have real bearing upon their individual lives. To Shannon as well as other Palahniuk characters, accountability becomes an individual measure, no longer pertaining to abstract markers perpetuated by bureaucratic entities of power. Paradoxically, Shannon is liberated at the end of the novel through her self-sacrifice, actually giving her name to her brother. Shannon reveals that she finally feels love, and through this, she is capable of giving without expecting anything in return, total and complete charity. She displays humility, and through this gesture she will become a "new story" (132) that will become her new life. In this way, Shannon and the stripper Merrick are new versions of their old selves, revitalized through the creation of new identities. She even mentions at the end of the novel that she has completely changed, no longer needing to be the center of attention. Shane will consequently also experience this transformation. Through parody as a rhetorical strategy, Palahniuk again effectively illustrates the process of personal empowerment.

In "The Power of Persisting: An Introduction," the first essay in *Burnt Tongues: An Anthology of Transgressive Stories*, Palahniuk discusses the nature of reading and writing. His essay is similar to Stephen King's "Why We Crave Horror Films," published over thirty years earlier. Palahniuk is almost parodying King by updating his predecessor's tone and style to discuss transgressive rather than horror fiction. Transgressive writing has had a similar rise in popularity comparable to that of horror fiction in the 1970s and 1980s. In his essay, King explains the statement introduced in his title regarding the purpose why audiences view movies in the horror genre: "To show that we can, that we are not afraid, that we can ride this roller coaster. Which is not to say that a really good horror movie may not surprise a scream out of us at some point, the way we may scream when the roller coaster twists through a complete 360 or plows through a lake at the bottom of the drop.... We also go to re-establish our feelings of essential normality; the horror movie is innately conservative, even reactionary" (*Little* 685–86). In his introduction, Palahniuk addresses transgressive writing through a similar approach, and the resemblance to King's essay is remarkable: "We return to troubling films and books because they don't pander to us—their style and subject matter challenge, but to embrace them is to win something worth having for the rest of our lives. The difficult, the new and the novel establish their own authority" ("Power" 3). In his discussion of why readers "are all mentally ill" (*Little* 685) and thus identify with what they view in horror films, King cites such horror genre hallmarks as *Die, Monster, Die!* and *Dawn of the Dead* and makes references to notorious serial killers (*Little* 686–87). Palahniuk offers a similar approach: "A hallmark of a classic long-lived story is how much it upsets the existing culture at its introduction. Take for example *Harold and Maude* and *Night of the Living Dead*—both got lambasted by reviewers and dismissed as distasteful, but they've survived to become as comforting as musty back issues of *Reader's Digest*" ("Power" 3). King and Palahniuk are both commenting on their own crafts, and, many years separating their essays, both delve into the paradox concerning why texts that seem so repulsive become so attractive to audiences. After mentioning his working-class background to indicate how he was not groomed to become a lover of classical literature or a connoisseur of great books, Palahniuk explains how he subsequently appreciated texts after neglecting them because he did not identify with the content. He states that he only understood Nick Carraway's situation in *The Great Gatsby* after reaching a certain level of maturity. Palahniuk confesses that only after life experience could he empathize with Fitzgerald's character ("Power" 5).

The word "empathize" is crucial. Palahniuk is getting at the heart of why readers identify with his own fiction. Palahniuk would probably not equate what he writes with rhetoric, definitely not in the sense of classical persuasion applying the emotional, ethical, and logical appeals or all that is associated with Aristotle, Plato, Cicero, and other major rhetorical forefathers. This said, Palahniuk certainly has an agenda in his writing, to give his readers incidences of how characters just like them have confronted their own marginalization and disenfranchisement. In "From the Editors: The Genesis of Burnt Tongues," the second essay in *Burnt Tongues*, Dennis Widmyer and Richard Thomas summarize the workshop experience that produced the stories included in their collection and give Palahniuk credit for the definition of "burnt tongue" chosen for their title: "Palahniuk defines *burnt tongue* as 'a way of saying something, but saying it wrong, twisting it to slow down the reader. Forcing the reader to read close, maybe read twice, not just skim along a surface of abstract images, shortcut verbs, and clichés'" (7). In his essay, Palahniuk reiterates this concept and provides substantiation for what has been asserted consistently throughout this book: through his transgressive approach, Palahniuk persuades readers to take action toward self-empowerment. What he says about *Burnt Tongues* applies to *Haunted*, *Snuff*, *Pygmy*, *Tell-All*, *Damned*, and *Invisible Monsters Remix*:

> The worst thing you could do is read this book and instantly enjoy every word. This book, the book you're holding, I hope you gag on a few words—more than a few. May some of the stories scar and trouble you. Whether you like or dislike them doesn't matter; you've already touched these words with your eyes, and they're becoming part of you. Even if you hate these stories, you'll come back to them because they'll test you and prompt you to become someone larger, braver, bolder ["Power" 4].

This statement reveals the rhetorical aim underlying Palahniuk's fiction, and it could serve as the critical touchstone through which to understand what Palahniuk is trying to accomplish in the six novels analyzed in the preceding chapters. Palahniuk infers that reading his books often necessitates a difficult and lengthy experience, thinking about his years of interacting with *The Great Gatsby*, and this corresponds perhaps to the ideology expressed through the stories. Readers internalize Palahniuk's ideas through the same process that Palahniuk underwent with *The Great Gatsby*. Even though Palahniuk's novels are not difficult to read, the subject matter is not all that easy to digest. A level of maturity is necessary.

Teenagers are frequently assigned *The Great Gatsby* in junior high and high school classes, but one wonders if they are capable of actually understanding the depth of despair Jay Gatsby, Nick Carraway, Tom Buchanan, Daisy Buchanan, George Wilson, Myrtle Wilson, and Jordan Baker all (literally all the characters) feel as a result of their envy. These characters strive to fill a personal emptiness with something they believe that others possess, coveting that something which they cannot even pinpoint, and they are motivated by the assumption that happiness could easily be achieved by gaining that particular undefinable something to which they feel entitled. The Valley of Ashes is the wasteland representing the sterility and aridity related to the spiritual emptiness within their souls. *The Great Gatsby* is canonized in American literature not because of the way it is taught in American schools but because of the way readers empathize, undergoing a process similar to Palahniuk, with the spiritual malady of those characters. The same is true for Palahniuk readers; almost everyone feels, no matter where one falls on the socioeconomic scale, marginalized and disenfranchised. Fitzgerald's characters feel entitled to prosperity, which seems to be defined monetarily through materialism, but they are uncertain exactly what they want or what they need, and their frustrations are manifested in their actions. Palahniuk's characters demand their share, whatever that share might be, and unfortunately this desire only exacerbates their dysfunction. Fitzgerald's wasteland has only shifted about a hundred years to the first two decades of the twenty-first century, and Fitzgerald's characters in *The Great Gatsby* do not fare much better than those in Palahniuk's six novels. Gatsby and Myrtle die, Wilson is a murderer, Daisy and Tom remain unhappy, and Nick, through his narrative retelling of what occurred, is grappling with his interpretation of what happened. The only person maybe to come out okay is Jordan, and she is a sexually manipulative, hedonistically motivated, compulsive liar who cheats at golf in the same way that she takes advantage of every situation for her own benefit. Jordan is not Hazie, and Nick is neither Shannon (such a comparison equates Brandy Alexander with Gatsby) nor Madison (Nick's hell could be a combination of West Egg and East Egg), but there are definitely several correlations between all of these. No wonder Palahniuk mentions *The Great Gatsby*. Palahniuk imitates King in his essay, but what he really does is establish *The Great Gatsby* as a master narrative that serves as the thematic basis for many of his novels. Fitzgerald's green light at the end of the Buchanan dock is inverted as Palahniuk's Nightmare Box in *Haunted*, both associated with impressions of reality.

In the six novels addressed in this study, Palahniuk successfully reacts to the exigencies, responds to audiences, and applies constraints. He also maintains an appropriate rhetorical stance throughout all of these narratives. Considering both Booth's and Bitzer's paradigms related to rhetorical responses, readers see how Palahniuk successfully maintains appropriate stances through his fictional personas, teetering into the pedant's stance and the advertiser's stance occasionally, but he neither tilts excessively toward concentrating on content in spite of audience interest nor leans markedly on effect while neglecting audience readability. Palahniuk has been accused of caring more for supplying needless factoids and relying too heavily upon stereotypes for his characterizations, as well as selecting details and descriptions for shock value instead of content development. If readers take into account the reasons why Palahniuk offers numerous facts, presents several stereotypes, and applies graphic images, they would recognize how he does so to accomplish his rhetorical purposes. The seemingly extraneous information actually substantiates his historical and cultural settings, the stereotypes enable audiences to more easily identify unorthodox personalities within the stories, and the pushing of moral and ethical boundaries relates directly to transgressive fiction. As has been asserted, Palahniuk does not experiment with form in a vacuum; his approaches to narrative style and document format have been predicated on how he wants his readers to respond toward a particular exigence. In the case of the six novels discussed in the preceding chapters, Palahniuk has responded to the marginalization and disenfranchisement of his audience—this is the overriding exigence toward which he reacts—and he has offered fictional illustrations through his characterizations, specifically through his literary personas of how people have become empowered through various means and move from the socioeconomic, cultural, and political outside to the inside. As has been mentioned, characters such as Shannon, Hazie, Madison, and others might not move to the apex of this power center, but they make headway toward that middle, moving at least inward by degrees. Moreover, Palahniuk does not place moral, ethical, or any other pronouncements on these characters—they are who they are, and their resemblance to the ordinary and the commonplace is what makes them relevant to readers. Palahniuk's constraints are these personas as well as other literary features in each novel, and, of course, he takes advantage of parody as a primary method of addressing his audience and responding to the exigence. Palahniuk uses parody to establish common ground with his audience as well as to maintain a connection with his literary heritage. Palahniuk depends on parody as a crucial constraint in all six novels, and without this rhetorical strategy, he would not have been capable in each rhetorical fiction situation of successfully responding to his exigence or effectively addressing his audience.

TEN

Future Postmodern Parody

Considering what Chuck Palahniuk has published recently, the point could be made that Palahniuk is not essentially a parodist and only applies parody when that device best serves his purpose. His most recent books, *Burnt Tongues: An Anthology of Transgressive Stories* (2014) and *Make Something Up: Stories You Can't Unread* (2015), are collections of short stories (one he co-edits and one includes his own works), and his latest novel, *Beautiful You* (2014), refers to other texts and to previous ideas but is not a parody as the novels addressed in the previous chapters fit that form. All of Palahniuk's recent works are unquestionably transgressive and are situated firmly in that genre of writing. Within the time period covered from *Haunted* (2005) to *Invisible Monsters Remix* (2010), Palahniuk also published *Rant* (2007), which is an extremely interesting book about time travel but is not distinctively a parody. Notably, *Rant* falls within the time frame of Palahniuk novels studied thus far, and although readers may notice this book's affiliation with previous texts, *Rant* is not a parody on the same level as the other works. There are certainly previous texts that offer narration similar to Buster Casey's (H. G. Well's *Time Machine* and Vonnegut's *Slaughterhouse-Five* come to mind, but they are not really referents). Granted, not everything Palahniuk writes is a parody, and not everything he publishes has a rhetorical purpose, and not everything he puts out must follow prescriptions, patterns, or paradigms. Palahniuk is a prolific writer, and he publishes a diverse range of texts.

This said, Palahniuk's "Fight Club for Kids" has gone viral, being mentioned in *USAToday* as a "hot clip" and getting countless views. In this video, Palahniuk parodies himself. He is never too pretentious to poke fun at himself, nor is he above ridiculing, lampooning, or satirizing his own previous creations. True, not everything that Palahniuk creates is a parody, but most of his popular texts in one way or the other imitate, simulate, or

Ten. Future Postmodern Parody

remake previously produced works. At the beginning of the video, Palahniuk jokes that he is actually only known as the author of *Fight Club*, exhibiting a self-deprecation characteristic of this personality. Considering *Fight Club* was published in 1996, almost twenty years earlier, Palahniuk states he has written *Fight Club 4 Kids* because his audience "is older, having children, and dying," so he has "to reintroduce the book to a whole a new generation." Palahniuk revises *Fight Club* to include an unnamed boy who befriends another boy who is "not really there." This other child says "silly things" such as "Quit your job!" "Start a fight!" and "Prove that you're alive!" All of these statements are in the form of rhymed lines, with cartoons illustrating what is read and appropriate music in the background setting the tone for a child-oriented presentation. Of course, Palahniuk gets excited while reading, raising his voice when he states, "You are not your fucking khakis." The profanity is bleeped, and Palahniuk apologizes with "I am so sorry. This is for kids. This is supposed to be for kids," although he says this smiling, foreshadowing that there will be similar mistakes, and there are. After introducing the "Horsing Around Club" and commenting how the children "fucking go to town on each other ... beating the shit out of each other," someone off camera reminds Palahniuk that this clip is for kids. Palahniuk then reads rules for fight club that have been tailored exclusively for this new venue, ending sarcastically with "Also, no weapons." Palahniuk concludes that everyone, especially the no-named boy, had fun participating in Horsing Around Club, and Palahniuk, unable to restrain his enthusiasm, summarizes a scene from the film version of *Fight Club* that was particularly brutal. After calling the pummeled fight club participant a "motherfucker," which is bleeped but is still heard, Palahniuk ends the children's story with "They all lived happily ever after. Believe it or not." His last words remind viewers *Fight Club 4 Kids* would serve as a nice Christmas gift.

Obviously, "Fight Club for Kids" is not for children, and viewers who assume this is for kids egregiously misunderstand Palahniuk's aim. A scan of online responses to the *USAToday* link to this clip reveals that many viewers do not catch the apparent self-parody. Just as with much of Palahniuk's fiction, and as has been cited in the preceding chapters, some people simply do not understand what Palahniuk is attempting. One only needs to compare "Fight Club for Kids" with Jonathan Swift's "A Modest Proposal" for a literary historical precedent concerning readers misinterpreting the intention behind a satirical discourse. In response to Irish hunger, Swift advocates the poor selling their children as food to the rich to ease suffering, and he makes extremely logical claims in a rational argument why this is a plausible proposition. Some readers actually believed Swift was promoting what is essentially cannibalism. Swift's intention was to expose social neglect of the poor and callous attitudes toward the impoverished, especially criticizing those who believed simple plans could solve complex problems associated with Irish poverty. Palahniuk is writing satire as Swift wrote satire, and there is absolutely no way he is approving a fight club for juveniles. Although, there are many comments from people who say that they will indeed show this clip to their children. Palahniuk is just having a little fun at his own expense. In other words, Palahniuk is definitely not calling for children to organize fight clubs, nor is he advocating child-on-child violence. He is just giving those familiar with the 1996 novel *Fight Club* or the 1999 film version something humorous to consider. This said, someone who knows nothing about *Fight Club* might become easily offended by this clip—just as readers looking at "A Modest Proposal" for the first time may have been appalled that anyone would propose such an unbelievable idea. Palahniuk is relying on his audience's familiarity with *Fight Club*, and without this knowledge of the referent, his viewers are not going to make the hilarious connections between this present text and the previous text. Concerning the six novels addressed in the preceding chapters, Palahniuk is counting on his audience making this kind of connection with previous textualizations.

"Fight Club for Kids" illustrates Palahniuk's parody process. Palahniuk is essentially taking a text that was addressed for adults and repackaging it, rather transparently, as something for children. Those who notice the references can better appreciate what Palahniuk is doing in this video. The core idea is already established as *Fight Club* is Palahniuk's most famous novel, and if viewers have not read the book, they probably have seen the movie or have heard references made to it in popular culture. Palahniuk adapts specific lines from the novel and movie for this children's literature context, and the characters are renamed, as is the title given to fight club. Palahniuk is clearly substituting nouns and adjectives to make the leap from one to the other context. What is extremely important, however, is the manner in which Palahniuk calls direct attention to this process, even lampooning the act of parody itself. His rants when he gets excited demonstrate this, and the choppy editing breaks, such as when he states his readers are getting older and then says they are dying, are intentional and point toward the self-reflexivity inside the imitation. Palahniuk pretends that he wants viewers to see this entire enterprise as his bungled and muddled attempt to capitalize on his remarketing a lucrative book concept, but he actually wants viewers to notice the blatant metacommentary concerning his making fun of himself. Palahniuk reads words loudly and expresses others quickly, especially those related to violence, and the illustrations become more graphic as the violence increases. Blood completely surrounds the body of one character in a cartoon visual, and seconds are devoted to showing this image. When Palahniuk chokes out the words referring to the fairy-tale ending of everyone living happily after, the tone betrays itself as self-deceptive and sarcastic. Palahniuk offers almost a one-to-one correspondence between *Fight Club* and *Fight Club 4 Kids*, stressing the comparisons and similarities between the two, but the importance of the parody rests with the differences. The concept of fight club is definitely not for children, and Palahniuk's parody reveals both the futility as well as the impracticability of one person in violent combat with another for the sake of fun. Viewers know that there is nothing fun about fight club's mature brutality.

Much attention was given in the first chapter to various theories of parody, and the trend is to strip this literary feature of humor, ridicule, and comedy to deem it postmodern. Moreover, parody is currently held to go beyond a point-by-point duplication of a previous text. Parody is not simply a remake. A current parody is not, for instance, a 2015 rote copying of something produced fifty years earlier in 1965, nor is it only a new version of an old product. A postmodern parody must not only show the similarity between two texts, the original and the revision, but it should also point out a difference that establishes the relevance or the significance of the reproduction. This difference should provide the rationale for the parody. In other words, copying the referent provides in marketing what would be similar to selling the same product with new wrapping. Postmodern parody offers something new as a result of the copying. Through her various publications laying out her literary critical theory, Linda Hutcheon offers an extensive discussion concerning the current treatment of postmodern parody, and her ideas have been the touchstones applied in this study to interpret Palahniuk's use of parody. In each chapter, Hutcheon's theory has been applied to *Haunted*, *Snuff*, *Pygmy*, *Tell-All*, *Damned*, and *Invisible Monsters Remix* to demonstrate how Palahniuk gives his readers new ways to understand old ideas presented through previous textualizations. The new ways are associated with ironic signaling and subversion, which means that Palahniuk's approaches at getting at these old ideas are from vastly different and unexpected directions from how previous authors or past texts have taken toward them. Palahniuk partially succeeds at this through his transgressive writing, but he also accomplishes his goal through his rhetorical selection of narrators, formats, and settings.

In *Haunted*, Palahniuk draws upon Boccaccio's *The Decameron* to show how a group of people realize that they cannot essentially escape their own character flaws. Just as Boccaccio's group of ten young people flee the biological disease of Black Death by seeking sanctuary at their country estates, Palahniuk's collection of personalities run away from the psychological disease within their current lives for the promise of something better through a writing retreat. Palahniuk imitates Boccaccio's frame narrative strategy, although he does not attach sections similar to the Italian author's introduction and conclusion. Instead of this narrative border structure, Palahniuk relies upon an unnamed narrator to provide commentary that connects the various poems and stories. Unlike Boccaccio, Palahniuk does not coordinate his participants' texts through male and female alternating turns. Instead, his participants' stories are much more personal and revealing to the point of being self-incriminating. Boccaccio asks his characters to tell tales that are indeed fictional; Palahniuk requires his speakers to present confessional accounts of past experiences masked as imaginative creations, more nonfictional than fictional. Boccaccio's young men and women seem to cohabitate successfully without any problems. On the other hand, Palahniuk's nineteen characters (seventeen guests plus the host and his assistant), are egotistical, duplicitous, and malicious, and most of them are in self-denial and are self-deceived concerning how their past actions influence their present predicaments. This group resorts to sabotaging their supplies and services in addition to self-mutilation and cannibalism to create what they believe is the necessary environment for media stardom when rescuers find them in the abandoned theater. The narrator is unnamed and is not included in the count of participants because he or she does not have any poem or story and is not included in the descriptions; however, this speaker uses the pronouns "we" and "us" to report what happens, so he or she would have been the twentieth character in the writing commune.

In *Snuff*, Palahniuk relies upon hyperreality to demonstrate the phases of simulation during Cassie Wright's monumental record-setting gang bang with 600 men. Jean Baudrillard's theory of simulacra helps clarify how Palahniuk begins with the original, provides a simulation of it, subsequently offers a simulation of that, then presents a simulation of that simulation, and, through this streaming of simulacra, eventually achieves hyperreality in which the last item is a complete distortion of the original. Palahniuk begins with Cassie having sex, then offers reproductions of Cassie having sex in porn films, which are basically imitations of Hollywood films. In addition, porn stars are compared to Hollywood stars, and this displays how their lives are relative simulations. Moreover, there are simulations outside of the novel that correlate directly to features inside of it. On the Internet, Palahniuk provides interviews with a transgendered Cassie as well as trailers of movies Cassie has made. There are actual porn movies that have plots that imitate the fictitious ones in which Cassie performed, which are imitations of actual films produced commercially in Hollywood. In terms of hyperreality, the image of a melted together Cassie and Branch Bacardi serves as the distortion Baudrillard claims is the result of the sequencing of simulacra. Palahniuk parodies the porn industry, but he also relies heavily on intertextuality to reinforce the various levels of simulation. This novel truly is a mashing of different kinds of imitations and various types of reproductions. The blending of the four narrative voices promotes the theme of simulation as the same scene is often described from several perspectives, and Cassie as the central figure is only constructed through the repetition of various character conversations and porn films shown on monitors.

In *Pygmy*, Palahniuk depends upon readers' knowledge of 1970s karate films to situate Pygmy's transformation from a potential foreign terrorist into a popular community hero. Although an understanding of the 1970s kung-fu movie genre is not a requisite for enjoying this novel, this background certainly helps readers situation most of the scenes within a context. Palahniuk assumes readers will bring to bear preconceptions concerning speech and violence to the text. In this sense, readers will prejudge Pygmy's stereotypically Asian way of talking in his dispatches. They will also relate Pygmy's reliance on karate kicks and chops through the interpretative lens of the B-movies featuring the representative good Asian hero combating (through hyperbolic physicality) bad adversaries. Pygmy imitates the broken English language and propensity to fight typical of these 1970s karate films. Pygmy interprets his world through the ideology instilled in him through education that is strictly anti–American and pro-totalitarian (probably based on communism). As he interacts with his host family and participates in school activities, Pygmy begins to assimilate into American culture, and he subsequently views the world through this frame of reference. More important, he begins to think for himself, shedding his allegiance to the foreign regime and Operation Havoc and basing his decisions on his own moral definitions of right and wrong. At the end of this novel, when he saves his community from biological contamination, Pygmy is Americanized, and Palahniuk completely subverts the prejudices applied to his novel based upon 1970s karate films. A critical point is, however, Palahniuk could not deconstruct what was not first constructed, so he initially had to support the Asian stereotypes before he could undercut them by elevating Pygmy as the American hero.

In *Tell-All*, Palahniuk again counts on his readers' past knowledge, in this case information about 1940s–1950s gossip journalism, to set up the action in this novel. Palahniuk uses boldface to highlight names of famous people, places, and objects to emphasize their importance, much the same way gossip writers dropped names in their celebrity columns. As Hazie Coogan writes her screenplay, she determines as narrator what celebrity is mentioned and in what context he or she is mentioned, so Hazie has the authority to control how these personalities are interpreted by readers. Through this process, Hazie determines, or at least influences, how the celebrities are perceived. This establishes what Mikhail Bakhtin terms a carnivalesque relationship between the names, and Bakhtin's theory helps to explain Palahniuk's purpose for boldfacing the names as well as reveals how power is distributed through this technique. As readers assign meaning to these boldfaced names through signification, they privilege these identities according to those interpretations. An actual celebrity's importance, for instance, depends upon where Hazie places him or her in the context of a paragraph, how readers respond to that placement, and how that celebrity's meaning interacts with the other celebrities' meanings inside that context. Lowly maid Hazie has power over these celebrities by deciding how they appear in her screenplay. Palahniuk essentially awards Hazie the status of gossip columnist, giving her the power to decide how these celebrities will be seen by readers. And, Palahniuk certainly displays how that power can easily be corrupted when the writer spreads falsehoods that are unfortunately taken as facts and truths. In this way, Hazie manipulates Katherine Kenton and Webster Carlton Westward III and consequently achieves her own dubious celebrity stardom. Palahniuk's insertion of Lillian Hellman into this story provides a parallel to Hazie's actions; Hellman creates her own version of American history through her plays, and in actuality, Hellman had her own battles with critics over literary license related to embellishing facts to serve her own purposes. The parody of gossip journalism provides the foundation upon which Palahniuk builds his story about Hazie's unscrupulous rise to fame.

In *Damned*, Palahniuk parodies both Dante Alighieri's *Inferno* and Judy Blume's *Are You There God? It's Me, Margaret* to address a young woman's rise to empowerment. Drawing from two extremely different texts, Palahniuk applies *The Inferno* as the dominant referent and the vehicle to ground his story. Hell determines the macro-level actions of his narrator, Madison Spencer, and the hierarchal structure of the underworld and the geography of the fictional landscape direct Madison's movements as a character. Palahniuk relies on *Are You There God? It's Me, Margaret* for the micro-level actions, everything related to the psychological and physical causes that motivate thirteen-year-old Madison. Palahniuk takes advantage of Dante's hell to design the landscape of swamps, rivers, lakes, and mountains, as well as the architecture of the city. He also relies on Dante to select his team of devils and demons and the range of punishments that they inflict on those damned for eternity. Palahniuk borrows from Blume to depict how Madison reacts toward events occurring in hell. Blume's "Dear God" daily meditations give Palahniuk a method of allowing readers a glimpse into Madison's thinking, while also placing Madison's thoughts into Margaret's context of a young female attempting to deal with tremendous change. Margaret's changes might appear minuscule compared to Madison's being in hell, but Palahniuk wants readers to recognize both are equally difficult situations. Palahniuk diverges from presenting only an imitation of these two referent texts by allowing Madison more freedom and granting her more assertiveness. Related to Naomi Wolf's third-wave feminist concepts of the "good girl" and the "bad girl," Madison relinquishes the good girl thinking that has previously informed her decisions and fostered all of her assumptions and embraces her inner bad girl. In this manner, Madison directs her energy toward her self-empowerment and defeats a Who's Who of historical evil personalities through physical combat. Madison's insecurities become manifested into a newfound confidence. Palahniuk might begin with Dante's version of hell as the location for endless punishment, continuous pain, and constant torture, but he completes his novel with Madison moving up the corporate level in a hell that operates on a business model. Ultimately, Madison becomes more empowered than Margaret, and she definitely asserts more control over her future than her literary counterpart.

In *Invisible Monsters Remix*, Palahniuk reformats his previous novel *Invisible Monsters*, adding Chapter 18 about the Elephant Man to influence how readers perceive Shannon McFarland. Palahniuk's first version of this novel is linear and straightforward, the traditional format of a novel; this version is back-and-forth, requiring a reader to begin in the front of the book, flip to the back of the book, and continue until the novel concludes somewhere in the middle. Not only is the arrangement changed, but Palahniuk includes several extra chapters, some of which do not seem to pertain to Shannon's story, and there is one that is even printed backwards on the page. Chapter 18 contains a description of the Elephant Man as a male dancer, more specifically a stripper, and even though he is still the deformed figure that is presented in both the play and the movie about Joseph Merrick, he is more confident, more agile, more attractive, and definitely a lot sexier, as women appear to enjoy watching him move. Applied to Shannon's narrative, this version of the Elephant Man calls into question her motivation. Compared to the Elephant Man in other media, who is the epitome of optimism, fortitude, and humility, Shannon is almost the binary, the opposite of these positive qualities, displaying self-loathing, ingratitude, vanity, and self-pity. This is not the Shannon at the end of the novel, however, when she performs an act of supreme self-sacrifice by giving her identity to her brother Shane. The Elephant Man in Chapter 18 is more the Shannon McFarland in this novel, and Judith Butler's theory of gender as performance helps explain this connection. Although physically challenged, this Joseph Merrick seems to overcome this by participating in a profession that demands sexual attractiveness. This Merrick has emphasized the positive in his life, although not exactly in the same way expressed through the Merrick in the play and the film. Through his placement of Chapter 18, Palahniuk suggests that this is how he wants Shannon to be interpreted, not as the selfish model but as the selfless sister. Although the parody is only related to one added chapter, it influences the entire reading of *Invisible Monsters Remix*. Without Chapter 18 in *Invisible Monsters*, Shannon is viewed differently.

Herman Melville is recognized in American literary history as one of the major humanist writers. He is known for portraying how people struggle in their lives to offer compassion, understanding, and sensitivity to those whom they know as well as to others whom they do not know. The theme of humanity—or basically what it truly means to be humane—is at the core of most of Melville's fiction. Ishmael grapples with this throughout *Moby-Dick*, and Captain Vere wrestles with this in *Billy Budd*. In the story "Bartleby, the Scrivener," Melville's elderly narrator explains his experience in his Wall Street law office with an employee who refuses to perform even the slightest task that he requests him to complete. Readers are shown numerous incidents during which Bartleby responds with the refrain "I prefer not to" when asked to perform duties attached to his copying job as well as those associated with social interaction. As the story progresses, the levels of refusal increase in importance to the point that Bartleby is not completing basic functions such as examining copies or retrieving mail. Eventually, he refuses outright to copy or to write anything. The narrator finally reaches a point when he begins to sympathize, if not empathize, with Bartleby: "For the first time in my life a feeling of stinging melancholy seized me. Before, I had never experienced aught but a not-unpleasing sadness. The bond of a common humanity now drew me irresistibly to gloom. A fraternal melancholy! For both I and Bartleby were sons of Adam" (1495).

Going so far as to close his business to avoid interaction with Bartleby, the narrator discovers the landlord has reported Bartleby's vagrancy to the police, and Bartleby is imprisoned at the Tombs, where he passively dies. The narrator learns that Bartleby previously worked at a menial job that most likely influenced his malaise. The narrator's famous last words express his frustration concerning the entire situation, "Ah Bartleby! Ah humanity!" (1509).

Readers might feel like this elderly lawyer when confronted with some of Palahniuk's characters. They might begin reading a Palahniuk novel with expectations that these figures will resemble ones they have come across in other stories, especially if they are unfamiliar with Palahniuk's writing, but they soon notice that the people described are not the ones they would usually run across at the grocery, at the mall, or in any other social context. This is especially the case just by looking at Shannon McFarland, and most people do not run across a porn star the caliber of Cassie Wright, a foreign exchange student such as Pygmy, or idiosyncratic personalities like Madison Spencer or Hazie Coogan, not even getting into the peculiarities of the people populating the writer's retreat. Readers understand, however, these seemingly different characters are a lot like them in various ways. They begin to identify with their socioeconomic and cultural situations, and this is because of Palahniuk's rhetoric in the form of fiction. Palahniuk manipulates readers into this initial reaction of seeing his characters as Others, much different from them, but then through his narrative strategies, he leads readers toward discovering that they share many of the same values, beliefs, and attitudes as these personalities. Granted, some readers might still share the same anxieties as Melville's narrator, continuously asking aloud why these characters make their decisions within the narratives, but these characters' struggles toward the fundamental humane right of personal empowerment is something with which every Palahniuk reader could identify. Readers might even shout, "Ah humanity!" while finishing a Palahniuk novel, especially after reading *Haunted*. The significance is that Palahniuk's characters are definitely not like Bartleby. Instead of saying, "I prefer not to," they demonstrate the mantra "I prefer to act," holding the idea of action over inaction. In this sense, Palahniuk updates Melville's fictional portfolio for a twenty-first-century audience. In all of his writing, even in "Fight Club for Kids," he addresses the universal principle of humanity and thus what it means to be humane. Of course, readers need to identify the parodic irony in what Palahniuk publishes to understand this. Palahniuk's transgressive approach is not Melville's romantic one, but Palahniuk nonetheless confronts the universal subject of humanity from a non-academic, popular, and egalitarian approach. Not to defame the American literary canon, but if one conducted a survey of how many people read anything written by Melville recently outside of an academic situation and how many people read one of Palahniuk's books, one would more than likely find Palahniuk would win this head-to-head competition.

This comparison between Melville and Palahniuk is not to suggest in one sweeping generalization that Palahniuk is parodying Melville, but it confirms several points introduced in the first chapter. It supports John Barth's contention that postmodern literature revitalizes previous literary presentations of ideas. It demonstrates T. S. Eliot's premise that great writing maintains a connection with the preceding literary heritage. It also refutes Lucy Ellmann's condemnation of Palahniuk (as well as most popular novelists) for producing inferior writing. Instead of Palahniuk and other writers, particularly those associated with transgressive fiction, being considered the Generation X slackers to the Baby Boom generation of responsible writers, they should be acknowledged for introducing new, vibrant, and interesting approaches to what could be considered worn out presentations of ideas. To return to comments that are cited in the first chapter, Ellmann states, "The country that produced Melville, Twain, James now venerates King, Crichton, Grisham, Sebold and Palahniuk. Their subjects? Porn, crime, pop culture and an endless parade of out-of-body experiences. Their methods? Cliché, caricature and proto-Christian morality. Props? Corn chips, corpses, crucifixes. The agenda? Deceit: a dishonest throwing of the reader to the wolves. And the result? Readymade Hollywood scripts." This extremely astute, knowledgeable, and intelligent critic fails to see that Palahniuk is putting Barth's and Eliot's theories into practice and discovering methods of continuing the tradition of American writers such as Melville, Twain, and James. One would expect Twain to chuckle at some of Palahniuk's satires, although James would likely grimace and scour at all the sexuality. In response to Ellmann's question about cliché, caricature, and "proto-Christian morality," the response is "postmodern parody." Ellmann is actually referring in her criticism to postmodern parody through transgressive fiction. Importantly, and this is essentially the overriding point of this entire book, Palahniuk is retextualizing what it means to be human for a twenty-first-century audience. He accomplishes this in the six novels that have been discussed in the previous chapters. Through "Fight Club for Kids," Palahniuk metaphorically holds up his middle finger in an obscene gesture to critics such as Ellmann, rebelliously proclaiming his literary place in the landscape of contemporary American writing.

In *Beautiful You*, Palahniuk refers peripherally to the famous 1953 *Sexual*

Behavior in Females produced by the Kinsey Institute. This novel is not a clear-cut parody. Palahniuk describes with Kinseyian precision the female sexual response. He does so to illustrate how C. Linus Maxwell studies Penny Harrigan's and other women's sexual reactions to a line of sexual products that will allow Maxwell to rule the world. Chances are reviewers such as Ellmann do not like this book. And, Palahniuk is fine with this. There are plenty of readers who appreciate how he applies postmodern parody in his transgressive fiction. These readers are more than willing to support Palahniuk by holding up their own middle fingers toward critics who question Palahniuk's significance as a cultural advocate for a large portion of the American population or who refute his position as a relevant literary voice worthy of inclusion within the diverse American literary canon. In "Fight Club for Kids," Palahniuk might say he is only really the author of *Fight Club*, but his wide range of work demonstrates that he is indeed one of the major writers in American transgressive fiction. A Palahniuk novel such as *Beautiful You* is about a lot more than what appears on the surface. Palahniuk definitely deserves more critical respect than what he has received, but as "Fight Club for Kids" suggests, Palahniuk does not seem motivated by what the critics, the academics, or anyone except his readers say about his writing. There will be plenty of readers who see literary merit in *Beautiful You* as well as in *Haunted, Snuff, Pygmy, Tell-All, Damned*, and *Invisible Monsters Remix*.

Chapter Notes

Chapter 1

1. In *Palimpsests*, Gérard Genette provides an insightful summary of Barth's "Literature of Replenishment" to inform his own famous study of parody:

> Each new age indulges in its own characteristic (and highly ambiguous) "refusal to inherit" and chooses its own predecessors, preferably from an age older than that in which the detestable previous generation lived. The Formalists might have spoken of a refusal of the father (Balzac, Dickens) in favor of some uncle unknown until then (Henry James, Herman Melville, Lewis Carroll), or of the grandfather (Fielding, Laurence Sterne, Diderot) or great-grandfather (Ariosto, Cervantes, the baroque). The father's turn will come (again) perhaps, when the following generation has exhausted the joys of "postmodern" baroque and seeks new inspiration, or references, in the works of—who knows?—its naturalist forebears, for example. This post-postmodern age will thus be a "return" to the "discreet charms"—for use very discreet indeed—of a Zola or a Theodore Dreiser [211–12].

2. Scholars elaborate on this general meaning. In *A Poetics of Postmodernism*, Linda Hutcheon claims the Greek prefix *para* suggests "counter" or "against" as well as "beside" or "near" (26). In *Theory of Parody*, she provides a more extensive definition:

> Most theorists of parody go back to the etymological root of the term in the Greek noun *parodia*, meaning "counter-song," and stop there. A closer look at that root offers more information, however. The textual or discursive nature of parody (as opposed to satire) is clear from the *odos* part of the word, meaning song. The prefix *para* has two meanings, only one of which is usually mentioned—that of "counter" or "against." Thus parody becomes an opposition or contrast between texts. This is presumably the formal starting point for the definition's customary pragmatic component of ridicule: one text is set against another with the intent of mocking it or making it ludicrous [32].

In *Parody*, Simon Dentith states *parodia* refers to the mock-heroic poem (11). Genette writes that *parodia* equates with "singing beside"—"para" refers to "besides" and "ode" equals "chant" (9).

3. Hutcheon asserts, "Parody is a perfect postmodern form, in some senses, for it paradoxically both incorporates and challenges that which it parodies. It also forces a reconsideration of the idea of origin or originality that is compatible with other postmodern interrogations of liberal humanist assumptions" (*Poetics* 11). Moreover, she points out, "Parody seems to offer a perspective on the present and the past which allows an artist to speak *to* a discourse from *within* it, but without being totally recuperated by it" (*Poetics* 35). There are other noteworthy critics who address parody and comment on the shift in the term's meaning. In *Parody: Ancient, Modern, and Post-Modern*, Margaret Rose writes, "In all of these specific and general uses parody may be defined in general terms as *the comic refunctioning of preformed linguistic or artistic material*" (52). Although, she clarifies, "In general the parodic method is the extension, in various directions and to various degrees, of the device of laying bare the device. In its attempt to expose that illusion which it originally tries to conceal, parody has a close affinity with irony" (83). Rose argues that the transgressive brings parody back to the comic but in a black, dark, and obscene way (94–95). In *Palimpsests*, Genette offers standard terminology for the work parodied and the work as parody: "I have deliberately postponed the mention of the

fourth type of transtextuality because it, and it alone, will be of direct concern to us here. It is therefore this fourth type that I now rebaptize *hypertextuality*. By hypertextuality I mean any relationship uniting a text B (which I shall call the *hypertext*) to an earlier text A (I shall, of course, call it the *hypotext*), upon which it is grafted in a manner that is not that of commentary" (5). He adds, "What I call hypertext, then, is any text derived from a previous text" (7). In *Parody and Taste in Postwar American Television Culture*, Ethan Thompson defines parody as traditionally "the comic refunctioning of performed linguistic or artistic material," making "its target part of its own structure, in order to somehow refunction it" (9). Conversely, Fredric Jameson states in his 1991 *Postmodernism, or, the Cultural Logic of Late Capitalism* that contemporary pastiche has become parody, a neutral or "blank" imitation devoid of comic intention (17). In *Parody*, Simon Dentith contends,

> At the level of popular culture, similarly, I have suggested the remarkable presence of parody and related forms in the endless and voracious circulation of cultural material that characterizes popular entertainment, to the extent that it can be spoken of as "karaoke culture," locked in an obsessive recycling or revoicing, driven by no other logic than the need to fill those endless broadcast or satellite hours and those newspaper column inches. In a world without cultural hierarchies, parody here certainly is not—or not only—parody of the "high" by the "low," for it more typically fixes upon other products of popular culture itself, as one comedian parodies another, as pop musicians and disc jockeys sample and remix each other, as indeed karaoke itself offers the chance to mimic or act out the incessantly reproduced voices of popular music [184].

There are certainly other theorists who address parody, and the flexibility and inclusiveness of this term will continue to be debated, especially considering its importance to postmodern imaginative writing. Two other noteworthy studies of parody are Joseph A. Dane's *Parody: Critical Concepts Versus Literary Practices, Aristophanes to Sterne* and Robert P. Falk's *American Literature in Parody: A Collection of Parody, Satire, and Literary Burlesque of American Writers Past and Present*. Falk's study of parody was published in 1955 and provides a historical coverage of American literary parody.

4. Hutcheon offers variations of this definition in several statements. Importantly, she comments, "Parody, therefore, is a form of imitation, but imitation characterized by ironic inversion.... Parody is, in another formulation, repetition with critical distance, which marks difference rather than similarity" (*Theory* 6). She posits, "Parody, according to the formalist theoreticians, is the result of a conflict between realistic motivation and an aesthetic motivation which has become weak and has been made obvious.... Parody is, therefore, an exploration of difference and similarity" (*Narcissistic* 24–25). Moreover, Hutcheon argues,

> Parody, then, is its ironic "trans-contextualization" and inversion, is repetition with difference. A critical distance is implied between the backgrounded text being parodied and the new incorporating work, a distance usually signaled by irony. But this irony can be playful as well as belittling; it can be critically constructive as well as destructive. The pleasure of parody's irony comes not from humor in particular but from the degree of engagement of the reader in the intertextual "bouncing" (to use E. M. Forster's famous term) between complicity and distance [*Theory* 32].

She also stresses the importance of readers recognizing the similarity: "To experience it as an adaptation, however ... we need to recognize it as such.... In the process we inevitably fill in any gaps in the adaptation with information from the adapted text. Indeed, adapters rely on this ability to fill in the gaps.... For an adaptation to be successful in its own right, it must be so for both knowing and unknowing audiences" (*Theory* 120–21).

5. Hutcheon's key term "historiographic metafiction" is presented in *A Poetics of Postmodernism*, in which she writes, "While all forms of contemporary art and thought offer examples of this kind of postmodernist contradiction, this book (like most others on the subject) will be privileging the novel genre, and one form in particular, a form that I want to call 'historiographic metafiction.' By this I mean those well-known and popular novels which are both intensely self-reflexive and yet paradoxically also lay claim to historical events and personages" (5). Hutcheon's *Theory of Parody* is her most thorough treatment of parody, and she offers this significant clarification between parody and similar forms:

> Parody, then, is related to burlesque, travesty, pastiche, plagiarism, quotation, and allusion, but remains distinct from them. It shares with them a restriction of focus: its repetition is always of another discursive text. The ethos of the act of repetition can vary, but its "target" is always with satire, which is extramural (social, moral) in its ameliorative aim to hold up to ridicule the vices and follies of mankind, with an eye to their correction? For the confusion certainly

does exist. Parody has been implicitly or explicitly called a form of satire by many theorists.... For some, this is a way of not limiting parody to an aesthetic context, of opening it up to social and moral dimensions.... Just calling parody satire seems a little too simple as an instant way to give parody a social function [43].

Significantly, in several commentaries, Hutcheon claims that irony, satire, comedy, or any other feature can be included within parody, with parody serving as the overriding form and the other quality determining tone or intent. Noteworthy is that she differentiates parody and intertextuality by claiming intertextuality is static and parody is dynamic, stating point blank, "My pragmatic perspective would not, however, make parody into a synonym of intertextuality" (*Theory* 23). Regardless, intertextuality is generally associated with parody in that two or more texts are interrelated by form, style, and/or content.

6. Moreover, Jenks writes,

An analysis of the concept "transgression" will take us along a series of continua, both vertical and horizontal, such as sacred—profane; good-evil; normal-pathological; sane-mad; purity-danger; high-low; centre-periphery and so on. It is critical to realize that these continua can be understood and acted in relation to as if they were absolute, as if they were indices of stratification, and as if they were dichotomies. Indeed, for a lot of the people for a lot of the time this is exactly how they are understood. Such paradoxes contribute further to the complexity of the idea. Although always appearing to make reference to clear-cut distinctions transgressions are manifestly situation-specific and vary considerably across social space and through time. Our analysis of transgression will take us through a variety of empirical contexts such as crime, sexuality, ritual, carnival, art, culture and madness [2–3].

Two other excellent books about transgression are Robin Mookerjee's *Transgressive Fiction: The New Satiric Tradition* and David Allison, Mark Roberts, and Allen Weiss's *Sade and the Narrative of Transgression*. Both are thorough in their treatment of transgression.

7. Laura J. Williams's "The Fresh Take" (2.2, 2004) once located at www.annarborpaper.com/content/issue24/palahniuk_24.html is no longer available online. Not only is Williams's review mentioned in the frequently referenced "Chuck Palahniuk" entry in *Wikipedia* and other online sites, but it is also cited in Thomas Austenfeld's "Can Terrorism Be Satirized? The Case of Chuck Palahniuk's *Pygmy*," Jesse Kavaldo's "The Fiction of Self-Destruction: Chuck Palahniuk, Closet Moralist," and other academic publications.

8. There are several extremely academic treatments of Palahniuk that focus on his philosophy, his writing, and his popularity. Three excellent collections of essays are Jeffrey Sartain's *Sacred and Immoral: On the Writings of Chuck Palahniuk*, Cynthia Rubin and Lance Rubin's *Reading Chuck Palahniuk: American Monsters and Literary Mayhem*, Francisco Collado-Rodriguez's *Chuck Palahniuk: Fight Club, Invisible Monsters, Choke*, and Read Mercer Schuchardt's *You Do Not Talk About Fight Club: I Am Jack's Completely Unauthorized Essay Collection*. Also worth consulting is the fall/winter 2005 issue of *Stirrings Still: The International Journal of Existential Literature* devoted to Chuck Palahniuk. These include helpful lists of the many Palahniuk interviews, and Palahniuk is certainly a loquacious, gregarious, and omnipresent celebrity popping up in various media venues. Schuchardt provides an excellent overview concerning Palahniuk's mass appeal in his introduction to the collected essays. This introduction, entitled "Chuck Palahniuk: Existentialist Paramedic," is worth reading for an insightful discussion of Palahniuk's mass appeal in contemporary American culture.

Chapter 2

1. The characters create essentially what Audre Lorde coined biomythography, a balance between objective and subjective presentation of autobiography. In *Postmodern American Fiction*, Paula Geyh, Fred Leebron, and Andrew Levy devote a chapter to the postmodern genre that blends fact and fiction, and in the introduction to this section, they provide this definition of biomythography:

The selections in this section also explore the combination of memoir and fiction, a hybrid that has been particularly prevalent during the postmodern era. An excerpt from Audre Lorde's *Zami: A New Spelling of My Name* (1982) illustrates how memoir often takes on narrative shape akin to that of fiction, while the content of the excerpt oppositely shows how individuals use fictional constructions to make order of real-life events. The result is a piece of literature that its author labels "biomythography," a form that seeks a balance between the mimetic and imaginative functions of autobiography [126].

2. Pertinent academic articles about *Haunted* include Steffen Hantre's "Blood on the Bookstore Floor: Chuck Palahniuk and the Case of

the Fainting Reader," Calum Kerr's "On Palahniuk's *Haunted*," and David Simmons and Nicola Allen's "Reading Chuck Palahniuk's *Survivor* and *Haunted* as a Critique of 'The Culture Industry.'" In "Hauntedness: Edgar Allan Poe and Chuck Palahniuk," Philip Coleman addresses Palahniuk's imitation of several of Poe's gothic literary strategies and spends time on the comparison between "The Masque of the Red Death" and *Haunted*. Coleman refers to Dara Downey's significant comments in her review of *Haunted* in the *Irish Journal of Gothic Horror Studies*: "[I]t is difficult to bring oneself to say that the book is an overall success.... Beneath its aggressive postmodern sensibilities, and its commitment to stylistic playfulness and rebellion, lies an assumption that [Palahniuk] is writing for a male audience, presenting woman in a manner that leaves the old dichotomies intact" (qtd. in Coleman 267).

3. In "The 'Guts' Effect," Palahniuk describes the creation of "Guts": "No one fainted the first time I read the short story, 'Guts.' This was on a Tuesday night, in the writer's workshop where my friends and I have shared our work since 1991. Each week, I would read another of the short stories I planned to include in a novel to be called *Haunted*. My goal was to create horror around very ordinary things: carrots, candles, swimming pools. Microwave popcorn. Bowling balls." He adds, "I told them how the three-act story of 'Guts' was based on three true anecdotes. Two had happened to friends, and the last had happened to a man I'd met while attending sex addict support groups to research my fourth novel. They were three funny, gradually more upsetting true stories about experiments with masturbation gone wrong. Horribly wrong. Nightmarishly wrong." Alan Slade discusses the interesting source for the most famous story in *Haunted*: "The story of St. Gut Free, for example, has its model in a legal case, famously pursued by 2004 Democratic U.S. Vice-Presidential candidate John Edwards. Edwards was vilified by conservatives in the press as a trial lawyer who enriched himself by pursuing frivolous suits like the case of a young girl whose intestines were sucked through her anus by a swimming pool pump. In our world, finding violence is easy since it is everywhere" (66). More than fifty people have supposedly either passed out or have vomited during Palahniuk's readings of "Guts," and per Internet reports, this number keeps increasing.

4. This citation was initially available from "Chuck Q&A: May 2004" from *The Cult: The Official Chuck Palahniuk Website*; however, this link currently no longer exists. This information about "hidden gun" and "ticking clock" is provided by 7zark7 at Quake3World.com at the following address: http://www.quake3world.com/forum/viewtopic.php?f=1&t=20871.

5. In my discussion of particular stories, I cite quotations from the Norton Critical Edition of *The Decameron* translated by Mark Musa and Peter Bondanella, but this edition only includes selections from Boccaccio's work. I also consulted but did not cite quotations from two notable editions of *The Decameron* by Richard Aldington (1930) and G. H. McWilliam (1972) that contained all one hundred of the tales.

6. Palahniuk states specifically, "In a way, that is the opposite of the American Dream: to get so rich you can rise above the rabble, all those people on the freeway or, worse, *the bus*. No, the dream is a big house, off alone somewhere. A penthouse, like Howard Hughes. Or a mountaintop castle, like William Randolph Hearst. Some lovely isolated nest where you can invite only the rabble you like. An environment you can control, free from conflict and pain. Where you rule" (*Stranger* xv). Referring to several of his other books, he adds, "After we're miserable enough—like the narrator in his Fight Club condo, or the narrator isolated by her own beautiful face in *Invisible Monsters*—we destroy our lovely nest and force ourselves back into the larger world.... You spend time alone, building this lovely world where you control, control, control everything. You let the telephone ring. The emails pile up. You stay in your story world until you destroy it. Then you come back to be with other people" (*Stranger* xv–xvi). The need for human connection, for community, is certainly the case in both Palahniuk's and Boccaccio's texts.

Chapter 3

1. Concerning reviews, Owen Williams and Brian Gallagher state in articles about the proposed movie version that the novel addresses male bonding. Worth acknowledging is Read Mercer Schuchardt's essay "A Copy of a Copy of a Copy." Although Schuchardt does not treat *Snuff*, he explains how *Fight Club*, *The Matrix*, and *American Beauty* correspond with Pink Floyd's *The Wall*.

2. Additional information may clarify this complex theory. Baudrillard comments that the idea of simulacra "is no longer a question of a false representation of reality (ideology) but of concealing the fact that the real is no longer real, and thus of saving the reality principle" (*Simulacra* 12–13). Baudrillard describes simulation as this process:

> Such is simulation, insofar as it is opposed to representation. Representation starts from the principle that the sign and the real are equivalent (even if this equiva-

lence is utopian, it is a fundamental axiom). Simulation, on the contrary, stems from the utopia of the idea of equivalence, *from the radical negation of the sign as value,* from the sign as reversion and death sentence of every reference. Whereas representation attempts to absorb simulation by interpreting it as false representation, simulation envelops the whole edifice of representation itself a simulacrum.

Such would be the successive phases of the image:
    it is the reflection of a profound reality;
    it masks and denatures a profound reality;
    it masks the *absence* of a profound reality;
    it has no relation to any reality whatsoever: it is its own simulacrum.

In the first case, the image is a *good* appearance—representation of the sacramental order. In the second, it is an evil appearance—it is of the order of maleficence. In the third, it plays at being an appearance—it is of the order of sorcery. In the fourth, it is no longer in the order of appearance, but of simulation [*Simulacra* 6].

This process is summarized by Richard Appignanesi and Chris Garratt as "(1) It is the **reflection** of a basic reality, (2) It *masks* and **perverts** a basic reality, (3) It marks the **absence** of a basic reality, and (4) It bears **no relation** to any reality whatever—it is its own pure simulacrum" (54–55).

3. Baudrillard adds about hyperrealism, "Never again will the real have the chance to produce itself—such is the vital function of the model in a system of death, or rather of anticipated resurrection, that no longer even gives the event of death a chance. A hyperreal henceforth sheltered from the imaginary, and from any distinction between the real and the imaginary, leaving room only for the orbital recurrence of models and for the simulated generation of differences" (*Simulacra* 2–3).

4. For the graphic definition, Branch states, "The legal standard for a gang bang is called 'instances of sex,' meaning any hole—her cunt, ass, or mouth—and any instrument—your dick, finger, or tongue—but for only one minute" (55).

5. The *Wikipedia* entry for Houston mentions the actual number of men may have been closer to 100 and provides the following background concerning the performer:

Houston is known for her work in Metro's *The World's Biggest Gangbang 3: The Houston 500* (1999), a movie in which she reportedly had sex with over 620 men without interruption on February 6, 1999. Although this claim is widely disputed by many eye witnesses, and the real number is said to have likely been around 100, [sic] Nevertheless, it broke the Guinness World Record of 521 men set by fellow big-bust porn actress/stripper Spontaneous Xtasy the year before, in 1998. Prior to this event, she spent 45 days in jail after turning herself in to Ventura County law enforcement for an outstanding DUI charge. Houston's on-screen performances cater heavily to anal sex, double & triple penetration, fellatio, and lesbian encounters. During 1999, she reportedly earned over one million dollars and brought in $20,000 a week from strip club appearances.

Houston also notes she gave proceeds from the film *United We Lay* to the Free Speech Coalition. She talks about her gang bang experience briefly in "After Porn Ends Houston 500 Gang Bang."

6. Articles referring to the proliferation of actual fight clubs include "Real-Life Fight Club in San Jose Pits Men Against Each Other in Dangerous Hand-To-Hand Combat," "Fight Clubs Hit High-School Locker Rooms," "Utah Shadowboxes with 'Fight Club' Phenomenon," and "Sixth-Graders Expelled for 'Fight Club.'" There are many accounts of the fight clubs starting all over the country in response to Palahniuk's novel. Neither *Snuff* nor any of Palahniuk's other novels has had such a grassroots following.

7. The sources reporting the upcoming film include Owen Williams's "Daryl Hannah Is Up to Snuff" in *Empireonline*, Brian Gallagher's "Daryl Hannah and Tom Sizemore Join *Snuff*" in *MovieWeb*, and Simon Reynolds's "Daryl Hannah to Play 'Snuff' Porn Star" in *Digital Spy*.

8. Baudrillard comments, "At the heart of information one finds history haunted by its own disappearance. At the hub of hi-fi, music is haunted by its disappearance. At the core of experimentation, science is haunted by the disappearance of its object. Pivotal to pornography is a sexuality haunted by its own disappearance. Everywhere it is the same stereophonic effect, the absolute proximity of the real: the same effect of simulation" (*Illusion*).

Chapter 4

1. Information about the crash is available through the "Asian Airlines Flight 214" entry in *Wikipedia*. In "KTVU Fires News Producers After Asiana Gaffe," Matt O'Brien reports what occurred at the television station after the names were misrepresented. Palahniuk would never do something as tasteless, tactless, and cruel as to state these names in any of his fiction. Palahniuk has discretion. The point is, however, Palahniuk is not afraid to recognize

incidents such as this occur in American media. The actual broadcast of these names can be located online.

2. Several postmodern theorists contend that nostalgia is only the backward glance into history, not necessarily applying the past, or what Fredric Jameson terms "pastness" (19), to the present. In *A Poetics of Postmodernism*, Linda Hutcheon defends parody, particularly its relationship with irony, against this kind of critical attack:

> Yet we have seen that [Fredric] Jameson and [Terry] Eagleton, in their recent writings on postmodernism, attack it for being nostalgic in its relation to the past. But if nostalgia connotes evasion of the present, idealization of a (fantasy) past, or a recovery of that past as edenic, then the postmodernist ironic rethinking of history is definitely not nostalgic. It critically confronts the past with the present, and vice versa. In a direct reaction against the tendency of our times to value only the new and novel, it returns us to a re-thought past to see what, if anything, is of value in that past experience. But the critique of its irony is double-edged: the past and the present are judged in each other's light [39].

In *Content of the Form: Narrative Discourse and Historical Representation*, Hayden White also provides an excellent study of postmodern nostalgia.

3. This definition of the hero corresponds, of course, to Joseph Campbell's seminal *The Hero with a Thousand Faces*, a benchmark study of mythological/archetypal criticism. Campbell explains how a hero moves from separation to initiation to return, during which the hero faces, aided by helpers, a series of tests, experiences a dark night of the soul, transforms through apotheosis, and may or may not achieve the boon or elixir.

4. Several 1970s karate films are available through *YouTube*. Other notable trailers available are "Sting of the Dragon Masters," "The Chinese Boxer," and "The King of Kung Fu" (featuring Bruce Lee). In particular, many full-length Shaw Brother productions are available through *YouTube*.

5. These films delineated Asians significantly as the Other in the Us-and-Them binary relations or attitudes toward subalterns described by Edward Said, Gayatri Chakravorty Spivak, and other postcolonial theorists. Said's theory is explained in *Orientalism* and *Culture and Imperialsim*; Spivak's theory is pronounced in "Can the Subaltern Speak?" Two helpful criticisms of these are Valerie Kennedy's *Edward Said: A Critical Introduction* and Mark Sanders *Gayatri Chakravorty Spivak: Live Theory*. An entire essay could be devoted to how these postcolonial theories apply to Pygmy, and more important, how they are demonstrated during the mock UN session.

6. In *Film and Stereotype*, Jorg Schweinitz draws on the 1920s study by Walter Lippmann and 1930s work of Daniel Katz and Kenneth W. Braly to define racial stereotypes: "To simplify ... stereotypes are standardized conceptions of people, primarily based on an individual's belonging to a category (usually race, nation, professional role, social class, or gender) or the possession of characteristic traits symbolizing one of these categories. This concept focuses on belief patterns and emphasized their guiding influence on attitudes and perceptions" (4–5). Schweinitz provides the following classifications of stereotypes:

> The different approaches within the social sciences attribute to these belief patterns an entire battery of optional characteristics weighing in differently on individual definitions. Stereotypes are thought to be (1) the relatively permanent mental fixtures of an individual (*stability*); (2) intersubjectively distributed within certain social formations, for which they assume the functions of consensus building and standardization (*conformity*); (3); therefore, (3) they do not, or only seldom, rely on personal experience but are primarily socially communicated (*secondhand nature*); in addition, (4) they are limited to the simple combination of a few characteristics (*reduction*) and (5) accompanied by strong feelings (*affective coloration*). Finally, (6) functioning automatically, stereotypes are considered to substantially interfere with the processes of perception and judgment, which they influence and even determine (*cliché effect*). Regarding the function of stereotypes, the term is therefore generally associated with making judgments, and (7) stereotypes are often ascribed the status of inappropriate judgments (*inadequacy*) [5].

The stereotyping of Asians has its base in the infamous defense of colonialism *La Réforme intellectuelle et morele* (1871) in which Joseph-Ernest Renan states, "The regeneration of the inferior or degenerate races, by the superior races is part of the providential order of things for humanity ... countries ... like China, are crying aloud for foreign conquest.... Nature has made a race of workers, the Chinese race, who have wonderful manual dexterity, and almost no sense of honor; govern them with justice, levying from them, in return for the blessing of such a government, an ample allowance for the conquering race, and they will be satisfied" (qtd. in "Postcolonialism").

7. The following paragraphs concerning Dorfman are modified from my dissertation

entitled "The Reification of History in the Novels of Ariel Dorfman" completed in 1994.

8. Dorfman posits that "the mass media have assisted the dominant class in trying to recover Paradise, and attain sin-free production ... and once innocence is processed by the entertainment media, it fosters the development of advanced capitalist society, it is identified as the center of innocence within this purified world" (*How* 97). This is a world in which there are strict differentiations, where "conflict has never a social base, but is conceived in terms of good versus bad, lucky verses unlucky, and intelligent versus stupid" (*How* 96), one in which those who fail to follow the capitalistic dream are exiled and left without a sense of history or of collectivity. Therefore, Disney's comics might seem targeted toward a child audience, but they are ultimately aimed at the entire populace and they reflect America's projection of an ideal Third World. To question the Disney allegory is comparable to committing cultural blasphemy, challenging a myth that has been trusted as factually correct. Tragically for the third-world population, to believe the Disney dream is synonymous with sacrificing any active role it may have in determining its present or its future.

9. *Pygmy* is organized as Pygmy's dispatches to his homeland. The following is an example how Palahniuk starts each epistolary: "Begins here first account of operative me, agent number 67, one arrival Midwestern American airport greater _____ area. Flight _____. Date _____. Priority mission top success to complete. Code name: Operation Havoc" (1).

10. An anti-capitalism motif clearly runs throughout this novel, and Pygmy views Wal-Mart as a microcosm of the American free-market consumer system:

For official record, squirrel maze of retail distribution center puzzle of competition warring objects, all improved, all package with fire colors. Area divided into walls constructed from objects, all tinted color to grab eye. All object printed: Love me. Look me. Million speaking objects, begging. Crown American consumer with power of king, to rescue choose and give home or abandon here for expire. Word label blow sharp into ear, loud into eye. Pander hand to take. Dying objects. All here, useful life winding down in clock ticks. Dying objects. Dying buyer. Dying slave woman "Doris." Desperate how sad [10].

11. Pygmy's final comment about the sodomy is sarcastic and repetitive of Trevor's own speech: "Electric-bolt eyes of bully bleeding water. Blue star of fighting anus leak blood into thin stripes down white legs. Everywhere patriotic. Here so great American nation" (18). Pygmy describes his response, and he perhaps unconsciously reveals anger by spitting back Trevor's profanity: "Weapon of this agent, stabbing, hollowing blue hold, scraping friction until full drive deep inside whole long of self. Next then retreating to pop free, dripping. Next again, stab full deep. All time, mouth of operative me flogging with English word *bitch*. Flogging close into cold blue ear, into curtain of clear-yellow hair swinging, flogging, 'Bitch' and 'Bitch' and 'Bitch'" (18).

12. Pygmy describes the baptism in all its frenzy, and this is clearly Palahniuk satirizing organized religion in this novel: "Mouth of worship leader say, 'We wash clean this child, born into the bogus faith of a false prophet. The misguided lies of a dead Mohammad or Buddha or Hindi.' Say, 'In this immersing, let this child die and be reborn in the name of the one true everlasting Lord.' Say, 'Let this death be not in vain, but many this tiny child arise in perfect union with Jesus Christ'" (27). Pygmy continues, "For official record, next American Christian vipers no able venture into water bin. Only witness, so fast occur. Vipers seated steps below bin level, below fake blood statue, below burning paraffin and bunched genital of plant life. View from vipers, witness leader man sunk into water. Gone. Next then water splash froth, wash out edge of bin. Next then, water smooth still flat. No bubble. No viper move, only await" (29).

Chapter 5

1. Other initial reviews of *Tell-All* include the following comments. Tim Robey points out, "There's a serious danger of smugness to Palahniuk's tone—we're invited to sneer at the vanity of awards ... but the more likely reaction is a shrug. What his caustic game never gives us is a reason to care." Corey Redekop writes, "A respected author with his best days behind him is a sad, depressing prospect. And with his 11th novel, American author Chuck Palahniuk has become very sad indeed." Lastly, Chris Talbott warns, "The obstacle in *Tell-All* is that most of the names being dropped belong to people who had their 15 minutes of fame 50 years ago, and without a passing knowledge of yesteryear's celebs, the humor can be lost in translation." A writer for *Kirkus Reviews* states, "Both the title and the boldface recall the golden age of the gossip columnist."

2. The term "carnival" is applied in a metaphorical manner as M. Keith Booker does in his study of transgression and the carnivalesque entitled *Techniques of Subversion in Mod-*

ern Literature: Transgression, Abjection, and the Carnivalesque:
I employ the notion of "carnival" in a strictly metaphorical sense. This use of the carnival is somewhat more general than that of Bakhtin, and is much closer to the view espoused by Peter Stallybrass and Allon White, who generalize the Bakhtinian "carnival" into their notion of "transgression," which involves a violation of the rules of hierarchies in any one of these categories of hierarchies.... [A violation] has important consequences in the others as well. In their opinion, then, "the idea of carnival as an analytic category can only be fruitful if it is displaced into the broader concept of symbolic inversion and transgression" [18].
Booker clarifies, "Stallybrass and White particularly emphasize the way in which oppressed, marginal groups are systematically identified with aspects of existence ... that are deemed unpleasant by the dominant group, which in turn seeks to distance itself from such facts of life through oppression and rejection of the group with which those facts are identified" (13).

3. Martinson describes the controversy surrounding "Julia":
The cauldron really boiled over in 1976–1977, when Muriel Gardner Buttinger came forth and accused Hellman of taking her life and fictionalizing it in "Julia," Hellman's depiction of a friend's martyrdom in Nazi Germany. Gardner's life, told in her book *Code Name: "Mary,"* seemed an exact parallel to Julia's. The furor gained momentum when it was discovered that a lawyer of Hellman's, Wolf Schwabacher, also was a close friend of Gardner's. This made it possible that Hellman heard of the outlines of Gardner's life through him, and then adapted into to her "memoir." Hellman stoutly denied the accusations and held firm as to the "shape" of the story, admitting she had changed names and details because many people in the story still lived. Gardner swore Hellman never contacted her to resolve the issue, but Blair Clark wrote that he and Hellman had an appointment to see Gardner, which Gardner canceled when she realized Hellman was going to bring a lawyer with her. Hellman, as litigious as she was confrontational, used legal means to settle disputes as her frailty diminished her capacity to fight back [353–54].

4. A summary of gossip journalism, comparable to what was offered for 1970s karate films in the preceding chapter, is not needed in this essay because the topic is treated throughout the novel. There are, however, several publications about gossip journalism that explore the tenaciously cut-throat mentality of reporters to uncover sensational stories. These publications are very interesting and are worth consulting: Samantha Barbas's *The First Lady of Hollywood: A Biography of Louella Parsons*, Simon Michael Bessie's *Jazz Journalism: The Story of the Tabloid Newspapers*, Daniel Cohen's *Yellow Journalism: Scandal, Sensationalism, and Gossip in the Media*, Jennifer Frost's *Hedda Hopper's Hollywood: Celebrity Gossip and American Conservatism*, John Langer's *Tabloid Television: Popular Journalism and the "Other News,"* Paula Morton's *Tabloid Valley: Supermarket News and American Culture*, and Henry Scott's *Shocking True Story: The Rise and Fall of* Confidential, *"America's Most Scandalous Scandal Magazine."* Also worth noting are Bob Batchelor's *Cult Pop Culture: How the Fringe Became Mainstream*, Bill Sloan's *"I Watched a Wild Hog Eat My Baby!" A Colorful History of Tabloids and Their Cultural Impact*, and Peter Dahlgren and Colin Sparks's *Journalism and Popular Culture*.

5. Palahniuk has the opportunity through these to play with taste and decorum. As Hazie continues, "What **Walter Winchell** calls 'stiff standing up'[at a funeral]" (25); "What **Hedda Hopper** calls a 'funeral flirtation.'**Louella Parsons** a 'graveside groom.' **Walter Winchell** a 'casket crasher'" (28); "Miss Kathie's goal to reduce until she becomes what **Lolly Parsons** calls nothing but 'tan and bones.'What **Hedda Hopper** calls 'lipstick skeleton.' A 'beautifully coiffed skull' as **Elsa Maxwell** calls **Katharine Hepburn**" (33). Hazie mentions, "This prattle, further example of what **Walter Winchell** means by the term 'toast-masturbating.' Or 'laud mouthing,' according to **Hedda Hopper**. According to **Louella Parsons**, 'implying gilt'" (58); "More 'projectile praise' and 'force fawning' or 'compliment vomit,' in the eyes of **Cholly Knickerbocker**" (59). In a longer passage, Hazie writes, "According to **Walter Winchell**, 'menoposture' refers to the ramrod straight backbone of a **Joan Crawford** or an **Ethan Berryman**, a lady of a certain age whose spine never touches the back of any chair. A **Helen Hayes**, who stands straight as a military cadet, her shoulders back in defiance of gravity and osteoporosis. That crucial age when older picture stars become what **Hedda Hopper** calls 'fossilidealized,' the living example of proper manners and self-restraint. Some **Katharine Hepburn** or **Bette Davis** illustration of noble hard work and Yankee ambition" (46–47).

Chapter 6

1. This was Palahniuk's plan. Madison is actually thirteen in *Damned*, and Margaret

starts out as eleven and has her twelfth birthday in Blume's novel.

2. These sections include Canto XXXI in which "The horrible giants, whom Jove menaces / E'en now from out the heavens when he thunders" (44–45); Canto XXXII in which Traitors are frozen in hell; and Canto XXXIV in which Lucifer is frozen but chews Judas, Brutus, and Cassius in his mouths.

3. Other demons include Astarte (50), Tartak (50), Mevet (51), Lilith (51), Reshev (51), Azazel (51), Behemoth (51), Cernunnos (81), Mastema (81), and Akibel (147). Similar to Dante's hell, Palahniuk's also has Harpies (115). Satirically, Palahniuk includes as demons Robert Mapplethorpe (51) and Charles Darwin (82).

4. Margaret also worries about menstruating. One exemplary section is *"Are you there God? It's me, Margaret. Gretchen, my friend, got her period. I'm so jealous God. I hate myself for being so jealous, but I am. I wish you'd help me just a little. Nancy's sure she's going to get it soon, too. And if I'm last I don't know what I'll do. Oh please God. I just want to be normal"* (100). When she begins menstruating, Margaret, always polite and courteous, states, *"Are you still there God? It's me, Margaret. I know you're there God. I know you wouldn't have missed this for anything! Thank you God. Thanks an awful lot...."* (149). This is the final paragraph in the book and displays Margaret as subservient whereas Margaret is openly defiant at the end of *Damned*.

5. Two other passages clearly show Madison is more defiant and reactionary than Margaret. In the first, Madison asserts,

> Are you there, Satan? It's me, Madison. I hope this won't sound too confusing, but I do hereby and forever abandon abandoning all hope. Honestly, I give up on giving up. I'm just not cut out to be some hopeless, disillusioned wretch with no aspirations for the rest of eternity, sprawled catatonic in my own feces on a cold stone floor. In all probability the Human Genome Project will, someday, find that I carry some recessive gene for optimism, because despite all my best efforts I still can't scrape together even a couple days of hopelessness. Future scientists will call it the Pollyanna Syndrome, and if forced to guess, I'd say that mine has been a way-long case history of chasing rainbows [113].

At the end of the novel, Madison gloats, *"Are you there, Satan? It's me, Madison. Whether you are or you are not, it hardly matters ... because I am here. The prodigal daughter. Little Maddy Spencer has come home to roost"* (200). This passage in particular demonstrates Madison has gone from timidity about her situation to belligerence and ultimately rebellion.

6. Nancy Wheeler's perceptions of *Playboy* and of kissing shape Margaret's sexual standards. There are several passages in which these mostly patriarchal standards are set: "'I'm growing already,' Nancy said, sticking her chest out. 'In a few years I'm going to look like one of those girls in *Playboy*.' Well, I didn't think so, but I didn't say anything. My father gets *Playboy* and I've seen those girls in the middle. Nancy looked like she had a long way to go. Almost as far as me" (6–7); "'Watch this.' Nancy grabbed her bed pillow and embraced it. She gave it a long kiss. When she was done she threw the pillow on the bed. 'It's important to experiment, so when the time comes you're all ready. I'm going to be a great kisser some day'" (7); and "'When you grow you'll change your mind,' Nancy told [Janie]. 'You'll want everybody to see you. Like those girls in *Playboy*'" (71). These are exactly the representations of femininity toward which Madison is responding, and she subsequently deconstructs these masochistic sexual objectifications of women and empowers herself as a third-wave feminist.

7. She continues, "Again here's a reference to my Influences of Western History textbook—for a long time after puberty, it's like the dark ages that fell between the Athenian Enlightenment and the Italian Renaissance. Girls get their boobs and forget they were ever so gutsy and smart. Boys, too, can display their own brand of clever and funny behavior, but let them get their first erection and they go complete moron for the next sixty years. For both genders, adolescence occurs as a kind of Ice Age of Dumbness" (13). An interesting comparison is between this note and the one preceding it about *Playboy* and kissing.

8. This crucial section of the novel alludes directly both to Blume and to *The Breakfast Club*:

> No matter how hard I try to resist the impulse, I keep hoping I'll still have my first menstruation. I keep hoping I'll grow really big boobs, like Babette in the adjacent cell. Or reach a hand into my short pocket and find a Xanax. I cross my fingers that if a demon dunks me in a vat of boiling lava I'll get thrown together naked with River Phoenix, and that he'll say I'm cute and try to kiss me.
> The problem is, in Hell there is no hope. Who Do I Think I Am? In a thousand words.... I don't have a clue, but I'll start by abandoning hope. Please help me, Satan. That would make me so happy. Help me give up my addiction to hope. Thank you [21].

9. Referring to sinners who can relinquish all hope, almost wishing she could do some-

thing similar, Madison mentions, "From another cell, fairly close by, someone begins to scream. Alone in their cells, other people slump in the classic postures of catatonic stupor, wearing the soiled costumes of Venetian doges, Napoleonic vivandiers, Maori headhunters. They've clearly been able to abandon all hope and clutch their filthy cage bars. They've flailed and thrashed in complete resignation, and now lie stained, staring, and motionless. The lucky bastards" (25). She also comments, "Increasingly, I'm not sure to which I was more addicted: hope or Xanax" (23), as well as "There it is, again—that nagging tendency to hope. My addiction" (33).

Chapter 7

1. There are several noteworthy academic articles concerning Shannon's motivation in *Invisible Monsters*: Sidney Sondergard's "Chuck Palahniuk and the Semiotics of Personal Doom: the Novelist as Escape Artist," Andrew Ng's "Destruction and the Discourse of Deformity: *Invisible Monsters* and the Ethics of Atrocity," Andrew Slade's "On Mutilation: the Sublime Body of Chuck Palahniuk's Fiction," Scott Ash's "Going to the Body: The Tension of Freedom/Restraint in Palahniuk's Novels," and James Dolph's "Behind the Queens' Veils: Power Versus Powerlessness in C. S. Lewis's *Till We have Faces* and Palahniuk's *Invisible Monsters*." Kathryn Hume also addresses this novel in *Aggressive Fictions: Reading the Contemporary Novel*.

2. There are, of course, the references to Shannon's father abusing Shane, and one cannot minimize or ignore the inappropriateness of this behavior. In one section, Brandy Alexander reveals to Shannon, "My father used to sit on my bed some nights ... and wake me up" (154). There is also the questioning of the father's integrity by feeding his hogs leftover snack cakes and other sweets before selling them at market (238) as well as his looting boxcars of a wrecked train, stealing many boxes of butterscotch pudding, which Shannon now hates (160). The father did other morally questionable actions—such as putting ice in meat and rigging potato sacks (152–58)—but he did so, Shane admits, to help provide for his family. Shane comments that his father was not a "bad person" but did what was needed to take care of his family (154).

3. *Fight Club* contains many pithy aphorisms broadcast all over the Internet. The conversation via cards on top of the Space Needle between Seth, Shannon, and Brandy provides some of the most famous lines in the novel about self-identity. Shannon states, "While I watch my future trapped in the suicide net, Brandy reads another card from Seth. '*We are all self-composting.*' I write on another card from the future, and Brandy reads it. '*When we don't know who to hate, we hate ourselves.*' An updraft lifts my worst fears from the suicide net and sails them away. Seth writes and Brandy reads. '*You have to keep recycling yourself.*' I write and Brandy reads. '*Nothing of me is original. I am the combined effort of everybody I've ever known*'" (39).

4. Furthermore, Johnson claims, "That the McFarland parents remain ignorant of the true events swirling around their family while overreacting to perceived threats reveals the conservative, reactionary nature of the nuclear family. Shannon marvels that the same parents who banished Shane from the house the evening they learned of his illness (telling him he could go to the health department the next day) could be the same one who march in the PFLAG parades" (69–70).

5. Johnson points out, however, "Shannon's perpetual desire for personal reinvention pushes her beyond Evie's shallow narcissism, and she begins to see the ridiculous role she and Evie play in the construction of beauty culture" (62).

6. Shannon continues, "And I remember my underwear. Sorry, Mom, sorry, God, but I was wearing just this little patch up front with an elastic string waist and just one string running down the crack and back around to the bottom of the patch up front. Flesh-tone" (260). The apology is tinged with sarcasm. In another section of the novel, Shannon admits her vanity: "Right now, looking at flashes of Brandy beside me in Manus's car, I know what it is I loved about her. What I love is myself. Brandy Alexander just looks exactly the way I looked before the accident. Why wouldn't she? She's my brother" (191). This egotistical self-pity is reiterated in another passage: '*I love Seth Thomas so much I have to destroy him. I overcompensate by worshipping the queen supreme. Seth will never love me. No one will ever love me ever again*" (39). The most famous line in the novel illustrates Shannon's sarcasm: "Birds ate my face" (256).

7. Butler states specifically,

> In this sense, *gender* is not a noun, but neither is it a set of free-floating attributes, for we have seen that the substantive effect of gender is performatively produced and compelled by the regulatory practices of gender coherence. Hence, within the inherited discourse of the metaphysics of substance, gender proves to be performative—that is, constituting the identity it is purported to be. In this sense, gender is always a doing, though not a doing by a subject who might be said to preexist the deed. The challenge

for rethinking gender categories outside of the metaphysics of substance will have to consider the relevance of Nietzsche's claim in *On the Genealogy of Morals* that "there is no 'being' behind doing, effecting, becoming; 'the doer' is merely a fiction added to the deed—the deed is everything." In an application that Nietzsche himself would not have anticipated or condoned, we might state as a corollary: There is no gender identity behind the expressions of gender; that identity is performatively constituted by the very "expressions" that are said to be its results [24–25].
8. Butler continues,
This perpetual displacement constitutes a fluidity of identities that suggests an openness to resignification and recontextualization; parodic proliferation deprives hegemonic culture and its critics of the claim to naturalized or essentialist gender identities. Although the gender meanings taken up in these parodic styles are clearly part of hegemonic, misogynist culture, they are nevertheless denaturalized and mobilized through their parodic recontextualization. As imitations which effectively displace the meaning of the original, they imitate the myth of originality itself. In the place of an original identification which serves as a determining cause, gender identity might be reconceived as a personal/cultural history of received meanings subject to a set of imitative practices which refer laterally to other imitations and which, jointly, construct the illusion of a primary and interior gendered self or parody the mechanism of that construction [138].
She concludes concerning gender parody, "Parody by itself is not subversive, and there must be a way to understand what makes certain kinds of parodic repetitions effectively disruptive, truly troubling, and which repetitions become domesticated and recirculated as instruments of cultural hegemony. A typology of actions would clearly not suffice, for parodic displacement, indeed, parodic laughter, depends on a context and reception in which subversive confusions can be fostered" (139).
9. This information was gathered from less-than-scholarly sites, but considering the subject matter, the sources were the only ones available. The sources included websites such as AdultDVDTalk.com and LukeisBack.com.

Chapter 8

1. In an article published in the spring 2012 issue of *Postscript: The Journal of the Philological Association of the Carolinas*, I argue *Fight Club* is a working-class novel. The fourth, fifth, and sixth paragraphs are adapted from that article.

Chapter 9

1. Summaries of Booth's and Bitzer's theories are taken from my thesis entitled "*Lady Chatterley's Lover* as a Rhetorical Response: Justification for D. H. Lawrence's Mask of Oliver Mellors." I have also applied Bitzer's theory concerning rhetorical situation in several papers related to F. Scott Fitzgerald's letters to his daughter Scottie, Fitzgerald's short story "An Alcoholic Case," and Raymond Carver's stories dealing with alcoholism.
2. While writing this chapter, I consulted several foundational studies related to literature as rhetoric. There are several works worth reading in this area. These include I. A. Richards's *The Philosophy of Rhetoric*, Kenneth Burke's *A Rhetoric of Motives*, Burke's *Language as Symbolic Action: Essays on Life, Literature, and Method*, Marie Hochmuth Nichols's *Rhetoric and Criticism*, Edwin Black's *Rhetorical Criticism: A Study in Method*, James Kinneavy's *A Theory of Discourse*, Donald Bryant's *Rhetorical Dimensions in Criticism*, Winston Weather's "The Value of Rhetoric to the Creative Artist," and Robert Scott and Bernard Brock's *Methods of Rhetorical Criticism: A Twentieth-Century Perspective*. Also worth noting are Lloyd Bitzer and Edwin Black's *The Prospect of Rhetoric: Report of the National Development Project* and William E. Tanner and J. Dean Bishop's *Rhetoric and Change*. Concerning voice, these should be consulted: Walker Gibson's *Persona: A Style Study for Readers and Writers*, Richard A. Larsen's "The Rhetoric of the Written Voice," and Walter Ong's "A Dialectic of Aural and Objective Correlatives," "The Province of Rhetoric and Poetic," "Voice as Summons for Belief: Literature, Faith, and the Undivided Self," and "The Writer's Audience is Always a Fiction."
3. Booth emphasizes the pedagogical relevance of this information: "I should like to suggest that it is this balance, this rhetorical stance, difficult as it is to describe, that is our main goal as teachers of rhetoric. Our ideal graduate will strike this balance automatically in any writing that he considers finished. Though he may never come to the point of finding the balance easily, he will know that it is what makes the difference between effective communication and mere wasted effort" ("Rhetorical" 111).
4. An Internet search will yield both sides of the debate about this video. Examples include Jonah Bromwich's "Sorority Video Generates Charges of Discrimination," Michael Kinney's "Alabama Sorority Recruitment Video

Draws Backlash, University Response," and Kristen Rein's "U. of Alabama Sorority Criticized for Recruitment Video." According to Rein, the University of Alabama administration "condemned the video." Rein also cites AL.com writer A. L. Bailey's volatile statements that might have begun this entire controversy:

> Remember all of those bikini-clad, sashaying, glitter-blowing, and spontaneous piggyback-riding days of college? Me either.... No, it's not a slick Playboy Playmate or *Girls Gone Wild* video.... It's a parade of white girls and blonde hair dye, coordinated clothing, bikinis and daisy dukes, glitter and kisses, bouncing bodies, euphoric hand-holding and hugging, gratuitous booty shots, and matching aviator glasses. It's all so racially and aesthetically homogeneous and forced, so hyper-feminine, so reductive and objectifying, so *Stepford Wives: College Edition*.

5. Palahniuk has guarded his sexuality, although he is now more open than he was in the past. He has broadcasted on *The Cult: The Official Chuck Palahniuk Website* his responses to media intrusion into his personal life. I do not plan to add to this discussion.

Bibliography

"After Porn Ends_Houston 500 Gang Bang." *YouTube*. YouTube, 8 June 2012. Web. 12 Sept. 2012. https://www.youtube.com/watch?v=-ut-cMwFcTs.
"Alabama Alpha Phi 2015 Recruitment Video." *YouTube*. YouTube, 17 Aug. 2015. Web. 22 Aug. 2015. https://www.youtube.com/watch?v=KudwS5U9ouA.
Alcoholics Anonymous: The Story of How Many Thousands of Men and Women Have Recovered from Alcoholism. 1939. 3rd ed. New York: Alcoholics Anonymous Services, 1976. Print.
Alighieri, Dante. *The Divine Comedy*. 1320. Trans. Henry Wadsworth Longfellow. 1867. Edison, NJ: Chartwell, 2008. Print.
All About Eve. Dir. Joseph Mankiewicz. Perf. Bette Davis, Anne Baxter, George Sanders, Celeste Holm, Thelma Ritter, and Gary Merrill, 1950. Twentieth-Century Fox, 1977. Film.
Allison, David B., Mark S. Roberts, and Allen Weiss, eds. *Sade and the Narrative of Transgression*. Cambridge: Cambridge University Press, 1995. Print.
Appignanesi, Richard, and Chris Garratt. *Introducing Postmodernism: A Graphic Guide to Cutting-Edge Thinking*. Cambridge, UK: Icon, 2007. Print.
Ash, Scott. "Going to the Body: The Tension of Freedom/Restraint in Palahniuk's Novels." Sartain 73–88. Print.
"Asiana Airlines Flight 214." *Wikipedia*. Wikipedia Foundation, 14 Mar. 2015. Web. 24 Mar. 2015.
Austenfeld, Thomas. "Can Terrorism Be Satirized? The Case of Chuck Palahniuk's *Pygmy*." *Terrorism and Narrative Practice*. Ed. Thomas Austenfelt, Dimiter Daphinoff, and Jens Herlth. Berlin: LIT Verlag Münster, 2011. 189–99. Print.
Bakhtin, Mikhail. *Rabelais and His World*. 1965. Trans. H. Iswolsky. Rpt. in *The Bakhtin Reader: Selected Writings of Bakhtin, Medvedev, and Voloshinov*. Ed. Emily Morris. London: Arnold, 1994. 195–206. Print.
Barbas, Samantha. *The First Lady of Hollywood: A Biography of Louella Parsons*. Berkeley: University of California Press, 2005. Print.
Barth, John. "Do I Repeat Myself? The Problem of the Already Said." *The Atlantic.com*. The Atlantic Monthly Group, 2011. Web. 24 June 2015.
———. "Literature of Exhaustion." 1967. *The Friday Book: Essays and Other Nonfiction*. New York: Putnam, 1984. 62–76. Print.
———. "Literature of Replenishment: Postmodernist Fiction." 1980. *The Friday Book: Essays and Other Nonfiction*. New York: Putnam, 1984. 193–206. Print.
Barthes, Roland. "The Death of the Author." 1967. *Image-Music-Text*. Comp. and trans. Stephen Heath. London: Fontana, 1977. 142–48. Print.
Barton, Chris. "'Damned' by Chuck Palahniuk." Rev. of *Damned*, by Chuck Palahniuk. *LATimes.com*. Los Angeles Times, 29 Nov. 2011. Web. 20 Mar. 2013.
Batchelor, Bob, ed. *Cult Pop Culture: How the Fringe Became Mainstream*. Vol. 1: Film and Television. Westport, CT: Praeger, 2012. Print.

Baudrillard, Jean. *The Illusion of the End or Strike of Events.* 1994. *The European Graduate School: Graduate & Postgraduate Studies.* European Graduate School EGS, 7 July 2015. Web. 7 July 2015. http://www.egs.edu/faculty/jean-baudrillard/articles/illusion-of-the-end-or-strike-of-events/.
_____. *Simulacra and Simulation.* 1981. Trans. Sheila Faria Glaser. Ann Arbor: University of Michigan Press, 1994. Print.
Bennett, Alice. *Afterlife and Narrative in Contemporary Fiction.* New York: Palgrave Macmillan, 2012. Print.
Bergin, Thomas. "An Introduction to Boccaccio." *The Decameron: A New Translation.* Comp., trans., and ed. Mark Musa and Peter Bondanella. New York: Norton, 1977. 151–71. Print.
Bessie, Simon Michael. *Jazz Journalism: The Story of the Tabloid Newspapers.* New York: Russell & Russell, 1938. Print.
Biele, Christian. "Utah Shadowboxes with 'Fight Club' Phenomenon." *Christian Science Monitor* 12 May 2000: 2. Print.
Bisch, Kevin. "The Gang's All Here: Hope Flickers at the World's Biggest Gangbang." *Salon.com.* Salon Media Group, 31 Aug. 1999. Web. 30 Sept. 2011.
Bitzer, Lloyd. "The Rhetorical Situation." *Philosophy and Rhetoric* 1.1 (1968): 1–14. Print.
Bitzer, Lloyd, and Edwin Black, eds. *The Prospect of Rhetoric: Report of the National Developmental Project.* Englewood Cliffs, NJ: Prentice-Hall, 1971. Print.
Black, Edwin. *Rhetorical Criticism: A Study in Method.* Madison: University of Wisconsin Press, 1978. Print.
Blume, Judy. *Are You There God? It's Me, Margaret.* 1970. New York: Atheneum Books for Young Readers, 2001. Print.
Boccaccio, Giovanni. *The Decameron.* 1353. Trans. G. H. McWilliam. 2nd ed. New York: Penguin, 1995. Print.
_____. *The Decameron: A New Translation.* 1353. Comp., trans., and ed. Mark Musa and Peter Bondanella. New York: Norton, 1977. Print.
_____. *The Decameron.* 1353. Trans. Richard Aldington. 1930. New York: Dell, 1962. Print.
Bomer, Paula. "Transgressive Fiction: Chuck Palahniuk's *Beautiful You* and More." Rev. of *Beautiful You,* by Chuck Palahniuk. *New York Times.com.* New York Times Company, 24 Oct. 2014. Web. 24 May 2015.
Booker, M. Keith. *Techniques of Subversion in Modern Literature: Transgression, Abjection, and the Carnivalesque.* Gainesville: University of Florida Press, 1991. Print.
Booth, Wayne. *The Rhetoric of Fiction.* 2nd ed. Chicago: University of Chicago Press, 1983. Print.
_____. "The Rhetorical Stance." *College Composition and Communication* 14.3 (1963): 139–45. Rpt. in *The Writing Teacher's Sourcebook.* Ed. Gary Tate and Edward P. J. Corbett. New York: Oxford University Press, 1981. 108–116. Print.
"Brandy Alexandre." *iadf.com.* Internet Adult Film Database, n.d. Web. 3 July 2015. http://www.iafd.com/person.rme/perfid=balexandre/gender=f/brandy-alexandre.htm.
"Brandy Alexandre." *LuckisBack.com.* LukeisBack, 2015. Web. 2 July 2015. http://www.lukeisback.com/stars/stars/female/brandy_alexandre.html.
Bromwich, Jonah. "Sorority Video Generates Charges of Discrimination." *New York Times.com.* New York Times Company, 18 Aug. 2015. Web. 24 Aug. 2015.
Bruccoli, Matthew J. *Some Sort of Epic Grandeur: The Life of F. Scott Fitzgerald.* 2nd ed. Columbia: University of South Carolina Press, 2002. Print.
Bryant, Donald. *Rhetorical Dimensions in Criticism.* Baton Rouge: Louisiana State University Press, 1973. Print.
Burke, Kenneth. *Language as Symbolic Action: Essays on Life, Literature, and Method.* Berkeley: Univerrsity of California Press, 1966. Print.
_____. *A Rhetoric of Motives.* 1950. Berkeley: University of California Press, 1969. Print.
Butler, Judith. *Gender Trouble: Feminisms and the Subversion of Identity.* New York: Routledge, 1990. Print.
Cafazzo, Debbie. "Sixth-Graders Expelled for 'Fight Club.'" *News Tribune* [Tacoma] 1 Mar. 2011: n. pag. *General OneFile.* Web. 16 Mar. 2011.

Campbell, Joseph. *The Hero with a Thousand Faces*. New York: Pantheon, 1949. Print.
Canterbery, E. Ray, and Thomas D. Birch. *F. Scott Fitzgerald: Under the Influence*. St. Paul: Paragon House, 2006. Print.
Carlaw, Darren Richard. "Damned." Rev. of *Damned*, by Chuck Palahniuk. *New York Journal of Books.com*. New York Journal of Books, 18 Oct. 2011. Web. 20 Mar. 2011.
"Cassie Wright." *Myspace*. Web. 18. Dec. 2011. http://www.myspace.com/cassiewrightlives.
"The Chinese Boxer." *YouTube*. YouTube, 6 Mar. 2012. Web. 12 July 2015. https://www.youtube.com/watch?v=yMztKtanc5Q.
"Chitty Chitty Gang Bang." *Creativity*. Crain Communications, 4 June 2008. Web. 18 Dec. 2011. http://creativity-online.com/work/snuff-chitty-chitty-gang-bang/1251.
Christopher, Renny, and Carolyn Whitson. "Toward a Theory of Working Class Literature." *Thought & Action: The NEA Higher Education Journal* 15.1 (1999): 71–81. Print.
"Chuck Palahniuk." *Wikipedia*. Wikipedia Foundation, 6 July 2015. Web. 6 July 2015.
"Chuck Palahniuk Interviews Cassie Wright-Part 1." *YouTube*. YouTube, 14 Apr. 2008. Web. 18 Dec. 2011. http://www.youtube.com/watch?v=jJF19qrFxLE.
"Chuck Palahniuk Interviews Cassie Wright-Part 2." *YouTube*. YouTube, 17 Apr. 2008. Web. 18 Dec. 2011. http://www.youtube.com/watch?v=ptdbl5stHmM.
"Chuck Palahniuk Interviews Cassie Wright-Part 3." *YouTube*. YouTube, 29 Apr. 2008. Web. 18 Dec. 2011. http://www.youtube.com/watch?v=gxNeAco5iBU.
Chun, Rene. "Naked Lunch and Dinner." *New York Times* 23 Apr. 1995: 49, 52. Print.
Cohen, Daniel. *Yellow Journalism: Scandal, Sensationalism, and Gossip in the Media*. Brookfield, CT: Twenty-First Century Books, 2000. Print.
Coleman, Philip. "Hauntedness: Edgar Allan Poe and Chuck Palahniuk." *The Ghost Story from the Middle Ages to the Twentieth Century: A Ghostly Genre*. Ed. Helen Conrad O'Briain and Julie Anne Stevens. Dublin: Four Courts Press, 2010. 266–78. Print.
Collado-Rodriguez, Francisco, ed. *Chuck Palahniuk: Fight Club, Invisible Monsters, Choke*. London: Bloomsbury, 2013. Print.
Crane, Stephen. "XXI." 1899. *The Norton Anthology of American Literature*. Ed. Nina Baym, et al. 8th ed. Vol. C. New York: Norton, 2012. 1007. Print.
Dahlgren, Peter, and Colin Sparks, eds. *Journalism and Popular Culture*. London: Sage, 1992. Print.
Dane, Joseph A. *Parody: Critical Concepts Versus Literary Practices, Aristophanes to Sterne*. Norman: University of Oklahoma Press, 1988. Print.
"Dead Porn Stars." *iadf.com*. Internet Adult Film Database, 13 May 2015. Web. 3 July 2015. http://www.rame.net/faq/deadporn/index.html.
"Dead Porn Stars Memorial Part 1." *YouTube*. YouTube, 5 May 2012. Web. 12 Sept. 2012. http://www.youtube.com/watch?v=oBx4lgieMAs.
"Dead Porn Stars Memorial Part 2." *YouTube*. YouTube, 8 June 2012. Web. 12 Sept. 2012. http://www.youtube.com/watch?v=G7YoXJ4eXr8.
"Dense the Ten Extreme 1978 English Dubbed-Kung Fu Movies." *YouTube*. YouTube, 29 Dec. 2013. Web. 12 July 2015. https://www.youtube.com/watch?v=3QId9J04NlU?.
Dentith, Simon. *Parody*. New York: Routledge, 2000. Print.
Denzin, Norman, K. *Reading Race: Hollywood and the Cinema of Racial Violence*. London: Sage, 2002. Print.
Dolph, James. "Behind the Queens' Veils: Power Versus Powerlessness in C. S. Lewis's *Till We Have Faces* and Palahniuk's *Invisible Monsters*." Sartain 102–15. Print.
Dorfman, Ariel. *The Empire's Old Clothes: What the Lone Ranger, Babar, and Other Innocent Heroes Do to Our Minds*. New York: Pantheon, 1983. Print.
Dorfman, Ariel, and Armand Mattelart. *How to Read Donald Duck: Imperialist Ideology in the Disney Comic*. 1971. Trans. David Kunzle. New York: International General, 1975. Print.
El Rey Network. El Rey Network, 2015. Web. 24 July 2015.
The Elephant Man. Dir. David Lynch. Perf. Anthony Hopkins, John Hurt, John Gielgud, and Anne Bancroft. 1980. Paramount, 2006. Film.

Eliot, T. S. "Tradition and the Individual Talent." *The Sacred Wood and Major Early Essays*. 1920. Mineola, NY: Dover, 1998. 27–33. Print.

Ellmann, Lucy. "Love the Ones You're With." Review of *Snuff*, by Chuck Palahniuk. *New York Times Book Review* 8 June 2008: 27. Print.

Falk, Robert P., ed. *American Literature in Parody: A Collection of Parody, Satire, and Literary Burlesque of American Writers Past and Present*. New York: Twayne, 1955. Print.

Faulkner, William. *As I Lay Dying*. 1930. Ed. Michael Gorra. New York: Norton, 2009. Print.

"Favorite Martial Arts Movies in the 70's (aka Martial Arts Movies of the 1970s)." *YouTube*. YouTube, 22 Dec. 2009. Web. 12 July 2015. https://www.youtube.com/watch?v=Dhrt32s9nTc.

Ferrante, Joan. "The Frame Characters of the *Decameron*: A Progression of Virtues." *Romance Philology* 19.2 (1965): 212–26. Print.

Fitzgerald, F. Scott. *The Great Gatsby*. 1925. New York: Scribner, 2004. Print.

Foucault, Michel. "Preface to Transgression." 1963. *Language, Counter-Memory, Practice: Selected Essays and Interviews*. Trans. Donald F Bouchard and Sherry Simon. Ed. Donald F. Bouchard. Ithaca: Cornell University Press, 1977. 29–52. Print.

Frost, Jennifer. *Hedda Hopper's Hollywood: Celebrity Gossip and American Conservatism*. New York: New York University Press, 2011. Print.

Gallagher, Brian. "Daryl Hannah and Tom Sizemore Join *Snuff*." *MovieWeb*. Watchr Media, 8 Feb. 2011. Web. 24 Sept. 2011.

"Gang Bang Pornography." *Wikipedia*. Wikipedia Foundation, 8 July 2015. Web. 10 July 2015.

Genette, Gérard. *Palimpsests: Literature in the Second Degree*. 1982. Trans. Channa Newman and Claude Doubinsky. Lincoln: University of Nebraska Press, 1997. Print.

Geyh, Paula, Fred Leebron, and Andrew Levy, eds. *Postmodern American Fiction: A Norton Anthology*. New York: Norton, 1998. Print.

Gibson, Walker. *Persona: A Style Study for Readers and Writers*. New York: Random, 1969. Print.

Graff, Keir. "Snuff." Rev. of *Snuff*, by Chuck Palahniuk. *Booklist* 1 Mar. 2008: 30. Print.

Graham, Sheilah. *College of One: The Story of How F. Scott Fitzgerald Educated the Woman He Loved*. London: Weidenfeld and Nicolson, 1967. Print.

———. *Confessions of a Hollywood Columnist*. New York: Morrow, 1969. Print.

———. *For Richer, for Poorer*. London: W. H. Allen/Virgin, 1975. Print.

———. *The Garden of Allah*. New York: Crown, 1970. Print.

———. *Hollywood Revisited: A Fiftieth Anniversary Celebration*. New York: St. Martin's, 1985. Print.

———. *How to Marry Super Rich: Or Love, Money and the Morning After*. New York: Grosset and Dunlap, 1974. Print.

———. *The Late Lily Shiel*. New York: Grosset and Dunlap, 1978. Print.

———. *My Hollywood: A Celebration and a Lament*. London: M. Joseph, 1984. Print.

———. *The Real F. Scott Fitzgerald, Thirty-Five Years Later*. New York: Grosset and Dunlap, 1976. Print.

———. *Rest of the Story: The Odyssey of a Modern Woman*. New York: Coward and McCann, 1964. Print.

———. *A State of Heat*. New York: Grosset and Dunlap, 1972. Print.

———, and Gerold Frank. *Beloved Infidel: The Education of a Woman*. New York: Holt, 1958. Print.

Grayson, Erik, ed. Issue devoted to Chuck Palahniuk. *Stirrings Still: The International Journal of Existential Literature* 2.2 (2005). Print.

Hammer, Kate. "Fight Clubs Hit High-School Locker Rooms." *Globe & Mail* [Toronto] 13 Nov. 2010: n. pag. *EBSCO*. Web. 16 Mar. 2011.

Hantre, Steffen. "Blood on the Bookstore Floor: Chuck Palahniuk and the Case of the Fainting Reader." Kuhn and Rubin 196–209. Print.

Harmon, William. *A Handbook to Literature*. 12th ed. New York: Longman, 2012. Print.

"Haunted." Rev. of *Haunted*, by Chuck Palahniuk. *Kirkus Reviews* 1 Feb. 2005: 143. *Literary Reference Center*. Web. 13 Feb. 2013.

"Haunted." Rev. of *Haunted*, by Chuck Palahniuk. *Publisher's Weekly* 2 Feb. 2005: 154. *Literary Reference Center*. Web. 13 Feb. 2013.
"Hawk and Chick." *Bob's Burgers*. Creat. Loren Bouchard and Jim Dauterive. Writ. Rich Rinaldi. Perf. H. Jon Benjamin, Dan Mintz, John Roberts, Kristen Schaal, Keisuke Hoashi, and Suzy Nakamura. Fox. WMBF, Myrtle Beach, 17 May 2015. Television.
Hellman, Lillian. Interview by Nora Ephron. "Lillian Hellman Walking, Cooking, Writing, Talking." *New York Times Book Review* 23 Sept. 1973: 2, 51. Rpt. in *Conversations with Lillian Hellman*. Ed. Jackson Bryer. Jackson: University Press of Mississippi, 1986. 132–37. Print.
———. *Pentimento: A Book of Portraits*. Boston: Little, Brown, 1973. Print.
Henley, William Ernest. "Invictus." 1892. 4th ed. Ed. M. H. Abrams, et al. New York: Norton, 1979. 1674. Print.
Henry, William, III, Jeanne McDowell, and Naushad Mehta. "Pssst... Did You Hear About? Ivana and Donald... Madonna and Warren... Where Does Gossip Come From? How Much Is It True? And Why Does America Love It?" *Time* 5 Mar. 5 1990: 46. *Academic Search Complete*. Web. 2 Sept. 2013.
Hollands, Neil. "Snuff." Rev. of *Snuff*, by Chuck Palahniuk. *Library Journal* 1 Apr. 2008: 78. Print.
———. "Tell-All." Rev. of *Tell-All*, by Chuck Palahniuk. *Library Journal* 1 May 2010: 69–71. *Literary Reference Center*. Web. 2 Sept. 2013.
Holman, Hugh. *A Handbook to Literature*. 4th ed. Indianapolis: Bobbs-Merrill, 1980. Print.
Houston. "Houston: An Intimate Portrait." Interview with George Gurley. *Observer.com*. Observer Media, 21 Aug. 2000. Web. 30 Sept. 2011.
"Houston." *Wikipedia*. Wikipedia Foundation, 12 Sept. 2011. Web. 30 Sept. 2011.
Hume, Kathryn. *Aggressive Fiction: Reading the Contemporary American Novel*. New York: Cornell University Press, 2012. Print.
Hutcheon, Linda. *Irony's Edge: The Theory and Politics of Irony*. New York: Routledge, 1994. Print.
———. *Narcissistic Narrative: The Metafictional Paradox*. Ontario: Wilfrid Laurier University Press, 2013. Print.
———. *A Poetics of Postmodernism*. New York: Routledge, 1988. Print.
———. *The Politics of Postmodernism*. New York: Routledge, 1989. Print.
———. *A Theory of Adaption*. New York: Routledge, 2006. Print.
———. *Theory of Parody: The Teachings of Twentieth-Century Art Forms*. 1985. Urbana: University of Illinois Press, 2000. Print.
Jameson, Fredric. *Postmodernism, or, The Cultural Logic of Late Capitalism*. Durham: Duke University Press, 1991. Print.
Jenks, Chris. *Transgression*. London: Routledge, 2003. Print.
Jess, Walter. "In This Tale, Teen Angst Really Is Hell." Rev. of *Damned*, by Chuck Palahniuk. *Washington Post* 9 Nov. 2011. *Points of View Reference Center*. Web. 19 Oct. 2012.
Johnson, Andy. "Bullets and Blades: Narcissism and Violence in *Invisible Monster*." Sartain 61–72. Print.
Katz, Daniel, and Kenneth W. Braly. "Racial Stereotypes of One Hundred College Students." *Journal of Abnormal Psychology* 28.3 (1933): 280–90. Print.
Kavaldo, Jesse. "The Fiction of Self-Destruction: Chuck Palahniuk, Closet Moralist." Schuchardt 13–33. Print.
Kennedy, Valerie. *Edward Said: A Critical Introduction*. Cambridge, UK: Polity, 2000. Print.
Kerr, Calum. "On Palahniuk's *Haunted*." *Stirrings Still: The International Journal of Existential Literature* 2.2 (2005): 139–42. Web. 3 Mar. 2013.
King, Stephen. "Why We Crave Horror Movies." *Playboy* Jan. 1981: 150–54. Rpt. in *The Little, Brown Reader*. Ed. Marcia Stubbs and Sylvan Barnet. Boston: Little, Brown, 1989. 685–87. Print.
"The King of Kung Fu." *YouTube*. YouTube, 6 Nov. 2011. Web. 12 July 2015. https://www.youtube.com/watch?v=ISK97vb9IPc.

Kinneavy, James. *A Theory of Discourse: The Aims of Discourse.* New York: Norton, 1971. Print.
Kinney, Michael. "Alabama Sorority Recruitment Video Draws Backlash, University Response." *The Moore American* [Norman, OK] 19 Aug. 2015. *Points of View Reference Center.* Web. 24 Aug. 2015.
Kuhn, Cynthia, and Lance Rubin, eds. *Reading Chuck Palahniuk: American Monsters and Literary Mayhem.* New York: Routledge, 2009. Print.
"Kung Fu Movie Trailers of the 1970's." *YouTube.* YouTube, 16 Sept. 2007. Web. 12 July 2015. https://www.youtube.com/watch?v=tw0JBjgPdhg.
"Kung Fu Trailers 1970's." *YouTube.* YouTube, 20 Apr. 2012. Web. 12 July 2015. https://www.youtube.com/watch?v=VYjN1sGgqEA.
Langer, John. *Tabloid Television: Popular Journalism and the "Other News."* New York: Routledge, 1998. Print.
Larson, Richard A. "The Rhetoric of Written Voice." *Rhetoric and Change.* Ed. William E. Tanner and J. Dean Bishop. Mesquite, TX: Ide House, 1982. 115–25. Print.
Linkon, Sherry. "Why Working-Class Literature Matters." *Working-Class Perspectives: Commentary from the Center for Working-Class Studies.* The Center for Working-Class Studies at Youngstown State University, 22 Feb. 2010. Web. 16 Mar. 2011.
Lippmann, Walter. *Public Opinion.* 1922. Sioux Falls: Greenbook, 2010. Print.
Lott, Ray M. *The American Martial Arts Film.* Jefferson, NC: McFarland, 2004. Print.
Lundgren, Suzanne. "Palahniuk Remix: A Review of *Invisible Monsters Remix.*" Rev. of *Invisible Monsters Remix*, by Chuck Palahniuk. *Utne Reader* Sept.-Oct. 2012: 80. Print.
Martinson, Deborah. *Lillian Hellman: A Life with Foxes and Scoundrels.* Berkley: Counterpoint, 2005. Print.
Maslin, Janet. "The Road to Hell, Paved with Telemarketers." Review of *Damned*, by Chuck Palahniuk *New York Times* 20 Oct. 2011: C1. *Newspaper Source Plus.* Web. 19 Oct. 2012.
Maxwell, Gloria. "Tell-All." Rev. of *Tell-All*, by Chuck Palahniuk. *Library Journal* 15 Sept. 2010: 36. *Literary Reference Center.* Web. 2 Sept. 2013.
McCracken, David. "Chuck Palahniuk's *Fight Club* as Working-Class Novel." *Postscript: The Journal of the Philological Association of the Carolinas* 27.12 (2012): n. pag. Web. 7 July 2015. http://pachome.org/wp/postscript/?page_id=665.
———. "*Lady Chatterley's Lover* as a Rhetorical Response: Justification for D. H. Lawrence's Mask of Oliver Mellors." MA thesis. Texas A&M University, 1988. Print.
———. "The Reification of History in the Novels of Ariel Dorfman." Diss. Texas A&M University, 1994. Print.
Melville, Herman. "Bartleby, the Scrivener." 1853. *The Norton Anthology of American Literature.* Ed. Nina Baym, et al. 8th ed. Vol. B. New York: Norton, 2012. 1483–1509. Print.
Miller, Laura. "Diary." Rev. of *Diary*, by Chuck Palahniuk. *Salon.com.* Salon Media Group, 20 Aug. 2003. Web. 6 July 2015.
Milton, John. *Paradise Lost.* 1667. Ed. Gordon Teskey. 3rd ed. New York: Norton, 2004. Print.
Mookerjee, Robin. *Transgressive Fiction: The New Satiric Tradition.* New York: Palgrave, 2013. Print.
Morton, Paula. *Tabloid Valley: Supermarket News and American Culture.* Gainesville: University Press of Florida, 2009. Print.
Murphy, Tim. "Soap Star: Chuck Palahniuk, Dude Novelist, Gets Campy." Rev. of *Tell-All*, by Chuck Palahniuk. *NYMag.com.* New York Media, 9 May 2010. Web. 23 May 2013.
Ng, Andrew. "Destruction and the Discourse of Deformity: *Invisible Monsters* and the Ethics of Atrocity." Kuhn and Rubin 24–35. Print.
Nichols, Marie Holcomb. *Rhetoric and Criticism.* Baton Rouge: Louisiana State University Press, 1963. Print.
Not The Wizard of Oz XXX. Dir. Will Ryder. Perf. Maddy O'Reilly, Brandy Aniston, and Nina Hartley. Pulse Distribution, 2013. *XVideos.com.* XVideos, n.d. Web. 10 July 2015. http://www.xvideos.com/video11045872/the_wizard_of_oz_full_porn_parody_movie_thisisntporn.com.

O'Brien, Matt. "KTVU Fires News Producers After Asiana Gaffe." *San Mateo County Times* [San Francisco] 25 July 2013: n. pag. *Newsbank*. Web. 10 Mar. 2014.

Ong, Walter. "A Dialectic of Aural and Objective Correlatives." *The Barbarian Within and Fugitive Essays and Studies.* New York: Macmillan, 1962. 26–40. Print.

———. "The Province of Rhetoric and Poetic." *The Province of Rhetoric.* Ed. Joseph Schwartz and John Rycenga. New York: Ronald, 1965. 48–56. Print.

———. "Voice as Summons for Belief: Literature, Faith, and the Undivided Self." *The Barbarian Within and Fugitive Essays and Studies.* New York: Macmillan, 1962. 49–67. Print.

———. "The Writer's Audience Is Always a Fiction." *Publication of the Modern Language Association* 90.1 (1975): 9–21. Rpt. in *Interfaces of the Word: Studies in the Evolution of Consciousness and Culture.* Ithaca: Cornell University Press, 1977. 53–81. Print.

Paglia, Camille. "It's a Jungle Out There." *New York Newsday* 7 March 1991: 83. Rpt. in *Patterns for College Writing.* Ed. Laurie G. Kirszner and Stephen R. Mandell. 8th ed. New York: Bedford St. Martin's, 2001. 538–41. Print.

Palahniuk, Chuck. "Afterword." *Fight Club: A Novel.* New York: Norton, 2005. 209–18. Print.

———. *Beautiful You.* New York: Doubleday, 2014. Print.

———. "Chuck Palahniuk Goes to Hell." Interview by Adam Weinstein. *MotherJones.com.* Mother Jones, Nov.-Dec. 2011. Web. 20 Mar. 2013.

———. "Chuck Palahniuk on Oprah's Diaphragm." Interview by C. P. Farley. *Powells.com.* Powell's Books, 5 July 2001. *Powells.com.* Rpt. in *Archive.org.* Web. 20 Feb. 2013. http://web.archive.org/web/20050310083951/http://www.powells.com/authors/palahniuk.html.

———. "Chuck Palahniuk: Tell-All." Interview by Nicole Powers. *SuicideGirls.* SuicideGirls, 27 May 2010. Web. 24 Mar. 2013. http://suicidegirls.com/interviews/Chuck+Palahniuk%3A+Tell-All/.

———. "Chuck Palahniuk Tells Time Out Why All Love the Idea of Apocalypse." Interview by Adam Lee Davies. *Time Out London.* Time Out Group, 28 July 2008. Web. 6 Mar. 2013. http://www.timeout.com/london/books/chuck-palahniuk-interview.

———. "Chuck Q&A: May 2004." *The Cult: The Official Chuck Palahniuk Website.* Cult Administration, May 2004. Web. 14 Mar. 2013.

———. *Damned.* New York: Doubleday, 2011. Print.

———. *Doomed.* New York: Doubleday, 2013. Print.

———. "Doubleday's 'Tell-All' Q&A with Chuck Palahniuk." *The Cult: The Official Chuck Palahniuk Website.* Cult Administration, n.d. Web. 20 Mar. 2013. http://chuckpalahniuk.net/content/doubledays-tell-all-qa-chuck-palahniuk.

———. *Fight Club: A Novel.* 1996. New York: Norton, 2005. Print.

———. "Fight Club for Kids (with Chuck Palahniuk)." *YouTube.* YouTube, 23 June 2015. Web. 30 Aug. 2015.

———. "Foreword: The Fringe Is the Future." *You Do Not Talk About Fight Club: I Am Jack's Completely Unauthorized Essay Collection.* Ed. Read Mercer Schuchardt. Dallas: BenBella, 2008. 7–11. Print.

———. "Fright Club." Interview by Sean O'Hagan. *The Observer* 8 May 2005: 14. Print.

———. "The 'Guts' Effect." *The Cult: The Official Chuck Palahniuk Website.* Cult Administration, 5 Jan. 2008. Web. 26 Feb. 2013. http://chuckpalahiuk.net/features/essays/guts-effect.

———. *Haunted.* New York: Doubleday, 2005. Print.

———. *Invisible Monsters.* New York: Norton, 1999. Print.

———. *Invisible Monsters Remix.* New York: Norton, 2012. Print.

———. Letter to the editor. Response to Laura Miller. *Salon.com.* Salon Media Group, 26. Aug. 2003. Web. 6 July 2015.

———. *Lullaby.* New York: Doubleday, 2002. Print.

———. *Make Something Up: Stories You Can't Unread.* New York: Doubleday, 2015. Print.

———. "Palahniuk Tells All of Shallow Hollywood." Interview by Paul Donoughue. *Courier Mail* [Brisbane] 3 July 2010: 25. *Points of View Reference Center.* Web. 2 Sept. 2013.

———. "The Power of Persisting: An Introduction." *Burnt Tongues: An Anthology of Trans-*

gressive Stories. Ed. Chuck Palahniuk, Richard Thomas, and Dennis Widmyer. Aurora, IL: Medallion, 2014. 1–6. Print.
_____. *Pygmy*. New York: Anchor, 2009. Print.
_____. *Rant: The Oral Biography of Buster Casey*. New York: Doubleday, 2007. Print.
_____. *Snuff*. 2008. New York: Anchor, 2009. Print.
_____. *Stranger Than Fiction: True Stories*. New York: Anchor, 2004. Print.
_____. *Survivor*. New York: Norton, 1999. Print.
_____. *Tell-All*. New York: Anchor, 2010. Print.
_____. "The Wish Book: A Reintroduction to *Invisible Monsters*." *Invisible Monsters Remix*. New York: Norton, 2012. v–ix. Print.
Palahniuk, Chuck, Richard Thomas, and Dennis Widmyer, eds. *Burnt Tongues: An Anthology of Transgressive Stories*. Aurora, IL: Medallion, 2014. Print.
"Palahniuk, Chuck: Invisible Monsters Remix." Rev. of *Invisible Monsters Remix*, by Chuck Palahniuk. *Kirkus Reviews* 1 June 2012: n. pag. *Literature Reference Center*. Web. 23 Nov. 2013.
Parkaboy (Fortean Mime). "*Haunted* by Chuck Palahniuk." *The Cult: The Official Chuck Palahniuk Website*. Cult Administration, 18 June 2005. Web. 7 Mar. 2013. http://chuckpalahniuk. net/forum/1000181/discussion-605-haunted-by-chuck palahniuk.
Peck, Claude. "Chuck Palahniuk's Latest An Empowering Inferno." Rev. of *Damned*, by Chuck Palahniuk. *Star Tribune* [Minneapolis] 9 Nov. 2011: n pag. *Points of View Reference Center*. Web. 19 Oct. 2012.
Pomerance, Bernard. *The Elephant Man: A Play*. New York: Grove, 1979. Print.
"Postcolonialism." *Wikipedia*. Wikipedia Foundation, 20 May 2015. Web. 12 July 2015.
"Pygmy." Rev. of *Pygmy*, by Chuck Palahniuk. *Publisher's Weekly* 2 Mar. 2009: 40–41. *Literary Reference Center*. Web. 2 Sept. 2013.
Redekop, Corey. "Palahniuk Running On Empty With 10th Novel." Rev. of *Pygmy*, by Chuck Palahniuk. *Winnipeg Free Press* 17 May 2009: D7. *Newspaper Source Plus*. Web. 2 Sept. 2013.
_____. "Palahniuk Shrugs with Indifference." Rev. of *Tell-All*, by Chuck Palahniuk. *Winnipeg Free Press* 22 May 2010: H8. *Points of View Reference Center*. Web. 26 Sept. 2013.
Reid, Craig. *The Ultimate Guide to Marital Arts Movies of the 1970s: 500+ Films Loaded with Action, Weapons and Warriors*. El Segundo, CA: Cruz Bay, 2010. Print.
Rein, Kristen. "U. of Alabama Sorority Criticized for Recruitment Video." *USAToday.com*. USAToday Network, 18 Aug. 2015. Web. 24 Aug. 2015.
Reynolds, Simon. "Daryl Hannah to Play 'Snuff' Porn Star." *Digital Spy*. Hearst Magazines UK, 9 Feb. 2011. Web. 24 Sept. 2011.
Richards, I. A. *The Philosophy of Rhetoric*. New York: Oxford University Press, 1936. Print.
Robey, Tim. "A Case of Celebrity Tourette's." Rev. of *Tell-All*, by Chuck Palahniuk. *Daily Telegraph* [London] 3 July 2010: 26–27. *Points of View Reference Center*. Web. 2 Sept. 2013.
Rose, Margaret. *Parody: Ancient, Modern, and Post-Modern*. Cambridge: Cambridge University Press, 1993. Print.
Rouse, P. T. J. *Martial Arts*. London: Virgin, 2005. Print.
Said, Edward. *Culture and Imperialism*. New York: Vintage, 1993. Print.
_____. *Orientalism*. New York, Pantheon, 1978. Print.
Sanday, Peggy Reeves. *Fraternity Gang Rape: Sex, Brotherhood, and Privilege on Campus*. 2nd ed. New York: New York University Press, 2007. Print.
Sanders, Mark. *Gayatri Chakravorty Spivak: Live Theory*. New York: Continuum, 2006. Print.
Sartain, Jeffrey, ed. *Sacred and Immoral: On the Writings of Chuck Palahniuk*. Newcastle, UK: Cambridge Scholars, 2009. Print.
Schuchardt, Read Mercer. "A Copy of a Copy of a Copy: *The Matrix*, *American Beauty*, and *Fight Club* as Retellings of Pink Floyd *The Wall*." Schuchardt 157–74. Print.
_____. "Introduction: Chuck Palahniuk: Existentialist Paramedic." Schuchardt 1–7. Print.
Schuchardt, Read Mercer, ed. *You Do Not Talk About Fight Club: I Am Jack's Completely Unauthorized Essay Collection*. Dallas: BenBella, 2008. Print.

Schweinitz, Jorg. *Film and Stereotype: A Challenge for Cinema and Theory.* Trans. Laura Schleussner. New York: Columbia University Press, 2011. Print.
Scott, Henry. *Shocking True Story: The Rise and Fall of* Confidential, *"America's Most Scandalous Scandal Magazine."* New York: Pantheon, 2010. Print.
Scott, Robert, and Bernard Brock, eds. *Methods of Rhetorical Criticisms: A Twentieth-Century Perspective.* New York: Harper, 1972. Print.
7zark7. "Writing Tips from Chuck Palahniuk." *Quake3World.com.* phpBB Group, 1 June 2006. http://www.quake3world.com/forum/viewtopic.php?f=1&t=20871.
Shapiro, Jonathan. "'Tell-All' by Chuck Palahniuk." Rev. of *Tell-All*, by Chuck Palahniuk. *LATimes.com.* Los Angeles Times, 27 May 2010. Web. 23 May 2013.
Silverblatt, Michael. "Shock Appeal—Who are These Writers, and Why Do They Want to Hurt Us? The New Fiction of Transgression." *Los Angeles Times* 1 Aug. 1993: 7. Print.
Simmons, David, and Nicola Allen. "Reading Chuck Palahniuk's *Survivor* and *Haunted* as a Critique of 'The Culture Industry.'" Kuhn and Rubin 116–28. Print.
Simon, Scott. "Real-Life Fight Club in San Jose Pits Men Against Each Other in Dangerous Hand-To-Hand Combat." *Weekend Edition Saturday* [NPR] July 30, 2005: n. pag. *Literature Resource Center.* Web. 4 Feb. 2011.
Slade, Andrew. "On Mutilation: the Sublime Body of Chuck Palahniuk's Fiction." Kuhn and Rubin 62–72. Print.
Sloan, Bill. *"I Watched a Wild Hog Eat My Baby!": A Colorful History of Tabloids and Their Cultural Impact.* New York: Prometheus, 2001. Print.
"Snuff." Rev. of *Snuff*, by Chuck Palahniuk. *Kirkus Reviews* 1 Mar. 2008: 213. *EBSCO.* Web. 29 Aug. 2011.
Sobel, Richard. *The White Collar Working Class: From Structure to Politics.* New York:Praeger, 1989. Print.
Sondergard, Sidney. "Chuck Palahniuk and the Semiotics of Personal Doom: The Novelist as Escape Artist." Kuhn and Rubin 9–23. Print.
Sontag, Susan. *Illness as Metaphor.* New York: Farrar, Strauss, and Giroux, 1977. Print.
Soukhanov, Anne H. "Word Watch." *The Atlantic* Dec. 1996: 128. Print.
Spivak, Gayatri Chakravorty. "Can the Subaltern Speak?" *Marxism and the Interpretation of Culture.* Eds. Cary Nelson and Lawrence Grossberg. Urbana: University of Illinois Press, 1988: 271–313. Print.
St. Andre, Ken. "Haunted." Rev. of *Haunted*, by Chuck Palahniuk. *Library Journal* 1 May 2005: 75–76. *Literary Reference Center.* Web. 13 Feb. 2013.
Stallybrass, Peter, and Allon White. *The Politics and Poetics of Transgression.* Ithaca: Cornell University Press, 1986. Print.
"Sting of the Dragon Masters." *YouTube.* YouTube, 26 Dec. 2012. Web. 12 July 2015. https://www.youtube.com/watch?v=tCm0lEGBkCE.
Swift, Jonathan. *Gulliver's Travels.* 1726. Ed. Albert J. Rivero. 3rd ed. New York: Norton, 2001. Print.
_____. "A Modest Proposal." 1729. *Patterns for College Writing.* Ed. Laurie G. Kirszner and Stephen R. Mandell. 8th ed. New York: Bedford St. Martin's, 2001. 648–55. Print.
Talbott, Chris. "It's Style Over Substance in Chuck Palahniuk's Slender New Novel, *Tell-All*." Rev. of *Tell-All*, by Chuck Palahniuk. *Canadian Press* [Toronto] 21 May 2010: n. pag. *Points of View Reference Center.* Web. 2 Sept. 2013.
Tanner, William, and J. Dean Bishop, eds. *Rhetoric and Change.* Mesquite, TX: Ide House, 1982. Print.
"Tell All." Rev. of *Tell-All*, by Chuck Palahniuk. *Publisher's Weekly* 22 Mar. 2010: 47. *Literary Reference Center.* Web. 2 Sept. 2013.
"Twilight Bone." *YouTube.* YouTube, 20 May 2008. Web. 18 Dec. 2011. http://www.youtube.com/watch?v=ymok-lh9XM4.
Vonnegut, Kurt. "Harrison Bergeron." 1961. *Literature and Its Writers: An Introduction to Fiction, Poetry and Drama.* Ed. Ann Charters and Samuel Charters. 6th ed. New York: Bedford St. Martin's, 2013. 604–09. Print.

Weathers, Winston. "The Value of Rhetoric to the Creative Artist." *Rhetoric and Change.* Ed. William Tanner and J. Dean Bishop. Mesquite, TX: Ide House, 1982. 31–41. Print.

Westbrook, Robert. *Intimate Lies: F. Scott Fitzgerald and Sheilah Graham: Her Son's Story.* New York: HarperCollins, 1995. Print.

"Where's Brandy Alexandre????" *AdultDVDTalk.com.* AdultDVDTalk, 28 June 2010. Web. 3 July 2105. http://forum.adultdvdtalk.com/wheres-brandy-alexandre.

White, Hayden. *The Content of the Form: Narrative Discourse and Historical Representation.* Baltimore: John Hopkins University Press, 1987. Print.

Widmyer, Dennis, and Richard Thomas. "From the Editors: The Genesis of Burnt Tongues." *Burnt Tongues: An Anthology of Transgressive Stories.* Ed. Chuck Palahniuk, Richard Thomas, and Dennis Widmyer. Aurora, IL: Medallion, 2014. 7–9. Print.

Williams, G. Christopher. "Nihilism and Buddhism in a Blender: The Religion of Chuck Palahniuk." Kuhn and Rubin 170–82. Print.

Williams, Owen. "Daryl Hannah Is Up to Snuff." *Empireonline.* Bauer Consumer Media, 9 Feb. 2011. Web. 24 Sept. 2011.

"The Wizard of Ass—Dorothy Is Not a Virgin Anymore." *YouTube.* YouTube, 7 May 2008. Web. 18 Dec. 2011. http://www.youtube.com/watch?v=gzY3r76Ax48.

Woodhead, Cameron. "Pygmy." Rev. of *Pygmy,* by Chuck Palahniuk. *The Age* [Melbourne] 4 July 2009: 26. *Newspaper Source Plus.* Web. 2 Sept. 2013.

Wolf, Naomi. *Fire with Fire: The New Female Power and How It Will Change the 21st Century.* New York: Random House, 1993. Print.

Wolfe, Tom. *I Am Charlotte Simmons.* New York: Picador, 2004. Print.

The World's Biggest Gangbang 3: The Houston 500. Dir. Greg Alves. Perf. Houston, Ron Jeremy, and Gina Adorabella. Metro Inc., 1999. Film.

Your Pretty Face Is Going to Hell. Creat. Casper Kelly and Dave Willis. Perf. Craig Rowin, Matt Servitto, and Henry Zebrowski. Adult Swim. Time Warner Cable, Hartsville, SC. 18 April 2013-Present. Television.

Zweig, Michael. "Six Points on Class." *Monthly Review* 58.3 (2006): 116–26. Print.

Index

academia 1–3, 6, 9, 16, 19, 145, 188–189
Achilles 104
Acker, Kathy 1
ADHD 132
adolescence 10, 85 90–93, 97, 99–103, 105–108, 125, 143–144, 162–163, 167–167, 170, 179, 184–185, 199*n*7
advertisement 7, 12, 16, 21, 71, 102, 110, 135, 139, 147, 159, 171–172, 176, 180–181
advocacy 141–143
AIDS 11, 114
Alcoholics Anonymous 133
Alexander, Brandy 116–122, 146, 172, 176, 200*n*2–6; *see also* McFarland, Shane
Alexandre, Brandy 118–119
Alighieri, Dante 10, 24, 26–27, 29, 90–109, 135, 148, 163, 166–170, 184–185, 199*n*3; *The Divine Comedy* 90–92, 95, 135; *Inferno* 10, 24, 90–109, 166–170, 184; Lady Fortune 26–27, 29; *Purgatorio* 26; Virgil 91, 95, 101, 107
All About Eve 78
All That Jazz 18
allegory 25, 27, 63, 154, 197*n*8
allusion 5, 39, 53, 55, 93–95, 119, 170, 192*n*5
American capitalism 56, 62–63, 92, 130, 135, 160, 162, 192*n*3, 197*n*10
American culture (contemporary) 12, 13, 55–58, 66, 67, 69–70, 90, 126, 131, 135, 149, 160–162, 165, 167, 183, 193*n*8, 198*n*4
American Dream 3, 56–57, 92, 124, 194*n*6
Americana 17, 66, 68, 125
Anderson, Sherwood 17
Are You There God? It's Me, Margaret 10, 91, 94, 99–108, 143, 166–171, 184–185, 198*n*1, 199*n*4–6; *see also Damned*; Margaret
art 7–9, 11, 19, 23, 31–32, 38–39, 41–43, 45, 49, 71, 77, 85, 137–140, 191*n*3, 192*n*3, 192*n*5, 193*n*6
artistic reproduction 8, 38, 40, 43, 45, 47–49, 52, 181–183
Asian culture 10, 56–59, 61
Asiana flight 214 54, 70, 195*n*1
assimilation 58, 69, 125, 161, 183
The Atlantic 11

B-films 55, 59, 61, 183
Bacardi, Branch 38–43, 46–48, 50–51, 69, 129, 131, 154–157, 183, 195*n*4; *see also Snuff*
Baker, Norma Jean 88
Bakhtin, Mikhail 75, 87, 89, 184, 198*n*2; carnival 75–76, 79, 80–81, 83, 86–89, 184, 198*n*2; grotesque 75–76, 89; realism 20, 24, 75–76, 79, 80–81, 83, 86, 89, 183
Barth, John 8–9, 11, 17
Barthes, Roman 151; "The Death of Author" 151
Barton, Chris 94
Baudrillard, Jean 38–40, 46, 48, 51–52, 182–183, 194*ch*3*n*2, 195*n*3, 195*n*8; artistic reproduction 8, 38, 40, 43, 45, 47–49, 52, 181–183; simulacra 38–41, 45, 48, 51, 182–183, 194*n*2, 195*n*3; *Simulacra and Simulation* 38–41, 45, 48, 51, 182–183, 194*n*2, 195*n*3; simulation 38–47, 51–53, 91, 159–160, 182–183, 194*n*2, 195*n*2, 195*n*8
Beautiful You 52, 68, 104–105, 131, 144, 147, 178, 188–189; Penny Harrigan 52, 104–105, 131, 144–145, 189
beauty 75, 80–81, 88 113–116, 123, 200*n*5
Bennett, Alice 91
Bergin, Thomas 24, 28
Birch, Thomas 84–85
Birch, Thora 51–52
Bisch, Kevin 48
Bitzer, Lloyd 137, 140–141, 176, 201*n*1–2; rhetorical situation 2, 137–177, 201*n*1
Black Death 10, 21–24, 26–27, 29, 35, 151, 182; *see also* Boccaccio, Giovanni; *The Decameron*
blue collar 124, 126, 127, 129
Blume, Judy 10, 91–93, 99–102, 105–108, 166–168, 170, 184–185, 199*n*1, 199*n*8; *Are You There God? It's Me, Margaret* 10, 91, 94, 99–108, 143, 166–171, 184–185, 198*n*1, 199*n*4–6; *Forever Amber* 105; *see also Damned*; Margaret
Bob's Burgers 55–56; "Hawk and Chick" 55–56
Boccaccio, Giovanni 10, 19–36, 135, 148, 150–154, 182, 194*n*5–6; Black Death 10, 21–24,

213

26–27, 29, 35, 151, 182; bubonic plague 22–23, 25, 153; *The Decameron* 10, 19–36, 54, 150–153, 182, 194n5; Florence 22, 24, 26, 29; Queen Pampinea 29–30; Villa Diodati 21, 24, 34–35
Bomer, Paula 131
Booth, Wayne 137–139, 148, 176, 201n1, 201n3; *The Rhetoric of Fiction* 137–139
Borges, Jorge Luis 8
Bouchard, Loren 56
bourgeois 69, 124–126
Bowles, Paul 24
The Breakfast Club 43, 91, 94, 146, 199n8
Brown, Larry 24
bubonic plague 22–23, 25, 153
Bukowski, Charles 24
Burnt Tongues: An Anthology of Transgressive Stories 7, 173–175, 178
Burroughs, William 11
Butler, Judith 117–119, 122, 186, 200n7, 201n8
Byron, Lord 24, 35

Canterbery, E. Ray 84–85
The Canterbury Tales 21
capitalism (American) 56, 62–63, 92, 135, 160, 192n3, 197n10
Carver, Raymond 17, 24, 201n1
Cardinal sin *see* Seven Deadly Sins
Cavett, Dick 77
Cedar family 57–58, 63–70, 125, 161–162
celebrity 10, 20, 48, 72–89, 101, 120, 125, 135, 146, 148, 155, 158, 163–165, 184, 193n8, 198n4
Cervantes, Miguel de 1, 191n1
Chambers, Marilyn 49–50, 159
Channing, Carol 155
Channing, Margo 78–79
character 13, 14, 138–140, 143–151, 153–160, 163–165, 167, 169–171, 173, 175–177, 179–187, 192n3–4, 193n1
Chaucer, Geoffrey 21; *The Canterbury Tales* 21
Chong, Annabel 44–46, 157, 159
Christianity 15, 63–65, 92–93, 101, 103–104, 135, 153, 162, 166–167, 188, 197n12
Christopher, Renny 127
Chun, Rene 11
church 13, 14, 27, 56, 65, 69, 92, 130, 132, 162; mega-church 56, 65
Clark, Tess 20, 23, 27, 31–34, 153; *see also* Haunted
class system 17, 28, 56, 60, 63, 113–114, 124–128, 170, 174, 179–180, 187, 196n6, 197n8, 201n1
Cold War 56
college 142–144
Colonel Sanders 66
confidence *see* self-esteem
Connors, Carol 52
Coogan, Hazie 10, 74–89, 125, 127, 129, 133, 135, 146, 148–150, 163–166, 176–177, 184, 187, 198n5; *see also* Tell-All
counterculture 37, 130, 145

Crane, Stephen 136; *War Is Kind* 136
The Cult: The Official Chuck Palahniuk Website 25, 49, 92, 194n4, 202n5

Damned 2, 7, 10, 52, 70, 90–109, 125, 129, 133, 136–137, 143, 146, 150, 166–170, 175, 181, 184–185, 189, 198n1, 199n4; adolescence 10, 85 90–93, 97, 99–103, 105–108, 125, 143–144, 162–163, 167–167, 170, 179, 184–185, 199n7; *The Aeneid* 108; Archer 98, 100, 134; *Are You There God? It's Me, Margaret* 10, 91, 94, 99–108, 143, 166–171, 184–185, 198n1, 199n4–6; Blume, Judy 10, 91–93, 99–102, 105–108, 166–168, 170, 184–185, 199n1, 199n8; Hell 10, 90–109, 125, 129, 146, 166–171, 176, 184–185, 199n2, 199n8; Hello Kitty 101, 108, 168; *Inferno* 10, 24, 90–109, 166–170, 184; Patterson 96–97, 168; Prophet Mahomet 98; Purgatory 91–92, 95, 99, 99, 101, 109; Satan 90, 93–95, 99–101, 103, 105–106, 108–109, 131, 146, 166–170, 199n4, 199n8; Spencer, Madison 91–109, 125, 127, 129, 131, 133, 146–147, 149–150, 167–171, 176–177, 184–185, 187, 198n1, 199n5–6, 200n9; *see also* Alighieri, Dante; puberty
Dante *see* Alighieri, Dante
Darwin, Charles 124, 199n3
Dauterive, Jim 56
Davies, Adam Lee 18
Davis, Bette 78, 198n5
The Decameron 10, 19–36, 54, 150–153, 182, 194n5; *see also* Boccaccio, Giovanni
deformity 111–113, 116–117, 200n1; *see also* disfiguration
Delivered 91
Denzin, Norman K. 58
Depression 15, 131
dialect (literary device) 57–61, 63–70, 162, 183, 201n2
dialogic 75, 79–81
Diary 16, 19, 145
The Dick Cavett Show 77
Die Hard 5
discrimination 14, 54–57, 59, 142–143, 160–163, 201n4
disenfranchisement 2, 7, 12, 14, 16, 29, 75, 89, 124–125, 127, 130–131, 141–142, 147, 152, 167, 171, 175–177
disfiguration 112, 115, 117, 119, 125, 129, 144, 172–173
Disney 17, 42, 48, 62, 197n8
distance (author to character) 148–151, 159
diversity 12, 15, 22, 54, 58, 125–127, 134, 147, 170; cultural diversity 12, 15, 54, 58, 125, 134, 170
"divine average" 7
The Divine Comedy 90–92, 95, 135
Don Quixote (Kathy Acker) 1
Donoughue, Paul 79, 81
Doomed 91–92, 105, 108
Dorfman, Ariel 62–63, 196n7, 197n7–8; *The*

Empire's Old Clothes 63; *How to Read Donald Duck* 62
Doubleday Publishing 49–50
drag queen *see* gender performance
drug use 11, 31, 64, 67, 69, 91, 99, 102, 107, 132, 143, 156, 167–168

Ebsen, Buddy 42, 50–51
Eco, Umberto 8
The Elephant Man (film) 10, 110–123, 173, 185–186; *see also* Lynch, David
The Elephant Man (theater) 111–112, 118, 120–121, 185–186
Elephant Man (Chuck Palahniuk character) 10, 111–113, 117–121, 173, 186
Elephant Man (Lynch/Pomerance character) 10, 111–112, 116, 118–123, 173, 185–186; *see also* Merrick, Joseph
Eliot, T.S. 6–7, 188; "Tradition and the Individual Talent" 6
Ellis, Bret Easton 24
Ellmann, Lucy 15–17, 188–189
Embellishment *see* fabrication
Empireonline 51, 195n7
empowerment 2–3, 10, 12, 14, 29, 44, 68, 77, 89, 91, 93, 102–103, 105–106, 120–121, 124–136, 141, 169–171, 173, 175–177, 184–185, 187, 199n6; self-empowerment 10, 92, 102, 106, 135, 141, 175, 185
English (broken) *see* dialect
Ephron, Nora 73
exploitation 12, 20, 23, 59, 66, 68, 93, 119–121, 156

fabrication 17, 30, 40, 76, 84, 87, 108, 158, 165–166, 184–185
family 10–11, 56–58, 63–64, 69–71, 102, 107, 111–119, 121–122, 125, 127–129, 131–135, 143–144, 146, 155, 172–173, 183, 186, 200n2, 200n4, 200n6; nuclear 10, 107, 112–116, 125, 200n2, 200n4; relationships 11, 112–115; *see also* siblings
fantasy 10, 45, 117, 160, 196n2
Farley, C.P 21, 93
Fate 24, 26–27, 29, 32, 102, 107, 134, 173
Faulkner, William 17, 149, 154–155; *As I Lay Dying* 154–155; Yoknapatawpha 17
feminism 25, 27, 44, 52, 77, 79, 87, 102–105, 108, 117, 122, 125, 131, 142, 159, 164, 169, 185, 199n6; first-wave 44, 77; post-feminism 52, 103–105, 159, 169, 199n6; third-wave 52, 103–105, 159, 169, 199n6
Ferrante, Joan 26
Fight Club 2, 12–13, 16, 50, 74, 113, 126–130, 132–134, 136, 141, 146–147, 154, 178–181, 187–189, 193n8, 194n6, 194n1, 195n6, 200n3, 201n1; Big Bob 134; Durden, Tyler 13, 127–128; "Fight Club for Kids" 178–180, 189; fight clubs 13, 126, 132,136, 154, 180, 195n6; Joe 13, 113, 127–128, 133–134, 147–148; Project Mayhem 12, 128; Singer, Marla 13, 129, 133

Fight Club 4 Kids 178–180, 189
fight clubs 13, 126, 132,136, 154, 180, 195n6
Fitzgerald, F. Scott 83–85, 174, 176, 201n1; *see also The Great Gatsby*
Fleiss, Heidi 52
Foucault, Michel 11; *see also* transgression
Frankenstein 21, 24, 35, 173
Franklin, Benjamin 124
fringe *see* marginalization

gang bang 1, 10, 18, 38–41, 43–49, 127, 146, 154–155, 158–159, 167, 182, 195n4–5
gang-bang queen 10, 48, 154
gender 10, 44, 52, 65, 77, 79, 100, 103–105, 113, 116–123, 125, 127, 144, 150, 152–153, 183, 186, 196n6, 199n7, 200n7, 201n7–8
gender performance 10, 77, 100, 103–104, 113, 116–123, 150, 183, 186, 200n7, 201n7–8; transgender 27, 116–121, 152, 183, 186 transvestite 49, 52, 117–119, 133; *see also* sexuality
Girls Gone Wild 142
Golden Harvest Productions 60
Google 159
gore 20, 25, 98, 102, 113, 152
gossip journalism 10, 72–89, 91, 148, 163–164, 166, 184, 198n4
Graham, Sheilah 83–85
Gray, Dorian 75
The Great Gatsby 174–176; Baker, Jordan 175–176; Buchanan, Daisy 175–176; Buchanan, Tom 175–176; Carraway, Nick 174- 176; Gatsby, Jay 175–176; Wilson, George 175–176; Wilson, Myrtle 175–176; *see also* Fitzgerald, F. Scott
Gurley, George 49

A Handbook to Literature 5–6, 9
Hannah, Darryl 51–52, 195n7
Hardy, Thomas 138–139
Hartley, Nina 50–51
Haunted 2, 7, 10, 13, 15, 19–36, 54, 106, 122, 125, 127, 129, 133, 136–137, 145–146, 150–154, 175–176, 178, 181–182, 187, 189, 193n2, 194n2–3; Agent Tattletale 25, 153; Baroness Frostbite 27; Brandon Whittier 19–20, 22–23, 27, 32–36, 126, 130, 150–151, 153; The Chef 26; Comrade Snarky 27, 152; Director Denial 152; Earl of Slander 30–31, 153; Lady Baglady 26, 125, 152; Matchmaker 27; Miss America 22, 26, 152–153; Missing Link 27; Mother Nature 22, 125; Nightmare Box 15, 31–35, 135–136, 153, 176; Saint Gut-Free 22–23, 25, 27, 106, 147, 152–153, 194n3; Tess Clark 20, 23, 27, 31–34, 153
Hefner, Hugh 158
hell 10, 22–23, 30, 90–109, 129, 146, 166–171, 176, 184–185, 199n2, 199n8; *see also* Damned
Hellman, Lillian 73–74, 76–79, 81, 83, 87, 164–165, 184, 198n3; *An Unfinished Woman* 76; *Pentimento* 73–74, 76–77; *Scoundrel Time* 76
Hemingway, Ernest 13, 17, 149

Index

Hempel, Amy 24
Henry, William III 89
hero 10, 55, 60–62, 64–66, 69–71, 76, 89, 104, 108, 124–125, 129, 160–161, 163, 183, 196n3
heroine 76, 105
Hershey, Barbara 18
heterosexuality 117–118, 156
Hilton, Perez 72
historiographic metafiction 9, 192n5
Hollands, Neil 38, 74
Hollywood 15, 31, 38–43, 45, 47, 50–52, 72–89, 93–94, 125, 135, 146, 158–160, 164, 166, 182–184, 188, 198n4; *see also Tell-All*
Hollywood and porn 39–40, 42–43, 45, 47, 50–52, 135, 160, 182
Homer 6–8, 104
homo viator 95
homosexuality 30, 65, 69, 114, 118, 126, 156
Hong Kong 60–61
hope 26, 83, 85, 88, 95–96, 100–101, 121, 123, 130–131, 133–134, 136, 199n5, 199n8–9, 200n9
horror 19–20, 23–24, 28–29, 106, 173–174, 194n2–3; *see also* King, Stephen
Houston 48–49, 195n5
hubris 69, 78, 103–105, 115–116, 119, 122, 153, 163, 165
humility 22, 31, 61, 120–121, 135, 173, 186
Hutcheon, Linda 2, 9–10, 17, 23, 55, 68, 92, 94, 106, 108, 154, 181, 191n2–3, 192n3–5, 196n2; *Irony's Edge* 23; *see also* parody
Hutchins, Christopher 72
hyperbole 55, 76, 144, 164, 183
hyperreality 37–53, 131, 154, 159, 182–183

I Am Charlotte Simmons 143–144
identity 10, 40, 101, 112–113, 116–118, 121–123, 125, 129, 143, 151, 172–173, 186, 200n3, 200n7, 201n7–8
imitation 5, 9–10, 38, 40–41, 43, 49, 85, 92, 107–108, 117, 120, 154, 160, 180, 182–183, 185, 192n3–4, 194n2, 201n8
In Touch 72
incest 11, 155
Inferno 10, 24, 90–109, 166–170, 184; *see also* Alighieri, Dante
intertextuality 2, 9, 24, 99–100, 106, 108, 120, 131, 144, 148, 154, 165–68, 181–185, 193n5
introspection 20, 34, 134
Invisible Monsters Remix 2, 7, 10, 19, 110–123, 125, 133, 136–137, 146 148, 150, 171–173, 175, 178, 181, 185–186, 189, 193n8, 194n6, 200n1; Alexander, Brandy 116–122, 146, 172, 176, 200n2–6; Barret, Rona 119; Chapter 18 111–113, 117, 119, 123, 148, 185–186; Cottrell, Evie 113–116, 118, 146, 200n5; *The Elephant Man* (film/play) 10, 110–123, 173, 185–186; Kelley, Manus 115, 146, 200n6; McFarland, Shane 10, 112, 114, 116–122, 125–126, 129, 133, 172–173, 186, 200n2, 200n4; McFarland, Shannon 6–7, 10, 111–116, 119–123, 125, 129, 131, 133, 135, 146, 148, 150, 171–173, 176–177, 185–187, 200n2–6; Merrick, Joseph (Chuck Palahniuk character) 10, 111–113, 117–121, 173, 186; Rhea sisters 118–119, 121–122; St. Patience, Daisy 111, 119, 122; Thomas, Seth 113, 116, 200n3, 200n6
irony 10, 14, 17, 23–24, 33–35, 48, 55, 57, 65–67, 70, 88, 93, 100–101, 105–106, 114, 119, 134, 144, 147, 151, 156, 171, 181, 187, 191n3, 192n4, 193n5, 196n2; parodic 23–24, 33–34, 65, 93, 101, 105–106, 147, 187, 191n3, 192n4, 193n5, 196n2

James, Henry 15, 17, 188, 191n1
James, Jesse 79
Jameson, Frederick 192n3, 196n2
Jenks, Chris 11, 193n6
Jeremy, Ron 48, 158
Johnson, Andy 114, 116, 121–122, 200n4–5
Johnson, Darin 40–41, 43, 45–47, 154–155, 157; *see also Snuff*
Johnson, Denis 24
journalism 10, 30, 32, 54, 62, 64, 72–89, 91, 148, 163–164, 166, 184, 198n4; gossip 10, 72–89, 91, 148, 64, 166, 184, 198n4; Hollywood reporters 72–79, 81–89, 163
Joyce, James 6, 138

karate 10, 54–71, 91, 148, 160–164, 167, 183, 196n4, 198n4; films (1970s) 10, 54–71, 91, 148, 160–164, 167, 183, 196n4, 198n4; hero 10, 54–71, 161, 163–164, 183; Hong Kong 60–61; martial art 10, 54, 57, 59, 61, 68–69, 162, 183
Kenton, Katherine 74–83, 85–88, 125, 146, 164, 166, 184, 198n5; *see also Tell-All*
Khakheperresenb 8; *see* Homer
King, Stephen 15, 23, 174, 176
Kinsey Institute 189
Kirkus Reviews 19, 38, 110, 197n1
KTVU 54, 57–58, 70, 195n1
Kuhn, Cynthia 24
kung fu 58–61, 64, 66, 70–71, 160, 162–163, 183, 196n4

Lawrence, D.H. 138–139, 148–149, 201n1
Lee, Bruce 60–61, 196n3
Levin, Harry 72
Life & Style 72
Lindgren, Suzanne 110
Linkon, Sherry 126
literary criticism *see* review
Little Nicky 90
Los Angeles Times 11
Lott, M. Ray 60–61
Lovelace, Linda 44
Lullaby 19, 145
Lynch, David 111, 114, 119–120; Elephant Man (character) 10, 111–112, 116, 118–123, 173, 185–186; *The Elephant Man* (film) 10, 110–123, 173, 185–186; *see also* Merrick, Joseph

Index

MacFarlane, Seth 5–6, 111; *American Dad* 5, 6; *The Cleveland Show* 5–6; *Family Guy* 5
magnum opus 21, 151
Make Something Up: Stories You Can't Unread 7, 178
Mankiewicz, Joseph 78–79
Margaret 99–108, 167–171, 185, 198n1, 199n4–6; *see also* Blume, Judy
marginalization 2, 7, 12, 14, 37, 56, 59–60, 67, 70, 75, 89, 107, 114, 124–127, 131, 141, 147, 167, 171–172, 175, 177, 187, 198n2; and disenfranchisement 2, 12, 14, 124, 127, 131, 141, 145–147, 167, 175, 177
marketing 12, 16, 19, 40–41, 49–50, 55, 62, 89, 102, 105, 110, 131, 159, 166, 172, 180–181, 197n10
martial arts (in film) 10, 54–55, 58–61, 65, 68–69, 162, 183, 196n4, 198n4; *see also* karate
Martinson, Deborah 77, 198n3
Marxism 62, 124, 126
The Mask 111
Maslin, Janet 91
Mason, Bobbie Ann 24
masturbation 22–23, 40–41, 51, 65, 68, 105, 154–155, 162, 194n3, 198n5
Maxwell, C. Linus 131, 189
Maxwell, Gloria 74
McCarthy, Mary 77
McDowell, Jeanne 89
media 7, 17, 20, 25, 33, 37, 45, 52, 54, 58, 62–63, 66, 72–89, 93, 107, 119, 125, 130, 141–144, 150, 157–159, 165–166, 182, 186, 193n3, 196n1, 197n8, 198n4, 202n5; *see also* journalism
Medoff, Marc 49
Melville, Herman 17, 186–188, 191n1; "Bartleby, the Scrivener" 186–187; *Billy Budd* 186; *Moby-Dick* 186
Merrick, Joseph 10, 110–123, 173, 185–186; *see also* Elephant Man; *The Elephant Man*; *Invisible Monsters Remix*
Messalina, Valeria 44–46, 147, 157
metacommentary 107, 144, 152, 180
middle class 28, 56, 113–114, 126–128, 170
Midwest 58, 161, 197n9
Miller, Laura 16
Milton, John 170; *Paradise Lost* 170
minimalism 17, 95
minority 59
modernism 9
Monroe, Marilyn 43, 46, 78, 84, 88
monster 112–113, 116, 122–123, 172
morality 15, 31, 92, 154
Moyer, Bill 128
Myspace 49, 52

name drop 74–75 79–82, 163–164, 166
narrator 20, 22, 25, 30, 33–35, 40, 57, 62, 78, 91, 104, 127–128, 137–138, 141, 143, 144, 147–155, 157, 160, 163, 167, 173, 181–187, 194n6
Naushad, Mehta 89
The New York Times 11, 15, 82, 88

Nightmare Box 15, 31–35, 135–136, 153, 176
nihilism 13, 14, 16
Norton Publishers 110, 194n5

O Brother, Where Art Thou? 6
The Odyssey 6, 8, 108; Odysseus 104, 108
O'Hagan, Sean 24, 28
OK! 72
O'Neill, Eugene 17; *The Iceman Cometh* 17
onomatopoeia 162
Operation Havoc 56, 69–70, 161, 183, 197n11
O'Reilly, Maddy 51–52

pain 12, 14, 25, 34–35, 65, 67, 122, 165, 185, 194n6
Palahniuk fans 2, 10, 25, 49, 54, 74, 92, 124, 130–131, 136–137, 141, 145–147, 149–150, 167, 172, 174, 176, 177, 180–181, 183–184, 187, 189; *The Cult: The Official Chuck Palahniuk Website* 25, 49, 92, 194n4, 202n5
Paradise 91–92, 95
Paradise Lost 170
parody 1–2, 5–11, 14, 17–18, 23, 29, 38–39, 45, 49–51, 54–59, 61, 63, 68, 76, 78, 81, 85, 89–94, 101, 106–108, 112, 117, 130, 136, 143–145, 147–150, 154, 160–161, 164–167, 170, 173–174, 177–189, 191n1–3, 192n3–4, 193n5, 196n2, 201n8; contemporary 1, 5–7, 9–11, 14, 17, 54–55, 61, 63, 68, 89–94, 130, 143–145, 147–150; postmodern 2, 5, 8–11, 18, 21, 23, 38, 101, 106–108, 136–137, 144, 154, 178–189, 196n2; transgressive 51, 92–94, 101; *see also* Hutcheon, Linda
Peck, Claude 91
Penny Harrigan 52, 104–105, 131, 144–145, 189
Penthouse 27
People 72
pigmy *see* Pygmy
plastic surgery 42, 48–49, 75, 81, 89, 115, 117, 120–121, 153
Playboy 23, 27, 52, 100, 102, 142, 158, 199n6–7, 202n4
Playgirl 111
Plymouth Rock 3
Poe, Edgar Allan 24, 35, 151, 194ch2n2; "The Masque of the Red Death" 24, 35
poetry 7, 9, 16, 20, 25, 30, 57, 66, 68, 95, 136, 140–141, 149–150, 152, 182, 191n2–3, 192n5, 196n2, 201n2
Polidori, John 24; *The Vampyre* 24
political correctness 11–12, 15, 114
Pomerance, Bernard 111; *see also The Elephant Man* (play)
popular culture (American) 2, 5–7, 9, 16, 23, 48, 52, 58, 60–63, 67, 71–90, 92–94, 111, 120, 127, 129–131, 143, 159, 162, 171, 174, 180, 188, 192n3, 192n5, 198n4
porn actors 37–53, 118,-119, 125, 135, 146–148, 154–160, 182, 187, 195n5–6
pornography 1, 11, 15, 18, 20, 22, 37–53, 67, 86, 93, 104, 118–119, 125, 128, 133, 135, 142, 144–

160, 167, 169, 182–183, 187–188, 195n5–8; actors 37–53, 118,-119, 125, 135, 146–148, 154–160, 182, 187, 195n5–6; Naughty America 43; New Sensations 43; the stud 44; suicide 43–44, 46–47; Vivid Entertainment 43; Wicked Pictures 43
post-9/11 56, 67
postmodern parody 2, 5, 8–11, 18, 21, 23, 38, 101, 106–108, 136–137, 144, 154, 178–189, 196n2
postmodernism 2, 8–11, 18, 23–25, 37–38, 52, 92, 101, 106–108, 137, 144, 154, 171, 178–189, 191n1–3, 192n3, 192n5, 193n1, 194n2, 196n2; literature 9, 92, 101, 171, 178–189; parody 2, 5, 8–11, 18, 21, 23, 38, 101, 106–108, 136–137, 144, 154, 178–189, 196n2
Pound, Ezra 8
power 10, 12–14, 23, 25, 31–32, 41, 57–70, 73, 78–81, 83, 85–89, 93, 96, 98, 103–105, 108, 124, 126, 128–134, 165, 169, 171, 173, 177, 184, 197n10, 200n1
Powers, Nicole 78–79
prejudice 10, 27, 55–57, 100, 130, 155, 158, 160, 163, 183
propaganda 13, 62–63, 65, 130, 135, 138, 145
puberty 92–93, 99–104, 106–108; see also adolescence
Publisher's Weekly 19, 57, 74
punishment 43, 93–97, 102, 106–107, 146, 185
purgatory 91–92, 95, 99, 101, 109
Pygmy 2, 7, 10, 17, 54–71, 73, 91, 125–127, 129, 135–137, 146, 148–150, 160–164, 166, 175, 181, 183, 187, 189, 193n7, 196n5, 197n9–12; Cedar family 57–58, 63–70, 125, 161–162; Operation Havoc 56, 69–70, 161, 183, 197n1; Pygmy 56–61, 63–70, 126–127, 129, 135, 146, 149–150, 160–164, 196n5, 197n9–12; Stonefield, Trevor 57, 64–65, 67, 69, 162, 197n11

Quek, Grace 44; see also Chong, Annabel

racism 17, 55, 57–59, 142
Rance, P.T.J. 61
Rant 178
reader see Palahniuk fans
Reader's Digest 62–63, 174
realism 20, 24, 75–76, 80
reality 10, 13, 15, 24, 31–35, 38–41, 43, 45–50, 52, 62–63, 87, 105, 116, 121, 134, 136, 146–147, 151, 153, 176, 194n2, 195n2
reality television 21, 34–35, 51–52; *Big Brother* 34–35; *Celebrity Rehab* 51; *Intervention* 34–35; *Naked and Afraid* 34–35; *The Real World* 21; *Survivor* 34–35
Redekop, Corey 57, 197n1
rehabilitation 51, 107, 129
Reid, Craig 59–60
religion 12–13, 31, 58, 69, 93, 99, 101–102, 106–107, 124, 126, 130, 162, 165–168, 170, 197n12
review (literary) 15–16, 19, 21, 38, 57, 74, 89, 91, 110, 131, 147, 152, 162, 165, 171, 174, 189, 193n7, 194n2, 194n1, 197n1; see also literary criticism
rhetoric 2, 7, 11, 20, 23, 58, 135, 137–178, 181, 187, 201n1–3; Aristotle 175; Cicero 175; Plato 174; "Rhetorical Situation" 2, 137–177, 201n3; see also Booth, Wayne
The Rhetoric of Fiction 137–139; "advertiser's stance" 139, 147, 171, 176; implied authors 138; "pedant stance" 139, 147, 159, 176; see also Booth, Wayne
Rinaldi, Rich 56
Ritter, Thelma 78–79
Rockwell, Sam 79
Roman Empire 44–45
romanticism 13, 17, 23, 39, 76–77, 98, 156, 170, 187
Rowlandson, Mary 17
Rubin, Lance 24

Sade, Marquis de 11
St. Andre, Ken 19
Saint Gut-Free 22–23, 25, 27, 106, 147, 152–153, 194n3
St. Patience, Daisy 111, 119, 122
Salon 16
Sartre 91
Satan 90, 93–95, 99–101, 103, 105–106, 108–109, 131, 146, 166–170, 199n4, 199n8
satire 5, 23, 45, 56–57, 65–66, 68, 74, 92, 100, 145, 160–161, 179–180, 188, 191n2, 192n3, 192n5, 193n5, 199n2
Saturday Night Live 129
Scylla 44
self-deception 20, 113, 115, 134
self-esteem 84, 92–93, 99–100, 102–106, 112–113, 116, 124–136, 170–171, 175–177, 184–185
self-mutilation 11, 20, 23, 65, 111, 113, 115–116, 119–122, 144, 182, 200n1
Seven Deadly Sins 25, 94–95, 102, 153
sex acts 11, 22, 27, 30, 38–41, 43–49, 51, 53, 68, 101, 106, 111, 114, 117, 125, 131, 143–146, 153–154, 156, 158, 160, 162–163, 183
sex toys 40–41, 47–48, 59, 67, 69–70, 125, 131, 143, 147, 158–160, 162–163; dolls 40–41, 47–48, 154; vibrators 41, 59, 68–70, 125, 131, 144, 147, 162–163
sexploitation 59, 68, 172
sexual development 10, 85 90–93, 97, 99–103, 105–108, 125, 143–144, 162–163, 167–167, 170, 179, 184–185, 199n7; see also adolescence
sexual expression 30, 59, 69, 85, 100, 117–119, 133 152, 156 183, 186; heterosexuality 85, 100, 117–118, 156; homosexuality 30, 59, 69, 118, 156; transgender 27, 116–121, 152, 183, 186; transvestite 49, 52, 117–119, 133; see also gender; gender performance
sexual intercourse 11, 22, 27, 29–30, 38–41, 43–49, 51–53, 59, 68, 76, 83, 6–87, 100–101, 106, 114–118, 125, 131, 142, 144, 146, 153–158, 160, 162–163, 165, 172, 186, 194n3, 195n4–5, 199n6; arousal 41, 52, 59, 100, 115, 117, 119, 125, 162–

163, 165, 172, 186, 199n6; attraction 22, 27, 41, 115, 119, 142, 165, 172, 186; romance 39, 86, 131, 156; *see also* sex acts
sexuality 11, 17, 22, -23, 26–29, 38–41, 46, 49, 52–53, 59, 65, 67–69, 79, 82–86, 91–93, 97–101, 103–108, 111, 114, 116–122, 126, 131, 139, 141, 143–144, 147–148, 155–156, 160, 162–163, 167–170, 172, 176, 185, 188–189, 193n6, 195n8, 199n6, 202n5; female 22, 26–27, 40, 46, 49, 67–69, 86, 92, 98–100, 103–106, 108, 118–120, 122, 125, 131, 141, 143, 145, 147, 156, 165, 168–170, 176, 189; male 17, 26–27, 40, 67, 111, 118–119, 121, 125, 131, 139, 143, 145, 155–156, 162–163
Shakespeare, William 32; *The Tempest* 32
Shapiro, Jonathan 74
Shaw Brothers Productions 59
Sheila 41, 43–44, 46–47, 50–51, 154–155, 157–159; *see also Snuff*
Shelley, Mary 24, 35, 105, 173; *Frankenstein* 21, 24, 35, 173
Shelley, Percy Bysshe 24
siblings 10, 111–114, 116–119, 121–122, 125, 129, 131, 133–135, 143–144, 146, 155, 172–173, 186, 200n6; *see also* family
Silverblatt, Michael 11
Simpson, Homer 6
The Simpsons 6
simulacra 38–41, 45, 48, 51, 182–183
Simulacra and Simulation 38–41, 45, 48, 51, 182–183, 194n2, 195n3
simulation 38–47, 51–53, 91, 159–160, 182–183, 194n2, 195n2, 195n8
sin 24, 26, 30, 92–96, 101–102, 106–107, 153–154, 197n8, 199n9
Sizemore, Tom 51, 195n7
Slaughterhouse Five 134, 178
Smith, John 17
Snuff 1, 2, 7, 10, 15, 18, 37–53, 55, 69, 118–119, 125, 129, 135–137, 145–148, 150, 154–160, 167, 169, 175, 181–183, 187, 189, 194n1, 195n4–7; Bacardi, Branch 38–43, 46–48, 50–51, 69, 129, 131, 154–157, 183, 195n4; Johnson, Darin 40–41, 43, 45–47, 154–155, 157; Mr. 72 40–41, 43, 45–47, 154–155, 157; Mr. 137 41–42, 45, 155; Mr. 600 43, 46, 154; Mr. Toto 41, 50, 155, 160; Sheila 41, 43–44, 46–47, 50–51, 154–155, 157–159; Terry 41–42; "true fact" 37–38, 40–44, 46–47, 53; Wright, Cassie 10, 38–53, 69, 119, 125, 127, 129, 131, 133, 135, 146, 154–160, 182–183, 187
Sobel, Richard 127
social decorum 7, 11, 15–16, 29, 52, 57, 103, 148, 169, 198n5
Socrates 13
Sondergard, Sidney 19, 200n1
sorority 142–145
Soukhanov, Anne H. 11
South Park 90
Spanbauer, Tom 18
Sparks, Lisa 48

Sparxxx, Lisa 48; *see also* Sparks, Lisa
Spencer, Madison 91–109, 125, 127, 129, 131, 133, 146–147, 149–150, 167–171, 176–177, 184–185, 187, 198n1, 199n5–6, 200n9; *see also Damned*
stance (author's) 137–139, 141, 143, 169, 171, 176, 201n3; advertiser's 139, 147, 171, 176; pedant 139, 147, 159, 176
Star 72
Star Wars 5
Steinbeck, John 77, 149
stereotype 7, 10, 20–21, 37, 54, 56, 58–62, 65, 67, 70–71, 91, 96, 100, 118, 135, 142, 144, 156, 158, 160–163, 177, 183, 195n8, 196n6; Asian 10, 54, 56, 58–62, 67, 70–71, 160–163, 183, 196n6; racial/cultural 10, 17, 37, 54, 58, 71, 196n6; sexual 100, 118, 135, 142, 144, 156, 158, 195n8; third-world 62–63, 65, 67
Stonefield, Trevor 57, 64–65, 67, 69, 162, 197n11
Stranger Than Fiction: True Stories 28, 92
stripper 110–112, 117–118, 121, 123, 173, 185, 195n5
style (literary) 6, 14, 17–18, 49, 59, 65, 74, 92, 95, 106, 110–111, 17, 131, 140, 162, 174, 17, 180–181, 184, 201n8, 201n2
subversion 11, 62, 75, 78, 93, 81, 117–118, 129, 141, 147, 166, 170, 181, 197n2, 201n8
suicide 31, 43–44, 46–47, 95, 123, 200n3
Sunset Boulevard 78
supermodel 112, 115–116, 118, 122–123, 172, 186
Survival 34, 124
Swift, Jonathan 105–106, 138, 161–162, 170, 179–180; Gulliver 161–162; *Gulliver's Travels* 161; Houyhnhnms 161–162; "A Modest Proposal" 179–180

Talbott, Chris 76, 197n5
Tarantino, Quentin 59–60
Tell-All 2, 6–7, 10, 17, 72–89, 91, 125, 127, 133, 135–137, 145–146, 148, 150, 160, 163–166, 170, 174–177, 181, 184, 187, 189, 197n1, 198n4–5; Baker, Norma Jean 88; Bankhead, Tallulah 42, 78; Birdie 78–79; Coogan, Hazie 10, 74–89, 125, 127, 129, 133, 135, 146, 148–150, 163–166, 176–177, 184, 187; Fitzgerald, F. Scott 83–85, 174, 176, 201n1; Graham, Sheilah 83–85; Hellman, Lillian 73–74, 76–79, 81, 83, 87, 164–165, 184, 198n3; Kenton, Katherine 74–83, 85–88, 125, 146, 164, 166, 184, 198n5; *Love Slave* 76, 84, 86–87, 148, 166; Mankiewicz, Joseph 78–79; *Paragon* 80, 83, 88, 166; Westward, Webster Carlton III 70, 76–79, 83, 86–88, 146, 165, 184; *see also* gossip journalism; Hollywood
The Tempest 32
terrorism 10, 56, 65, 67, 70, 133, 160, 163, 183, 193n7
Tillotson, Kathleen 138
torture 20, 35, 66, 94, 96–98, 111, 168, 185
Tourette's Syndrome 79
transcendentalism 13

220 Index

transgender 118, 152, 183; *see also* gender performance
transgression 2, 7–8, 10–12, 17, 20–22, 27–28, 51, 53, 68–70, 82, 92–94, 106, 114, 124, 130–131, 143–145, 148–149, 152, 167–169, 173–174, 177–178, 187–189, 191*n*3, 193*n*6, 197*n*2, 198*n*2; literary device 2, 7, 10–11, 13–14, 20–21, 27–28, 53, 70, 82, 92–94, 106, 114, 130, 145, 148, 152, 167–168, 170, 174–175, 177–181, 187–189, 191*n*3, 193*n*6, 197*n*2, 198*n*2; *see also* transgressive fiction
Transgression 1, 193*n*6
transgressive fiction 2, 8, 11–13, 17, 21–22, 27, 51, 68–70, 92–94, 106, 114, 124, 131, 148–149, 173–174, 178–189
transvestite 49, 52, 117–119, 133; *see also* gender performance
true fact 37–38, 40–44, 46–47, 53; *see also* Tell-All
Twain, Mark 15, 17, 188
twelve steps 132–134
twenty-first century America 2, 7, 11, 15, 17, 21, 93–94, 103, 124, 126, 130, 176, 187–188
Twitter 92

Ulysses 6
underworld *see* hell
United Nations (model) 65–66, 68, 162–163
University of Alabama 142, 144; Alpha Phi Sorority 142, 144
US 72
USAToday 178–179

victim 2, 12, 20, 34, 44, 52, 65, 114, 116, 120, 152–153
Victorian era 104, 111, 113, 117, 120, 171; geek show 104, 111, 117
villain 60–61, 64, 77–78, 104, 125
violence 11, 56, 59–61, 64–65, 68, 88, 94–98, 102, 113–116, 120–122, 125, 127–130, 144, 148, 168–169, 174, 179–181, 183, 188, 194*n*3

Virgil 91, 95, 101, 107
Vogue 110
voiceover (film) 59–60
Vonnegut, Kurt 134, 178; *Slaughterhouse-Five* 134, 178

War Is Kind 136
Weeks, Clair 48
Weinstein, Adam 91
westerns 60, 62, 67
Westward, Webster Carlton III 70, 76–79, 83, 86–88, 146, 165, 184; *see also Tell-All*
Whitman, Walt 7; "divine average" 7
Whitson, Carolyn 127
Whittier, Brandon 19–20, 22–23, 27, 32–36, 126, 130, 150–151, 153; *see also Haunted*
Wikipedia 16, 81, 193*n*7, 195*ch*3*n*5, 195*ch*4*n*1
Williams, G. Christopher 13
Williams, Laura J. 13, 193*n*7, 195*ch*3*n*5, 195*ch*4*n*1
The Wizard of Oz 49–51
Wolf, Naomi 103–104, 169, 185
Wolfe, Tom 1430144; *I Am Charlotte Simmons* 143–144
women's rights 24–25, 169
Woodhead, Cameron 57
working class 17, 28, 60, 124, 126–127, 174, 201*n*1; literature 127, 201*n*1
World War II 45, 76–77
Wright, Cassie 10, 38–53, 69, 119, 125, 127, 129, 131, 133, 135, 146, 154–160, 182–183, 187

You Do Not Talk About Fight Club: I Am Jack's Completely Unauthorized Essay Collection 13, 193*n*8
YouTube 44, 58, 60, 142, 150, 196*n*4

Zelda Zonk *see* Sheila; *Snuff*
Zweig, Michael 126

www.ingramcontent.com/pod-product-compliance
Ingram Content Group UK Ltd.
Pitfield, Milton Keynes, MK11 3LW, UK
UKHW041952140426
5217IPUK00015B/770